ABANDONED

The Untold Story of the Abortion Wars

ABANDONED

The Untold Story of the Abortion Wars

MONICA MIGLIORINO MILLER

SAINT BENEDICT✝PRESS
Charlotte, North Carolina

Cover design by Chris Pelicano

Cataloging-in-Publication data on file with the Library of Congress.

ISBN: 978-1-61890-394-5

Published in the United States by
Saint Benedict Press, LLC
PO Box 410487
Charlotte, NC 28241
www.saintbenedictpress.com

Printed and bound in the United States of America.

PRAISE FOR *ABANDONED*

"Quite simply, this is the best book ever written on abortion. Beautifully written, this is about the consequences of *Roe v. Wade*, as seen through the eyes of one woman, who tells a clear and compelling story with passion but without fanaticism. On a subject that is often heavy and depressing, this is a hard-hitting yet compassionate and moving book. Honestly, I wouldn't have thought such a narrative could be done, only now it has been done."

> —Dinesh D'Souza, best-selling author of
> *Ill-liberal Education*, *What's So Great About America*,
> *What's So Great About Christianity*, and
> *The Enemy at Home*.

"*Abandoned* is a kind of shocking immersion into the depths of the American battle over abortion. Here is preserved up close and in detail an important historical moment that reveals at once the commitment, the fears, the frustration and the hope of those who oppose abortion and the darkest truth about the practice of abortion itself. This book is unprecedented, provocative and will leave its mark on all who read it."

> —Jill Stanek, nurse, columnist, blogger, and
> winner of the 2009 Life Prizes Award.

"As a pro-life activist leader who has fought for decades in the battle for the unborn I can honestly say that Miller's book is one of the most important ever written on the subject of abortion. It is a masterpiece of passion and unique insight. There are few books that can change a person's life-but this is one of them. Its compelling historical narrative takes you places you have never been, makes you see things you have never seen. As no other book has done, Miller's true story lays bear what's at stake in the war over abortion."

> —Joe Scheidler, National Director of
> The Pro-Life Action League

"*Abandoned* grabs you from the very first paragraph and takes you not only deep into the history of the pro-life movement but deep into the harsh, brutal realities of the abortion industry. It's a must read for anyone interested in a subject that remains the hot button issue of our times. You will not be able to put this book down but you will definitely need to pass it on to as many people as possible."

> —Teresa Tomeo, Syndicated Catholic Talk Show Host
> and best-selling Catholic Author

"I am involved in every aspect of the pro-life movement on the national level, and it is very clear to me that one of the key educational needs is precisely to help people, starting within the movement, and reaching outside that movement, to understand the history of pro-life work– especially in the area of activism. This book is a unique literary contribution—revealing like no other book, what those opposed to abortion did for life."

—Father Frank Pavone,
National Director of Priests for Life

"Raw. Gritty. Real. *Abandoned* is to abortion what *Uncle Tom's Cabin* was to slavery and *Night* was to the Nazi Holocaust."

—Jack Ames, Founder and Director of Defend Life

"Shocking discoveries. Daring rescues. Inspiring stories. Miller's compelling book has it all. *Abandoned* chronicles the experiences of one courageous activist who has dedicated her life to protecting innocent children and their mothers. This must-read story provides a deep understanding of the blessings and challenges faced while speaking up for those who cannot speak for themselves and serves as a rallying cry to a new generation of activists. At this pivotal moment in history Monica's testimony will motivate you-and countless others-to be part of the solution to the abortion crisis."

—David Bereit, National Director of Forty Days for Life

"A completely compelling story told with a beautiful narrative voice. The reader is treated to an underground of activists that the public rarely sees or hears. The personal tone of the narrative, the vividness of the illustrations, the avoidance of cliché and sloganeering, the empathy for women seeking abortion make this a report that should get wide readership and generate new light on an old familiar issue."

—Al Kresta, President and CEO, Ave Maria Radio;
host of *Kresta in the Afternoon*

*For Joe who helped set me
on the path—and for Edmund
who came with me.*

TABLE OF CONTENTS

PART I
RADICAL ACTS

PART II
THE EDGE OF THE WORLD

PART III
A DANGEROUS PERSON

Creon has ordered
That none shall bury him or mourn for him;
He must be left to lie unwept, unburied
For hungry birds of prey to swoop and feast
On his poor body.

*   *   *

No one shall say *I* failed him! I will bury
My brother—and yours too, if you will not.

Antigone, by Sophocles

AUTHOR'S NOTE

EVERYTHING written about in this narrative actually took place. From the years 1979 through 1982 the author kept a diary of her pro-life activity and some conversations in the book are reconstructed from those diary entries, otherwise the author has relied on her memory or the memory of others who have first-hand knowledge of the episodes recounted in this book. In addition, many incidents are historically supported from newspaper articles, official court transcripts or legal documents.

Only one person who appears in this book has asked for anonymity and out of respect for that wish the author has used a pseudonym. The author also took the liberty of not using the true names of the owners of "Pet Haven" cemetery—nor the true name of the cemetery—to spare these persons any further public scandal that involved their business.

Other than these few changes, the author has tried to be as historically faithful as possible to the conversations and episodes as they occurred.

PROLOGUE

THE STORY I *HAVE* TO TELL

WHEN I was nine years old I made a peace treaty with the animals. I wrote it out on a sheet of wide-ruled notebook paper—the kind of paper used by a grade school student. Attempting to make the lettering as fancy as I could manage and using a ball point pen rather than a pencil, I intended the treaty to be permanent. The treaty was a perpetual commitment that I would never harm an animal as long as I lived. After writing out my pledge, I punctured my finger with a pin and signed the treaty in blood, thinking treaties were signed that way. I rolled it up as if it were composed on the finest parchment and tied a piece of red ribbon around the scroll. I even crumbled the paper slightly to make it look old as most important documents seemed worn in appearance. I placed the sacred document in a cigar box where most of my precious possessions were secretly stowed. Eight months later I lifted the lid of the box, rolled open the scroll and wrote:

> I Monica do hereby and on this 10th day of July in the year 1962 re-ratify this treaty for the reason that I killed an animal.
>
> Kind of animal: Snail
>
> Reason: Reproduction
>
> I do from this day forward promise never to harm another animal.

I then signed my name in pen since it seemed to me that the solemnity which attended the first signing in blood could not be repeated.

I had killed a very small snail in my aquarium because, whether it was true or not, a school-girl friend had told me that snails reproduce on their own and soon my whole aquarium would be overrun with them, crowding out the angel fish and gouramis. So that little snail had to go. In my quest to rid the sea world of this menace I forgot all about the treaty only to recall a few days later, to my horror that I had made such a pact and had now shamefully broken it. There was nothing else to do but re-ratify the document and start again.

As I got a bit older I eventually gave up on the treaty, noticing that I swatted flies and mosquitoes and occasionally trampled on ants. The treaty was a lofty ideal but totally impractical in the real world.

However short-lived my official peace treaty with the animals was, it nonetheless indicated an early sensitivity toward living things. Even before composing the treaty, I recall traveling in the car with my parents, stuffed into the backseat with my brothers and sister. Luckily I sat next to the window. We were driving down a residential street when I spied suddenly a wounded bird in someone's driveway. It seemed to be an odd place for a bird, even a wounded one. I was convinced the bird, which looked like a robin, needed our help and asked my father to stop the car. He didn't. He was not inclined to do such things and probably thought I was overreacting anyway. As we sped on, I was filled with anxiety and craned my neck to see the bird, hoping to be mistaken—that the bird was just a toy left in the driveway by a child.

Whenever a resident of my aquarium died I held fish funerals for them. One such funeral was held in the middle of the fall, and I used a small, white cardboard jewelry box lined with cotton as a coffin for an expired angel fish. My brothers and sister and a few neighborhood children formed the impromptu funeral party. We walked the short distance to the abandoned apple orchard down the street and selected a gravesite. With our mother's garden trowel borrowed from the garage, my older brother Paul dug the tiny five-inch-deep grave. With great solemnity I placed the tiny coffin into the earth and covered it with dirt. The ceremony concluded with a reverent recital of the Our Father over the grave of the expired fish.

Even in adulthood this sensitivity toward living things stayed with me. Seeing a stray cat, I feed it. Coming across a dead dog on the side of the road, I bury it. Most insects can live in my house with impunity, and those I wish to be rid of are simply scooped into a napkin and placed safely outside.

Once, while walking through a field in the dead of winter, the grass and bushes covered with snow, I came upon the bloody footprints of a rabbit. Obviously there was a wounded animal out there somewhere that needed attention. My dear friend Edmund—who would one day become my husband—was with me, and together we followed the red trail on the white snow. For over an hour we diligently followed the path it made, but the animal was not to be found alive or dead and we at last gave up the search.

The seeds laid in childhood sprang forth later in life. My defense of animal life in childhood matured into a deeper defense of life in adulthood. And this is the story I have to tell. As it turned out, I threw myself into the defense of a people nobody wanted, the unborn marked for abortion.

This story begins in 1976, the year I became aware of something called the "Pro-life movement" and takes the reader through 1994—the year that the anti-abortion clinic blockades basically came to an end, an activity that I pioneered, for which I went to court, and for which I served time in jail. Thus this story is a slice of time—an important episode in the history of the anti-abortion movement seen through a narrative microscope. Here you will be taken to the dark places and see things very few people have beheld. You will also be taken to the high places, full of light, when babies were saved and the truth about the dignity of the human being was recognized. Certainly, I expect those who are already active in the pro-life cause, to be attracted to this narrative. This is one of the rare books that presents the issue of abortion through the experience of those who are engaged in the anti-abortion struggle. But I believe that this story will be helpful to those outside the movement, as they will be introduced to pro-life people, see what we did, why we did it, and perhaps, even should they support legalized abortion, come away with a more profound understanding of what is at stake in the abortion war.

As this prologue is written, Barack Obama is the president—a supporter of legalized abortion. Someone else will take his place, but the battle over legalized abortion will continue. After nearly forty years of controversy, it appears that the war over abortion will not come to a quick and easy end. My hope is that this book will shed a light on one of the most desperate moments in the history of the world—a moment in which we have before us that great struggle over life itself and the meaning of human existence.

PART I

RADICAL ACTS

CHAPTER ONE

THE BODIES

I think we are in rats' alley where the dead men lost their bones.
—T. S. Eliot, *The Wasteland*

WE PULLED our cars slowly into the dark alley. Rats scurried before our headlights, frightened by the noise of our intrusion. We parked our three-vehicle caravan in the alley off Monroe Street, near Michigan Avenue in downtown Chicago and stopped in front of a loading dock upon which stood three garbage dumpsters and a filthy blue trash barrel. The address, 30 South Michigan, was crudely painted on the barrel in white lettering. It had rained in the Loop earlier that day, and the alley pavement shone with a slimy oil. We turned off our engines and headlights, paused for a moment, and looked around to make sure no one else was about. The stench of rotting garbage nearly overwhelmed the eight of us as we slowly and quietly got out of our cars. We climbed onto the loading dock, lifted the dumpster lids, and began to sift through the trash. I opened the lid on a bright red dumpster and yanked out a bag of garbage. Peering into the very bottom of the dumpster I saw a bag that was baby blue in color. As I hauled the bag out, I noticed it was heavier than the others. I rested it on the loading dock and opened it. The top of the bag was stuffed with bloody surgical paper, and underneath was a small, heavy cardboard box, about the size of two shoe boxes, sealed in duct tape. I pulled the box out, carefully cradling it in my arms, and placed it in the backseat of one of the cars. We returned the rest of the bags to the dumpster to look as though nothing had been disturbed. As we pulled out of the alley, rats again darted in front of our headlights. One scampered across the top of a dumpster as our car made its way down the wet and oily path and out into the street.

We made the short drive to the northwest side of Chicago and parked our cars outside Joseph Scheidler's garage. I lifted the cardboard box, carried it into the garage, and set it down on a card table beneath a bright utility light. We all gathered around the table and stood in apprehension as the duct tape was carefully peeled off the box and the flaps opened. I peered inside and saw small plastic specimen bags, known as Whirl-Paks, each filled with a dark reddish liquid. We took the bags out and laid them on the table. There were forty-three altogether.

Several bags were marked with a woman's name, age, a date, and two numbers. The smaller number told us the gestational age of the aborted fetus contained within. We thought the other number indicated the amount of abortions performed at the Michigan Avenue Medical Center since the beginning of the year. As of this Saturday night, March 14, 1987, the number was in the three thousands.

On this cool evening, six of us made the midnight run to the alley behind the abortion clinic and then to Joe Scheidler's garage. Joe, the founder and executive director of the Pro-Life Action League, had already attracted national media attention for his passionate, no-nonsense approach to pro-life activism. My successor as executive director of the Illinois Right to Life Committee, Dick O'Connor was there. Peter Krump, a young father of four children who made a living as a carpenter made the trip with us, as had the quiet and reserved Jerry McCarthy. Tim Murphy, clever, quick-witted, and rough around the edges, was there that night, and so was Andy Scholberg, the soft-spoken intellectual. Rudi, who worked at Rush-Presbyterian-St. Luke's Medical Center, was the pathologist in our company. He had many years of experience handling the bodies of aborted and miscarried fetal children, and helped us verify the gestational age of the fetal remains. And then there was me—Monica Migliorino, thirty-four years old, a graduate student, active in the pro-life movement since 1976.

This was the first time I had ever seen the remains of aborted babies. As Rudi examined each of the forty-three bags, he concluded that most of the children were between six and fourteen weeks. Despite the small size of the remains, the tiny hands, feet, ribs, eyes floating free of their sockets, and sometimes even an intact face were plainly visible through the plastic windows of the specimen bags. The body parts loomed up through their murky world of formalin and blood like the inky prophecies of a Magic 8 Ball.

At the very bottom of the box lay an oblong plastic bag, much larger and heavier than the others. I picked it up and held it in my hands to examine it. The bag was stuffed with an unrecognizable material, and the weight of the oddly-shaped parcel made me apprehensive. I turned it over and over in my hands, staring at it, trying to make sense of it. At last my eyes recognized a shape crammed tightly against the plastic. It jumped out at me—an arm, disconnected from anything else that would have helped me see it for what it was. And then my eyes distinguished another arm, and then a severed foot, a full inch in length.

I had been staring at arms but did not see arms. I had no prior context by which my brain could recognize them. They were the dismembered limbs of a completely torn and mutilated body and, up until that day, my eyes had never been confronted with such a reality. It was as if an alien word had been spoken, a word I could not at first fully understand until, after much straining, I finally comprehended the message. Someone was trying to speak to me through the silent, shocking vestige of this broken body.

We took the remains out of the bag, separated the limbs that had become enmeshed in the placenta, and assembled the body parts. The child, a boy, was at least six months gestational age, perhaps older. He had been aborted by the dilation and evacuation, or D&E, method. His body was well-formed, and his red and purple veins were visible through his translucent skin. I began to imagine how Regaldo S. Florendo, the clinic's owner and abortionist, had seen every part of this fetal child's body as he removed him from the womb limb by limb. It seemed as though the clinic wanted to hide this child as he was placed on the bottom of the box, buried beneath others who shared a similar fate. And, unlike his brothers and sisters, not a single piece of identifying information was scribbled on his plastic shroud. His identity, as well as his body, had been effectively concealed. Perhaps Florendo had blundered somehow in the performance of this late-term abortion and, in panic, felt as though he needed to cover it up. Maybe he miscalculated the unborn child's stage of development, started the abortion, and once begun, believed he had no choice but to see the grisly deed completed.

Joe Scheidler was with us in his garage when the shattered remnants of this child were brought to light. Andy Scholberg, who worked for Joe at the Pro-Life Action League, began the process of photographing the body, arranging the torn limbs into a hideous parody of a living baby. Joe stared, transfixed, then said tightly, "I can't look at him anymore." He turned around and went back into the house.

This was not the first night we had retrieved the bodies of aborted children from the garbage dumpster behind the Michigan Avenue Medical Center, and it would not be the last. The retrieval efforts began February 28, 1987, and lasted until April 25. Tim Murphy was responsible for organizing the late-night runs to the alley. In those two months we recovered about six hundred bodies, packed tightly into their cardboard coffins like the ones we had first discovered. Some nights, sometimes twice in a week, Tim went to the alley alone and emerged with a single silver-ducted taped box.

Joe Scheidler found out about the dumpster babies in a most unexpected way. Cas Bogdon, an advertising agent for the abortion clinic who designed its advertisements for the Chicago Yellow Pages, had a falling-out with the clinic management. But Cas knew a secret. He knew that the clinic disposed of the aborted babies in the dumpster behind the building. The disgruntled Cas took his news to Tom Bresler. Tom, a very outgoing, friendly man, a Catholic convert and an ordained deacon, had opened a crisis pregnancy center at 18 South Michigan Avenue, just a few doors north of Florendo's clinic. Bogdon thought pro-lifers might wish to retrieve fetal remains and do some advertising of their own—advertising that would bring negative publicity to the clinic. Tom Bresler made some calls, and a meeting was arranged. Bogdan told Joe Scheidler and Tim Murphy where the bodies could be found.

* * *

I was living in Milwaukee when we first discovered the bodies of the aborted in the 30 South Michigan dumpster, but I had lived in Chicago for eight years before moving to Wisconsin in August of 1985 to pursue a Ph.D. in Theology at Marquette University. I still had many close friends in the Windy City, including Joe Schiedler and others in pro-life circles. While a graduate student at Loyola, I spent countless hours standing in front of the building that housed the Michigan Avenue Medical Center to try to talk women out of abortion—a practice commonly referred to as "sidewalk counseling." Jerry McCarthy had informed me of the discovery of the fetal remains and I decided to join my friends in the Chicago retrievals. Week after week I made the trek from Milwaukee to the alley off Monroe Street to find, in the dead of night, the bodies of aborted babies. My good friend Edmund, a graduate student in English at Marquette who later became my husband, often accompanied me as we sped south along Interstate 94 in his 1973 cream-colored Super Beetle.

I was living an unusual life, digging through trash dumpsters on a Chicago loading dock and picking the bodies of human beings out of the trash. I kept boxes of aborted children, draped with a rosary, in my closet. Edmund and I spent hours painstakingly photographing the tiny, broken corpses. We rented equipment and set up a makeshift photography studio, sometimes in his apartment, sometimes in mine. We knew this was a rare opportunity. We had the remains of the aborted unborn in our own hands and felt it was vital to make a record of legalized abortion. My mind became forever etched with the memory of hundreds of dismembered, broken bodies—their blood, intestines, and torn skin.

I came to know some of those bodies very well in my attempts to get the photographs just right. I named some of the children. The child we found in the oblong bag in Joe Scheidler's garage was named David. Another fetal child, whom I called "Baby Face" was a five-month-old who, from skin tones and facial features, appeared to be black. He or she was killed by the D&E method. But unlike most of the fetal children, the face of this baby was almost entirely intact. Although the baby's lower jaw was gone, and one eyeball was missing from its socket, this was a beautiful, well-formed face.

Nearly as much as the sight of the bodies, the chemical smell of the formalin preservative solution remained in my memory. The aborted babies were packed in a twenty percent solution. The odor was sharp and penetrating; it made my eyes water and irritated my nostrils. Because I often had to be very close to the bodies to photograph them, the inside of my nostrils and sinuses soon became dry and burnt.

Tim Murphy, Peter Krump, Edmund Miller and I sometimes rendezvoused at nine or ten-o'clock on Saturday nights. We met at Blackie's, a bar on the corner of Clark and Balboa at the south end of the Loop, popular with young singles. One Saturday night Edmund, Peter, and I sat at a table at Blackie's waiting for Tim Murphy to arrive. Earlier that week, Tim had gone alone to the dumpster behind the Michigan Avenue Medical Center and retrieved another box of remains. Edmund and I intended to take the box of aborted babies back to Milwaukee and photograph them.

The bar was crowded. Loud music was playing, the heavy rock of the eighties. Tim finally walked into the bar carrying a large paper bag which concealed the familiar smallish, duct-taped cardboard box. Rock singer, Robert Palmer's deep, raspy voice piped into the bar and drowned out our conversation as Tim explained how he had found the box in the dumpster on Wednesday night.

Tim set the paper bag on the table where we were seated. At first we were rather amused by Tim's absolute brazenness. But we soon felt very ill at ease with a box of mutilated body parts sitting on a table in a hip singles bar. The bar was populated by young, attractive men and women, most of them professionals of one kind or another, talking, drinking beer, playing pinball, watching sports, and laughing together. In the midst of all this we sat around a box that contained a secret. It enveloped a silent sorrow and as it lay on a table in this gay and noisy bar, and no one apart from our small group knew it. The aborted unborn bore the weight of their hidden lives and their hidden deaths. I picked up the box and we all stood. Silently we processed in single file out of the bar and into the cool night air. The heavy door closed slowly behind us and the sounds of laughter and music faded away.

CHAPTER TWO

BEGINNING

"Fear not that life shall come to an end, but rather that it shall never have a beginning."

—John Henry Cardinal Newman

M Y PRO-LIFE journey began twelve years before it finally brought me to the edge of a loading dock and face-to-face with the aborted unborn. In January, 1976, I sat in the kitchen of a small, shabby student apartment in Carbondale, Illinois. The following announcement propelled me into the world of abortion:

"Listen, kiddo, I have no intention of keeping this baby."

My friend Sheila's declaration seemed calculated to smash my naïveté.

"Huh?" I said, still determinedly obtuse.

"I'm getting an abortion."

Wrapped in a cranberry-colored bathrobe, Sheila's small frame occupied the chair across the table from me. She looked tired and disheveled. She had been back in the United States for almost three weeks after her month-long trip to Mexico. While I slowly sipped on a mug of instant coffee, she told me about the handsome young man she had met in Mexico City.

"Does he know you're pregnant?" I asked.

"Nope."

"Aren't you going to tell him?"

"Nope," said Sheila with a nervous giggle.

She must have caught the expression of horror that passed over my face.

"Aw, don't worry, Mon. It's not like this is my first abortion, you know." She gave another nervous giggle.

It sometimes seemed that Sheila, knowing my moral sensitivity, took pleasure in saying things that shocked me. Now I was even more distressed. This was new to me. It had never occurred to me that someone would actually have more than one abortion. Frozen with pain and fear, all I could do was utter a faint: "You know, Sheila, I don't think you should do it."

I left her apartment and stood on the dark sidewalk. I felt dazed and suddenly sick to my stomach. My head and heart pounded with the news of an impending death that I felt powerless to prevent. How could one person stop another from having an abortion anyway?

I walked the short block to my own apartment, entered the bedroom without turning on the light, and collapsed on the floor. I begged God that somehow this baby might not die. But I felt lost and helpless, utterly ignorant as to what I could do. The next day Sheila's roommate, Liz, drove her to the Reproductive Health Services Clinic in St. Louis where she aborted her second baby.

Sheila and I were close friends, both theatre majors at Southern Illinois University in Carbondale. When I had arrived there four years earlier, I was eighteen years old, away from home for the first time, dropped into the middle of a decadent place. I came with a shred of innocence and moral sensitivity still left in me from my Catholic upbringing. In 1972 my father drove me to campus and, with tender and fatherly worry, said goodbye to me outside of a tall, modern, sterile-looking structure—a dormitory in a cluster of three on the east side of the SIU campus. I was going to be an actress and, as much as an eighteen-year-old can be, I was consumed by the ambition to become a great and famous one.

Drugs, drinking, casual sex, cohabitation, open homosexuality among students and faculty alike were pervasive in the cultural milieu of the Theatre Department. Abortion was also a part of college life. SIU students provided a steady flow of customers to Reproductive Health Services in St. Louis, fifty miles away. Many of those students were theatre majors who either got abortions there or accompanied friends on the trek to rid themselves of unwanted pregnancies.

In many ways Sheila was the living icon of Carbondale's dissolution. She was a heavy drinker, very foulmouthed and extremely promiscuous. I liked her. We got along in the strange way that opposites occasionally do. Sheila was open, funny, generous, affectionate and pretty. She also had a cynical side, but she tolerated my frequent sermons about her lifestyle. I was sober, quiet, intellectual, and for a time, had even considered a religious vocation. Sheila seemed to enjoy my company precisely because I was so very different from her.

Despite Sheila's abortion, we continued to be friends. A few months later she moved in with an older man who was separated from his wife. Sheila became something very close to a kept woman. Her man, twenty years older than she, gave her all the material things she could want. After Sheila had settled into her new surroundings, I went to visit her at her new apartment outside of Carbondale. We went to lunch at a restaurant nearby, and after a pleasant meal and chat she drove me to her place to pick up my car. While we were driving back, there was a pause in the conversation. Suddenly Sheila spoke.

"You know, Mon, this has been a hard year for me. My grandmother died. She practically raised me. And one of my good friends from high school OD'd on drugs."

She paused again.

"I guess it's true what they say—that death comes in threes."

"What do you mean?" I asked. "Who else died?"

"Well . . . you know . . . my baby."

Sheila's gaze was fixed on the road ahead. I looked at her and then looked away. I didn't know what to say, so I said nothing. But I was amazed that she acknowledged the death of her unborn child. I foolishly thought that the abortion had not affected her in any way—but indeed, like the loss of her grandmother and her friend, Sheila mourned the loss of that unseen child.

*   *   *

In May, 1976, five months after Sheila's abortion, I graduated from SIU with a Bachelor of Science in Theatre. The month before my graduation I went on a two-day retreat at the Newman Center during Holy Week in preparation for Easter. There I met Shirley Parks, who gave a short testimony about her involvement with something called "the pro-life movement." A whole new reality opened up before me about life and death, justice and injustice, and the quest to save the unborn. I became good friends with Shirley. She gave me a number of books about abortion and I embarked on a very different program of education. I was particularly influenced by *Abortion and Social Justice* edited by Thomas Hilgers and Dennis Horan, first published in 1972, a year prior to the Supreme Court's *Roe v. Wade* decision, which, on January 22, 1973, legalized abortion on demand in the United States.

This book peeled away the veil of the womb and introduced me to the hidden world of the unborn child. The first chapter, written by Dr. Bart T. Heffernan, was entitled "The Early Biography of Everyman." The second, written by the "father of fetology," Albert W. Liley, transported me to a reality I never knew existed:

> The prerequisites for motion are the muscles and nerves. In the sixth to seventh week, nerves and muscles work together for the first time. If the area of the lips, the first to become sensitive to touch, is gently stroked the child responds by bending the upper body to one side and making a quick backward motion with his arms. . . . By the beginning of the ninth week, the baby moves spontaneously without being touched. Sometimes his whole body swings back and forth for a few moments. By eight and a half weeks the eyelids and the palms of the hands become sensitive to touch. If the eyelid is

stroked, the child squints. On the stroking of the palm, the fingers close into a small fist.

. . . Every child shows a distinct individuality in his behavior by the end of the third month. This is because the actual structure of the muscles of the face, for example, follows an inherited pattern. The facial expressions of the baby in his third month are already similar to the facial expressions of his parents.

. . . Further refinements are noted in the third month. The fingernails appear. The child's face becomes much prettier. His eyes, previously far apart. now move closer together. The eyelids close over the eyes. Sexual differentiation is apparent in both internal and external sex organs and primitive eggs and sperm are formed. The vocal cords are completed. In the absence of air they cannot produce sound; the child cannot cry aloud until birth, although he is capable of crying long before.

The words of these authors revealed the unseen, silent, yet thoroughly fascinating and dynamic universe of the unborn baby. While I had been opposed to Sheila's abortion, her baby, so impersonal to her, was also impersonal to me. The books Shirley Parks lent me were my formal introduction to the child in the womb. The unborn were now alive and personal to me: living, real, and present. By the time I finished *Abortion and Social Justice* I had become completely aware that to kill an unborn child was to end the life of another *someone*, another self, a person-in-relation to me.

Shirley and I hung around with each other from April of 1976 to September of 1977. We attended several meetings at which I was able to learn the current political strategies to restore to the unborn their right to life. At this point I was really just getting my feet wet. Not until I moved to Chicago would I become an active, front-lines participant in the right-to-life struggle.

Even though I had already graduated from SIU, I stayed on in the small college town for several months afterwards, trying to sort out my life. I was twenty-three years old. For the last two years I had hoped to enter a Discalced Carmelite monastery in Des Plaines,

Illinois, but after much difficult discernment I decided that I was not called to that life. What, then, was I going to do? I decided, for the time being, to go on to study theology. I was accepted into the graduate program at Loyola University of Chicago. So I said goodbye to my wonderful ninety-dollars-a-month, one-bedroom apartment in Carbondale, packed my meager worldly possessions into the back of a bright-yellow 1968 Volkswagen squareback, put my dear black cat Hector into the passenger seat, and headed north for the big city.

In Rogers Park I rented a small, one-room apartment on the basement level of a large, old courtyard building on Loyola Avenue, a block away from the Loyola campus. The apartment had all the aesthetic qualities of a dungeon. It was tucked into the back of the courtyard, and its only source of light was two small windows that hung about three feet above my head. They were too high to look out of, and they let in only the thinnest rays of natural light. The rent was one hundred and twenty-five dollars a month. It was not much of a trade for my old apartment, but Hector made a smooth adjustment from pampered, country-town cat to big-city tom. He would roam the alleys and bring home what looked to be either very large mice or very small rats.

I attended St. Ignatius Church, a Jesuit parish just down the block from my dark, dreary quarters. It was a majestic Romanesque church filled with architectural beauty and graced by original Charles Bosseron Chambers paintings of Mary, Joseph and the infant Jesus at the side altars and Chambers' Stations of the Cross. Outside of special shrines and basilicas, the splendor of this church could only be found in a major city. The church gave the appearance of something true and solid, a kind of stone-and-glass witness to the faith for which it stood. And it was here in this parish, and in this city, that I found an army of true and solid pro-life activists.

I moved to Chicago in October of 1977, and by the end of the year I found myself standing outside Chicago abortion clinics trying to persuade women not to abort their babies. After the *Roe v. Wade* decision, clinics opened virtually overnight and abortion was advertised openly in the Yellow Pages. Many pro-lifers responded by stationing themselves outside of abortion facilities to talk to the women as they arrived for their appointments.

Nearly every Saturday morning I stood on the pavement outside of the Michigan Avenue Medical Center hoping to talk to mothers entering the building. One cold Saturday morning in April of 1978 found me standing alone near the door to the building. I was not dressed warmly enough for the frigid spring air. The chilly Chicago wind whipped my face as I scanned the long, wide sidewalk with apprehension, waiting for customers to arrive. Across the street and a little farther south, I could easily distinguish the giant bronze lions that welcome visitors to the Art Institute of Chicago. I had been doing this for five months, but I wasn't sure that I had ever actually saved any unborn children from the fate that awaited them.

The Michigan Avenue Medical Center was owned by Regaldo S. Florendo. Later that year Florendo would be featured in a *Chicago Sun-Times* exposé entitled "Abortion Profiteers." Authored by Pam Zekman and Pamela Warrick, the sixteen-part series uncovered the unscrupulous practices of abortion providers in a string of Michigan Avenue clinics. Beginning with the headline "Making a killing on Michigan Avenue," the series first hit newsstands on November 12, 1978. It ran for fifteen days, chronicling the lies, greed, callousness, welfare fraud, physical mutilations and even the deaths of women in the business of legalized abortion. The authors were assisted by four undercover investigators from the Better Government Association, who actually took jobs in the clinics. The story was spread across the front page of a paper read by millions. Zekman and Warrick won a Pulitzer for the series.

In the dozens of hours I spent outside of Florendo's clinic I saw him only once. It was a usual Saturday morning when I first caught sight of his slender frame approaching from down the street. As he came closer to the building, he eyed me coldly before walking through the narrow single-door entrance. I recognized him from his picture on the front page of the *Sun-Times*.

Florendo's wife was often at the abortion clinic as well. She was a short, plump, well-dressed woman, cold and utterly humor-less. Once or twice I tried to speak to her. She responded with her delicate oriental features fixed in a mask of stone. I sometimes saw their teenaged children at the clinic along with cousins and in-laws. Their abortion clinic was kind of a family business.

Florendo was born in the Philippines and educated there. He came with his wife and children to America to make his fortune. He put his medical knowledge and skill to work by doing abor-tions, and in the era of *Roe v. Wade*, Florendo *did* make his fortune. He made his home in Kenilworth, the most exclusive suburb of Chicago, and a long way from the poverty he had known in the Philippines.

On this particular April Saturday, rain had fallen the night before, leaving slick patches of ice on the Michigan Avenue side-walk. I anxiously awaited the arrival of Donna Rozewski, my skilled and experienced sidewalk counseling partner.

Finally Donna appeared, harried and flustered, around the cor-ner of Monroe Street. I was relieved to see her. As soon as Donna planted herself next to me, a Yellow Cab pulled up to the curb in front of the building. As the young black woman in the back-seat paid the driver and waited for him to count out her change, Donna and I walked over to the idling car. As soon as the woman got out, Donna handed her a "Life or Death" brochure, a full-color pamphlet crammed with information on fetal development, descriptions of the various abortion procedures, and graphic photos of aborted children. Donna showed the woman the photo of an unborn baby at eight weeks gestation and said, "Did you know the heart of the baby is beating eighteen to twenty-one days past con-ception? And brain waves can be detected as early as six weeks?" A look of horror spread across the woman's face. "God, that's awful! Awful!" she cried as she stared at the photo of a baby aborted at ten weeks, clearly visible in Donna's open pamphlet.

There was a Burger King next door to 30 South Michigan. "Come on," I said, "let's go over to the restaurant and talk. We want to help you—give us a chance." I was astonished, the woman immediately said "Yes, okay!" To us. A pair of complete strangers! We walked into the Burger King and settled into a booth in the least populated part of the restaurant.

The woman's name was Jackie. She was twenty-six years old, unmarried, and already caring for a ten-year-old daughter. She lived in South Bend, Indiana, and had taken the South Shore train to Chicago. While Donna continued to talk with Jackie I went to the counter and ordered three coffees. When I returned, Jackie was in tears. "I don't believe it," she said, dabbing her eyes with a paper napkin. "When I was in the cab I prayed to God—'send me a sign if you don't want me to get this abortion'—and as soon as I get out of the cab, there you are! Man, that's something!"

I knew as I sat in the booth listening to Jackie that other women were coming to Florendo's clinic and no one else was out on the sidewalk to talk to them. Knowing that Jackie was in Donna's very capable hands, I went back outside. Three women arrived for their appointments within fifteen minutes. Each one ignored everything I said to them and refused the pamphlet. In another fifteen minutes two more women arrived, each accompanied by a young man. I tried to say something about the humanity of their babies, and that they might come to regret their decision. One of the men took the "Life or Death" brochure I held out to him. He angrily tore it into several pieces and flung it back at me. "Mind your own shit!" he said as he and the woman went through the glass door.

Caught by a gust of Chicago wind, the shredded pieces of the pamphlet fluttered down the sidewalk. At that moment a sudden vision of what was happening upstairs sprang into my mind: A woman was lying on the operating table, her feet in the stirrups, ready for her abortion. Florendo, expressionless, was seated at the end, removing her child from her womb piece by piece.

The bits of paper were driven into the street by the wind. They scattered across the pavement. Abortions were happening right now, right there, six floors above my head. Gripped by a horrid sense of frustration and urgency, I said to myself: "Go! Go in. Go in the building. Go upstairs and try again. Try to talk them out of it. Why are you afraid? What do you have to lose? I turned around, yanked open the single glass door, and crossed what had been, to my mind, a forbidden threshold. I went through the tiny foyer of the building, entered the main lobby, and headed straight for the elevators. Two young black men in security guard uniforms were there. As soon as I got close enough, one of them grabbed me around the waist, yanked me off my feet, backed himself out of the inner door, then through the glass entry door, and heaved me onto the sidewalk. I stumbled but managed to catch my balance on the icy pavement. I was hit by a wave of humiliation. I turned around and stared at him in amazement. He stood on the other side of the glass door, breathing heavily but holding it firmly shut against reentry.

I shouted at him in my frustration. "Babies are being butchered upstairs! Don't you care? You're helping the murder of those babies." This was the first time I had ever said such a thing to anyone associated with an abortion clinic. The guard stared at me in silence, still holding the door shut. I retreated back into the Burger King, where, still trembling from the experience, I slumped into the booth next to Jackie and burst into tears. I explained what had just occurred. Jackie looked at me with concern and sympathy and put her arm around me. The counseled became the counselor. With a reassuring smile she said, "Don't feel bad about all that, honey. I'm keeping this baby."

Later that day I rode the El back to Rogers Park. I was lost in thought as the noisy train curved behind apartment buildings, past Wrigley Field, past Graceland Cemetery. I pondered what had just happened outside of the Michigan Avenue Medical Center. Today I knew a baby had been saved—rescued. It seemed unreal—a life delivered from death. I savored Jackie's words: "I'm keeping this baby." I felt a strange lightness. Suddenly I found myself transported back to the night I had sat in Sheila's kitchen. The sound of her words echoed in my brain: "Listen, kiddo, I have no intention of keeping this baby." Sheila's baby was forever gone. But somehow I felt Jackie's words unraveled the death of that child.

CHAPTER THREE

RAPHAEL

"Anyway, I keep picturing all these little kids playing some game in this big field of rye and all. Thousands of little kids, and nobody's around—nobody big, I mean—except me. And I'm standing on the edge of some crazy cliff. What I have to do, I have to catch everybody if they start to go over the cliff—I mean if they're running and they don't look where they're going I have to come out from somewhere and catch them. That's all I'd do all day. I'd just be the catcher in the rye and all. I know it's crazy, but that's the only thing I'd really like to be. I know it's crazy."

—J. D. Salinger, *Catcher in the Rye*

DONNA and I had met each other on a bleak winter day in February, 1978, only a few months before we counseled Jackie at the Michigan Avenue Medical Center. Marcita Hecht, a fellow parishioner of St. Ignatius, invited me to attend what she described as "a very special pro-life meeting" at the Illinois Right to Life Committee. I did not know what the meeting was about, but I assumed it involved some sort of important pro-life initiative, so I told her I would go. With a handful of other St. Ignatius parishioners, Marcita and I took the El train to the Chicago Loop, then walked a short distance to the historic Monadnock building on Jackson Street. There was no way I could know that the invitation of this kindly, spinsterish woman would turn out to be the real starting point of nearly all my pro-life activist work in the years to come. I was headed to a gathering that would forever change how I perceived my place in society, my sense of self-sacrifice, and my view of civil law. Moreover, I was about to enter the ground floor of one of the most significant dimensions of the right-to-life movement—a form of activism that would stir the most controversy and thus attract the most attention to the pro-life cause for years to come.

I walked into a spacious conference room where about thirty people had already gathered. A largely-built, very tall man with a well-trimmed beard stood in front of a row of seats. Behind him was a green portable chalkboard. Marcita leaned over to me and said in a low voice, "That's Joe Scheidler." This was the first time I had ever seen him. Joe was the executive director of the Illinois Right to Life Committee.

I soon learned that Joe had called the meeting to plan a sit-in at a Chicago abortion clinic. In Joe's mind, the pro-life sit-in was a strategy whose time had come. In the pro-life movement, thus far, it was a tactic that remained untried on a large scale, but it had worked for civil rights activists across the country, and we all firmly believed that the pro-life movement was essentially a civil rights cause. But our goal was not merely civil disobedience. We didn't believe that the pro-life sit-in was simply a protest or a symbolic action. It was intended to save the lives of the unborn.

"They've been done in D.C. and St. Louis," said Joe. "It's an effective way to save babies and I think we should do one here. Also, there's something else to consider. We want to establish that the unborn baby is a person, same as you and me, and we can do that once we get to court. We've got to challenge abortion in the courts. When we go into court, we say that the law had to be broken to save human life. It's called a defense of necessity, and we can bring in all kinds of photos and movies on fetal development. The unborn will have their day in court. *Roe v. Wade* said the unborn child is not a person. When we go to court we will reveal their personhood—show their humanity."

Many of those present were excited about doing a sit-in. The idea was new. It was bold. We were encouraged by the thought that our court case would be a forum to chip away at the law that denied the unborn their right to life. Joe explained what had been done in the few sit-ins that pro-lifers had conducted in other cities. Protesters entered the abortion facilities and sat or stood in front of the doorways or halls to the procedure rooms. With arms locked together they would not permit women, staff members, or the doctor into that area of the clinic. Anyone inside the procedure rooms when the sit-in began would be allowed back through the human shield-wall, but nobody was allowed into the rooms. If any women were in the waiting room, two or three designated pro-lifers would speak to them in the hope of persuading them out of their decision to abort.

Joe paused for a moment. "If we're going to do this, we need people who are willing to risk being arrested. You have to know that there is a definite possibility of spending some time in jail. Is anyone here willing to take that chance?"

Nine hands went up, including mine. It seemed that blocking clinic doors was a natural response to the impending murder of human lives. I wanted to be a part of this action. Perhaps my youthful zeal and idealism drowned out my doubts, but oddly I was not particularly anxious over the possibility of arrest. After all, I was only twenty-four years old and unmarried. I had no major family responsibilities to hold me back. Little did I realize that the decision I made that day would decide the course of my pro-life journey. Fifteen years later it would not be so easy when, married and with two small children, I would serve a lengthy jail term for similar activity.

But today things were much less complicated. Filled with optimism that our sit-in could save lives and contribute to social change, I was excited to be a part of the first pro-life sit-in held in Chicago. But an important question remained: which clinic would it be? Most of those at the meeting were seasoned sidewalk counselors. As a relative new-comer to pro-life work, I listened as others discussed the pros and cons of the various physical layouts of downtown abortion clinics. Most of them wanted to do the first sit-in at the Concord Medical Center at 17 West Grand Avenue, just west of State Street. The clinic had a storefront-type entrance which would make getting inside a swift and simple operation. Also, some noted that Concord was a "high-volume" clinic, and did a large number of abortions on Saturday. One woman stated that she had counted twenty-two women entering the clinic that very morning.

Concord Medical Center was actually located below ground level and was accessible by a staircase immediately off the clinic's street entrance. The procedure rooms were situated down a hall that led directly from the center of the waiting room. We planned to position ourselves at the entrance to the hall to block access to the rooms. It was agreed that the sit-in would take place on Saturday March 11, 1978, just one month away.

When the meeting was over, people hung around to chat over doughnuts and coffee. Marcita introduced me to Joe. He held a Styrofoam cup filled with coffee in his left hand and shook my hand with his right. His six-foot, four-inch frame loomed over me. He smiled and looked at me intensely with his bright sky-blue eyes. "Welcome to Chicago!" he boomed in a jovial tone. He asked what brought me to the city, and I told him about my graduate studies at Loyola University. "Loyola!" he said. "I used to teach journalism at Mundelein College, you know, right next to Loyola. I even met my wife Ann there."

Someone else came up to introduce himself to Joe. I turned and saw a young, heavyset woman who wore wide-rim glasses and whose thick black hair was pulled behind her head into a bun. She wore a flowing dress with a delicate flower print. The whole effect gave her the vague aura of a flower child left over from the sixties.

Marcita noticed I was looking at the woman.

"That's Donna Rosewski," Marcita said softly. "She had an abortion but now she's an active pro-lifer. She even became a Catholic a few years ago."

Marcita was eager to introduce me to Donna. She told me that Donna was a "sidewalk counselor," and was one of the very first people in the nation to do this sort of work. Donna was also the co-founder of a group called Women Exploited. Known as WE, the organization operated as a support group for women who came to regret their abortion. Donna and her group believed that abortion not only victimized the unborn but attacked the intrinsic dignity of women as well. WE became the prototype for the later and much larger post-abortive women's groups such as Women Exploited by Abortion, Victims of Choice, and the Silent No More Awareness Campaign.

Donna and I became fast friends. We got together several times in the weeks following the meeting at the Illinois Right to Life Committee. We especially liked going out to eat at restaurants in downtown Chicago. After one such meal we decided to stroll along the Chicago lakefront. It was chilly, but the waves of Lake Michigan were calm. They gently lapped the shore as we walked along the densely packed sand. It was on this evening that Donna told me about her abortion experience.

"My boyfriend's name was Raphael. He was Mexican—born there. It's because of him that I became interested in Hispanic culture and learned to speak his language. I loved him, and we had intercourse—once! And wouldn't you know it—I got pregnant from just that one time. He was scared. He didn't really want the baby. I had a roommate who said abortion was the best thing. My mother was totally against my having the baby because she thought that a baby would keep me from getting an education and having a good career."

Donna told me that she and Raphael went to the Concord Medical Center together. It was 1975. The clinic had opened its doors only a few weeks after the 1973 *Roe v. Wade* decision. A *Chicago Sun-Times* article reported on the clinic's opening, stating: "The facility is clean and bright and reassuring-looking: the walls and furniture are done in soft pastel colors, and the center looks more like a brand new suburban school than the stereotype of a place where abortions are done."

The *Chicago Daily News* also ran an article about Concord in its October 20–21, 1973 editions, praising the care women received there and comparing it to another Chicago abortion center, Midwest Population, on the Loop's north end. While Midwest Population was described as "sleazy" and "informal," Concord was described as "bright, color-coordinated," "lavish," and "surgically antiseptic":

> The physician scrubs his hands and arms between each abortion and then puts on a new pair of sterile gloves, just as surgeons do in hospital operating rooms. At the Midwest clinic gloves are changed but doctors don't scrub between abortions. At Concord, the plastic hose attached to the vacuum aspirator used in abortions and its plastic tip are discarded after each use. At Midwest, they are washed in disinfectant and re-used.

The clinic—located in the basement level of the building that housed it—seemed plain and utilitarian to Donna on the day she descended the stairs and entered the large waiting room. Every seat was taken. Donna stood at the counter and filled out the intake form. She checked the box that indicated she was not sure if she wanted an abortion. She was hoping to receive at least some counseling before she made her decision.

"I wanted to know how abortion might affect me physically and mentally and I wanted to know if the fetus was human," Donna explained to me with bitterness in her voice. "But before I received any counseling Raphael and I had to pay for the abortion. My blood was drawn, and I was told to undress, and they gave me a hospital gown and those paper slippers to wear. I was prepped for an abortion I wasn't even sure I wanted! Then they took me into a counseling room with seven other women

"We were treated like guinea pigs. The whole manner of treating their patients was to make the woman unthinkingly follow one step after another. I felt like they didn't want me to think, like the whole process was designed to inhibit thinking about what you're doing. Their attitude was one of 'Now let's behave properly,' as if we had been naughty children who had done something wrong and now we were going through the necessary surgery to clear up the problem we had caused. They acted like, 'Let's get this done as fast as possible with no complications, no complaining.'"

The group of waiting patients was given a short lecture by a woman who told them she had had an abortion herself. She described the mechanics of the surgery.

Donna continued: "The counselor said, 'Abortion is simple. A tube is inserted and you'll feel a gentle suction. Afterwards you can lie down for a while and then go home.' She never mentioned any possible physical complications except for 'you can expect a little cramping—something like menstrual cramps.' Of course, no mention was made of the baby whatsoever."

"I listened as if I was alienated from her and from everything else. I felt like I could not talk with this counselor. I felt intimidated by her detached manner and matter-of-fact approach to abortion. This woman was not a counselor. She was not sympathetic to my problem. She showed no compassion toward us even though she'd had an abortion. But what could I do? I couldn't go back. I couldn't say no. There I was in my gown ready for an abortion. It's hard to explain—once you're in there, you don't get out. You're there. What's the answer? If you leave, what do you do?

"I felt very vulnerable and very alone. Raphael didn't want the baby and I was too afraid of disappointing my parents to back out. Most of the blame is mine. I didn't have the courage to go on with the pregnancy."

Donna first saw the doctor who performed the abortion when she was lying on the surgical table, even though she had already signed a form that said, *I have seen the doctor and he has explained the abortion procedure to me.*

"When the doctor finally did come into the room," Donna told me, "one of the first things he said to me was, 'Who was your partner in crime?' I told him, 'My husband.' I did not want him to think I was not married. He gave me a strange look, as though he somehow disapproved of abortions for married couples.

"The abortion was extremely painful. I grasped the nurse's hand in a vice-like grip. She said 'My goodness but you're upset.' I moved on the table because it hurt so much. I wondered if the doctor waited long enough for the anesthetic to take effect."

"It was over in a few minutes. I got off the table. I could hardly walk. I was hanging on to the nurse. They put me in a bed. I couldn't move. I felt paralyzed from the waist down. I was in a state of total shock. While the abortion was happening it finally hit me—I was destroying my baby. The clinic was piping music from some radio station into the room. The music was low, but I remember it distinctly. How absurd it all was." Donna gave a short, bitter laugh and shook her head. "They were playing 'Stairway to Heaven.'"

We had already walked a long distance and decided to sit down on the cold sand. For a few moments we just listened to the sound of the waves and watched them creep up and retreat from the shore. Donna then said, "I know that if only one person had talked to me, calmed my fears, and extended a helping hand, I would not have killed my unborn child." Donna knew that many post-abortion support groups recommended, as a part of the healing process, that a woman give a name to her aborted child. Donna named her baby Raphael.

Donna's experience with abortion drove her into the arms of the pro-life movement. But other post-abortive women, some whose experiences were very much like Donna's, went in the entirely opposite direction.

A year after Donna had her abortion, Susan Wicklund, who also felt she was not ready to have a baby, had an abortion at a Portland, Oregon clinic. She might as well have had it at Concord, as her experience is a near mirror-image of Donna's. In her autobiography *This Common Secret: My Journey as an Abortion Doctor*, Wicklund recounts the day of her abortion:

> The first thing they wanted in the tiny office was my money. Pay in advance, all of it, in cash. I was so frightened and unaware. What was supposed to happen? No counseling took place, no explanation of procedures or options: no one tried to understand my circumstances or my questions.

In another tiny room the nurse told me to undress and lie down on the table.

"What are you doing?" I wanted to know.

"Just be still," she said. She sat in front of me and put a cold speculum into my vagina. I could feel tugging and pulling, but no real pain. She was done quickly, took out the speculum, and then told me to get dressed.

"Am I done?" I asked.

"Done?" she slapped the words at me. "No. I just put something in your cervix that will make it open up for the abortion. You should leave now and come back at three this afternoon."

. . . When we returned the same woman took me back to the small room, again had me get undressed and used the speculum to examine me. She removed something she had put inside me earlier, but was impatient with me when I asked questions.

I was moved into a much larger room. It seemed huge, filled with machines and trays of exposed instruments and syringes and needles. Two other women came in. They had me strip naked, lie on a table, and put my feet in stirrups. They put a paper sheet over my upper body and told me to lie still. Then all three of them walked out. No advice, no preparatory explanation, no squeeze of the hand. For a long time I lay there in that vast, cold room, utterly exposed and as vulnerable as I'd ever been in my life.

Finally the door opened, and a very large man, the doctor, came towards me. . . .

He said nothing, didn't even tell me his name, asked no questions, but abruptly started to work. . . .

"What are you doing?" I asked. "Please tell me what you are doing!"

I could feel instruments inside me, a harsh invasion and pain I hadn't expected. "Is it supposed to hurt?" I pleaded.

"Shut up and lie still!" His voice was rough, angry, as if I had no right to intrude. I started to squirm away from him, trying to make him stop long enough to talk to me. . . .

> He called for nurses to hold me down. . . . I writhed and
> fought as nurses grabbed my arms and shoulders. I heard
> myself scream. . . .
> They injected something into my arm, and I faded away
> from the nightmare. . . .

When Susan awoke and was ready to leave, the only advice she
was given as she walked out the door was that she could go to an
emergency room if she experienced any problems. She explains:
"Something very terrible had been done to me. I felt abused and
violated and beaten."

Several years after her abortion Susan decided to enter the
medical profession and she vowed that what had happened to her
would never happen to other women. To avenge her own nightmare she committed herself to doing abortions full-time to ensure
that women would be treated with dignity and respect.

While Donna's abortion took her outside the clinic to persuade women not to enter, Susan's took her inside the clinic where
she confirmed women in their decision to abort. How could two
women with such similar experiences end up fighting on opposite
sides of the abortion war? Donna realized: "When the abortion was
happening it finally hit me that I was destroying my baby." Susan
reasoned: "I had been about eight weeks pregnant when I had my
abortion . . . an eight-week embryo is about the size of a thumb-
nail. It cannot feel pain or think or have any sense of being. I have
never regretted that abortion." When Susan had her abortion she
believed there was no baby, there was no life, there was no *someone*,
no personal *other* with whom she had a connection.

How different was Susan's attitude toward Sonya, her daughter to whom she gave birth a few years after the abortion. Indeed,
Susan's entire birth-experience was the complete opposite of her
abortion nightmare. She wrote: "In stark contrast to my abortion
experience, during Sonya's birth I was surrounded by people I loved
and who loved me."

The essence of giving life through birth is family, community, the end of isolation. Susan wrote of her unborn child, whom she did not want, as merely tissue "with no sense of being" with whom she had "not felt attached." Donna, however, knew she was somehow attached to the life growing within her, that she was actually destroying the life of her baby.

Donna was driven to abortion primarily because there was no encouragement to keep the baby by her boyfriend, family, or friends. She felt trapped into an abortion. Now her Saturday mornings were spent standing outside of the Concord Medical Center, trying to be that voice and helping hand, trying to spare women the same anguish she experienced.

In 1976, while I was just being introduced to pro-life work, Donna's commitment to the unborn would be seriously tried.

One Saturday at Concord, Donna persuaded a woman to stop and talk with her. They stood across the street from the clinic as Donna explained to the woman the stages of fetal development. A tall, thin woman with a lean face, who was dressed in a white lab coat came out of the clinic and walked across the street. It was Ruth Osgood, who worked at the clinic as an assistant manager and counselor. Ruth knew that Donna had come to her clinic for an abortion a year earlier.

Toting a clipboard and a pen, she planted herself firmly a few feet away from Donna. Every time Donna said something to the woman, Ruth scratched something down on the clipboard. Donna was annoyed, but she did not want to be distracted and continued to speak with the woman. After a few minutes of her note-taking, Ruth suddenly strode forward and wedged herself between Donna and the abortion-bound woman.

"What are you trying to do here, Ruth?" said Donna. "This woman and I were talking." Donna nudged Ruth out of the way, trying to maintain her conversation with the woman, who was by now completely bewildered that two people were fighting over her. Lured by the authority of the clipboard, lab coat, and Ruth's reassuring hand on her shoulder, the woman turned her back on Donna and walked across the street and through the clinic door.

Donna stood alone, outraged but resigned to the loss. She walked across the street and stood outside the clinic to wait for another woman to arrive. Within minutes a squad car and police van pulled up to the curb. Two officers got out of the vehicles.

"Are you Donna Rozewski?" one officer asked her.

"Yes," Donna replied, slightly apprehensive.

"You're under arrest for assault and battery," the officer stated. He grabbed Donna's wrists, pulled them behind her back, and handcuffed her.

"What are you doing?" Donna shrieked. "I didn't assault anyone!"

"The lady in the clinic says you did."

Donna was escorted to the back of the police van and told to climb in. Humiliated, she stumbled inside.

"Why don't you listen to my side of the story? Are you just going to take the word of the abortion worker?" Donna asked as the policeman began to close the wagon doors.

"She made a complaint against you," the officer explained.

"Well, maybe I'll make one against her," Donna muttered, not knowing what else to say as the officer secured the doors and shut her in the darkness. Donna heard the other officer get into the driver's seat. In another moment the engine rumbled loudly, and with a jolt the van began its noisy, bumpy ride to the Chicago police station at 13th and State. She was escorted to a cell and subjected to a strip search. Three hours later she was released and given a court date.

Several weeks before the trial, Donna did indeed file a complaint of disorderly conduct against Ruth. On the day of the trial, in the hallway outside of the courtroom, the Chicago city prosecutor told Donna that the charge against her would be dropped if she agreed to withdraw her complaint against Ruth. Donna agreed, and walked out of the courtroom with a deep sense of sadness. The whole episode was an absurd game. She was, of course, relieved that the charges against her were dropped, but she had already paid a price in time, fear and humiliation. Nonetheless, Donna had won the respect of every pro-lifer in town. She was one of the first people in the nation arrested for trying to save the unborn. As we planned the Concord sit-in, Donna's experience proved very valuable. As the only member of our group ever arrested she coached the rest of us on what to expect.

* * *

Ted Moran was tall, lean and almost always angry. As a security guard for Concord Medical Center, he took his job very seriously. In front of pro-lifers he put on a show of bravado. He seemed to love the badge, the cap, the dark blue uniform that came with the job. On Saturday mornings he would often strut back and forth in the small courtyard space in front of the clinic or stand near the door with his arms crossed in front of his chest, his shallow face cast in a menacing expression.

But on the morning of March 11, 1978, he was caught off guard. Twenty-seven pro-lifers managed to get past him into the clinic, descend the staircase that led to the waiting room, and block the hallway to the procedure rooms. We assembled ourselves four ranks deep and plugged the hall with our bodies. I stood in the rear of the group huddled between Rosy Stokes, a plump good-natured Irish woman, and Carol Makita, a divorced single mother of four.

Donna stood at the head of the human wall. Here in this very room she had awaited her own abortion and, like that day, every seat in the waiting room was taken. She held a leaf of notebook paper, and I saw that her hands trembled. But it was with a steady voice, full of conviction, that she addressed the women assembled for their abortions:

> My name is Donna and I know how you feel. I had an abortion at this very same clinic three years ago. I cannot begin to tell you the pain and hurt I have suffered since that day. All of us here want to spare you that hurt. Maybe you find this hard to believe, but we care about you. That's why we are here today.

We ask you, we beg you not to kill your children. We ask this clinic to stop killing children. I know from my personal experience with abortion that this clinic will not tell you the truth. This clinic will not tell you the truth about your baby and it will not tell you the truth about the real consequences of abortion—the tears, the anguish, the guilt, the loss that you will feel when that baby is taken from your body. We are here to help you—please let us help you.

Donna walked over to a couple and began to talk with them. I too made my way into the waiting room. The women—some with boy-friends, some with husbands, others who had come alone, appeared nervous, embarrassed and uncomfortable. I felt their vulnerability. I tried to pass out the "Life or Death" pamphlet. One woman took it. I tried to speak with another woman, but her boyfriend held up his hand. "She's got nothin' to say to you—leave us alone."

I saw Donna talking with a woman in Spanish. The woman seemed to be listening. I decided to return to the group. As I crossed the waiting room Ruth Osgood was on the phone and I heard her say "Our clinic has been invaded by protesters. They won't leave and they're upsetting the women." About twenty minutes later police arrived, arrests were made, and we spent the day in jail.

The sit-in attracted enormous media attention. That evening we were the lead story on several Chicago television stations and stories appeared the next day in the major Chicago papers. A cor-ner had been turned in the direction of the pro-life movement and I had certainly turned a corner in my own life. The sit-in experience cemented my commitment to saving the unborn as if I had endured a kind of initiation that would mark me forever. I was disappointed that the women in the waiting room hadn't listened to me, but I felt that I had, nonetheless, confronted abortion in the very place where it occurred. I had crossed boundaries—not only legal, but social and cultural—boundaries that protected the practice of abor-tion. While standing with my arms locked with Rosy and Carol's, I was very aware that, as long as I could maintain my position, my presence was a barrier to the deaths of the unborn.

*   *   *

After that day, Donna and I became a sidewalk counseling team. Not only did we frequently sidewalk-counsel at the Michigan Avenue Medical Center, but many Saturday mornings found us outside of Concord.

On one such morning, only two weeks after the sit-in, Donna and I arrived at the clinic. As usual Ted Moran stood outside. The sit-in at Concord made him even more hostile and sarcastic toward us. As Donna and I approached the building, he eyed us coldly. I knew he detested us, but I decided to talk to him anyway. I naively hoped that we could have a real human conversation. I thought that Ted, and other clinic staff, believed that pro-lifers only cared about the unborn child and did not care about the woman, that we had no concern for the woman's own personal problems, that in this way we were merely zealots.

Ted moved to where the edge of the courtyard met the sidewalk. He leaned against the end of the black wall and stuffed his hands into his front trouser pockets. I stepped over to him while Donna kept her eye on the sidewalk.

"Hey, Ted. Let's talk," I said in as friendly a tone as I could.

"I ain't got nothin' to say to you. I'm here to protect this clinic from people like you."

"We're here to offer women help."

"No, you're not. You make the women feel guilty—you stick your nose in their private business. Once a woman came here who needed an abortion or she was gonna die and you guys harassed her too. You don't think a woman should have an abortion no matter what the situation."

"Here's the problem, Ted," I tried to explain. "You don't think the unborn baby is worth anything—no matter *what* the situation."

"You know what you are?" Ted responded seething with hostility and anger. "You're terrorists!"

"Terrorists!" I exclaimed. This was the first time I heard that word applied to pro-life activists. Not until years later would advocates of legalized abortion routinely refer to pro-lifers this way. Apparently Ted was ahead of his time.

"You terrorize women, You show them bloody pictures of dead fetuses, for God's sake. That's a terrorist tactic!"

"We are here to help women—and tell them the truth about abortion."

"The women who come here have a right not to be bothered by you."

"Ted, would you feel the same way about us if these women were killing babies already born?"

Ted's response to my question was very strange.

"Just flush them down the toilet and be done with it."

Ted did not make it clear whether he was referring to the born or the unborn. He then continued: "You condemn women. Maybe if you were more polite, more of these women would listen to you."

"I try to be as kind as I can. We're not perfect. Maybe we sometimes say things that aren't right. But Ted, I really try hard to be kind."

"Oh, sure," his voiced dripped with sarcasm, "You're good Christians and you love everybody. So why don't you get in bed, get f-----, and don't bother us. Besides you're not only terrorists, you're criminals. You broke the law. You got arrested. These women are acting within the law. What the clinic does is legal—but you're a law-breaker. You should be in prison and I'm gonna do what I can to put you there."

I looked at Ted. He flared his nostrils and shut his lips tightly together. We stared at each other for a few seconds. He folded his arms across his chest and leaned against the black wall.

"You know if you keep coming around here something bad is gonna happen to you. If you want to be a martyr then just keep coming around."

"What do you mean?" I asked.

"If you break the law again, I'll be sure you become a martyr."

Ted unfolded his arms, pushed himself away from the wall and walked into the abortion clinic. I didn't have the conversation I had hoped for and now perhaps things were worse than ever. I tried not to be discouraged and joined Donna who had by now stationed herself several feet east of the clinic.

She was the first to notice the large blue van parked at the curb. A Hispanic couple sat in the front seat. We quickly walked over to the vehicle. By the time we reached it, the man had gotten out of the van and stood on the sidewalk, waiting for the woman to emerge. Donna, speaking to them in Spanish, learned that their names were Marcello and Irene. I started to talk with Marcello, who spoke English fairly well. "The doctor told her she cannot have anymore children," Marcello explained. "She had an abortion a year ago because she was too sick."

Marcello and Irene, immigrants from Mexico, were in their early thirties. They had six daughters; the eldest was fourteen years old, and the youngest six. They were both very religious people; they came from a country that was culturally Catholic but had been, like many others in the Chicago Hispanic community, successfully proselytized by Pentecostals. Irene's last abortion seemed to still weigh on Marcello's conscience. "She had to have it," he told me. "The doctor said her life was in danger. I don't like it. I know abortion is wrong. It's murder. But the doctor said she had to have it."

Donna and I persuaded the couple to come with us to Kamar's, a small, greasy-spoon at the corner of Grand and State. The four of us settled into a booth by the window and ordered coffee. Irene was a quiet woman. As Donna spoke with them, I studied her face. She never smiled. She had a somber look, and her complexion was pale and blotchy. It troubled me that she seemed unhappy.

Marcello, on the other hand, was talkative and extroverted. We hoped to convince Irene and Marcello to cancel the abortion they had planned for that day and at least give Irene a chance to be seen by another physician.

Marcello explained: "My wife was very sick in the last pregnancy—she had to be in bed all the time."

Perhaps it was the language barrier, but Marcello never really explained the nature of Irene's illness except that she was constantly nauseated. "Come on," I persuaded. "Certainly your baby is worth the time to see another doctor."

They agreed to wait and see a pro-life doctor whom we recommended. "Confia en Dios—trust God," Donna said to them before they left. They climbed back into the van and drove away.

In the following weeks Donna and I kept in close contact with Marcello and Irene. For the next two months of her pregnancy Irene was again ill with nausea and fatigue. But into the fifth month the sickness and fatigue passed. There was certainly nothing life-threatening about the pregnancy. Following only two hours in labor, Irene gave birth to their seventh child. On a Sunday afternoon Donna and I went to the neighborhood where the family lived, a Hispanic community on Chicago's south side. The eldest daughter opened the door to their flat and welcomed us. The smell of fresh sausage cooking on the stove greeted us as we walked through the door. The apartment was cozy and well-kept.

I peered into the small kitchen where Marcello, Irene, and their five other daughters sat around the kitchen table. Marcello rose and came into the living room, followed closely by Irene.

Marcello's whole face was lit by a joyful, radiant smile. He was giddy with laughter as he hopped from one foot to the other, appearing not to stand but rather to levitate over the floor. I had never seen a happier human being.

"Come, come see the baby," he said as he led us to a small room off the living room. Inside was a white bassinet which cradled the sleeping baby. "This is our son!" Marcello exclaimed, flashing a large smile full of teeth. Irene, in her quiet way, looked at her son with a serene, happy expression. It was the first time I had seen her smile. She appeared content, filled with the deep, warm satisfaction of having brought this boy into the world.

I glanced over at Donna. She could not take her eyes off the sleeping baby. She seemed to study him, and her eyes were moist with tears. The sight of the baby took her back to the day she passed through the door of Concord. The child she had left there seemed to have come back to her. Marcello and Irene named him Raphael.

CHAPTER FOUR

ABORTION AND THE EL TRAIN ADS

"Power is not only what you have, but in what your enemy thinks you have."

—Saul Alinsky, *Rules for Radicals*

I STOOD on the old wooden platform of the Howard elevated train line at the Loyola stop and waited for the train to arrive. I was headed for my evening theology class at the Loyola Water Tower campus located at the north end of the Loop. It was April, 1979. It had been over a year since our arrest at Concord and six months since the short, even perfunctory bench trial that took place in Cook County Circuit court. Our attorney Carmen Speranza planned it that way. We had asked for a defense of necessity—the common law defense whereby conduct that would otherwise be considered criminal is justified as necessary to avoid a public or private injury. For example, in case of fire, a person could break into a private residence in order to conduct a rescue. This person would not be guilty of breaking and entering, even if he had to smash a window or break down a door to get inside the burning building. Furthermore, the defense did not require that a threat to life actually exist—only that the defendant had a reasonable belief that such a threat did exist. In short, the law permitted a legal transgression for the sake of preventing a greater evil.

Carmen predicted that the lower court would deny us this defense; thus, he placed all of his legal strategy into winning a reversal on appeal, and he was confident that we would prevail. Meanwhile, we were sentenced to a lenient six months court supervision. That sentence had come to an end at the beginning of April. I was frustrated by the conviction and the delay, yet all of us remained very hopeful that we—and most importantly—the unborn would have our "day in court." The court supervision in no way interfered with my sidewalk counseling efforts—and this activity had become my principle pro-life routine—but, as I rode the El that day, this routine was about to be disturbed.

I enjoyed riding the El trains in Chicago. I looked forward to the free time to read a book or to have the rhythm of the train rock me into a light nap. Riding the El was actually a way for me and many other Chicagoans to chill out as the business day paused while we were transported from one destination to the next. On this particular Thursday, I ascended the stairs to the platform and stopped dead in my tracks. I felt as though someone had just punched me in the face. Standing before me was a large blue signboard. On it was written "Albany Women's Medical Services," and it advertised a "full-service reproductive health clinic." While the facility hid behind euphemism, I knew Albany was an abortion clinic located on Elston Avenue. My mind was punctured by the thought that murder was being peddled on the El lines.

While my gaze was still fixed on the poster, the train arrived. The doors of the car folded open in front of me and, in a trance, I walked through and flopped down in a seat by a window. I turned my head. Out of the window I could still see the sign: stiff, immovable; it seemed to mock me. When the Howard El approached the Loop, it plunged its riders into a deep dark hole and, underground now, the cars twisted us through dank tunnels hidden in the bowels of the city. The Albany signs had been posted at nearly every stop along the line—even in the subway, the posters were hung at each of the stops. Here they were pasted up on metal backboards affixed to the walls of the tunnels. Feeling as if a legion belonging to the enemy had defiantly invaded the town, I thought to myself, *How would we get them?* I was already plotting a way to destroy the abortion clinic's advertising venture. The signs on the elevated portion of the line could be simply blotted out with the old-fashioned spray paint method. A sign could be painted out quickly and easily in the darkness of night, as long as no one was standing nearby.

But the use of spray paint would not be a swift enough method of obliterating the signs on the subway walls. A person standing across the track would be out in the open and easily seen by others who might come along to wait for the train. Some means of blotting out the sign, something that would only take seconds, would have to be devised. I thought of pasting pro-life flyers over the name of the clinic and the clinic's phone number, but it would be far too clumsy to handle flyers and glue at the same time. It occurred to me that I had half a roll of contact paper at my apartment, the kind that simulated wood. If the contact paper was cut into rectangular strips wide enough and long enough to cover the abortion clinic's name and phone number, all a person had to do was jump down into the subway gully, cross over the rails, and slap two of these precut strips over the name and phone number. The backing could be peeled off before descending into the pit. The whole job would not take more than a few seconds from start to finish.

The subway mission, though, would be dangerous. First, there was the obvious danger of being hit by an approaching train. Els are extremely noisy, however, and the rattling and screeching of cars coming down the line can be heard several hundred feet away. There would be plenty of time to do what needed to be done before any trains arrived. Secondly, a person had to get down into that subway gully and cross over the tracks. Anyone who regularly rides the El knows about the infamous "third rail," which runs alongside the second track and is understood to be the live rail—alive with electricity. To touch the third rail was potentially lethal.

I recruited two people to help obliterate the abortion center ads. The first volunteer was Anna, a young woman in her early twenties who lived in a sparsely furnished, one-room apartment across from St. Ignatius Parish. Ironically, Anna was going to a trade school to learn lettering for sign-making.

The other person was my friend Jerry Zealy, also in his twenties. A devout Catholic, he was the head of the St. Ignatius chapter of the Legion of Mary. Jerry came from an interracial home—still rare enough in the late seventies—and he happily described himself as "bright-skinned." He had light gray-green eyes and curly, reddish-brown hair. He was nice-looking with a wonderful, handsome smile.

But Jerry did not smile very often. He was a tormented soul. His mother died when Jerry was ten and her death always seemed to bother him. He grew up with a keen awareness of racial injustice and often spoke to me about his anger. He was also unhappy with his job. He worked for the Illinois Bell telephone company and was resentful and frustrated that he seemed to be passed over for raises and promotions, blaming it on racial prejudice. Jerry perceived his job as nothing more than paper-pushing and he hated it. His surly attitude was undoubtedly obvious to his bosses and co-workers.

Jerry was also a recovering drug addict. After graduating from high school he attended the prestigious Northwestern University, a school known for its tough entrance requirements. Jerry told me that in his college days he was a self-proclaimed rebel, a civil rights activist, keenly aware of his own heritage and just plain mad about discrimination. He may have joined the Black Student Union and attended a civil rights demonstration or two. But while at Northwestern, Jerry also got heavily involved in the drug scene. He started out smoking marijuana, but soon progressed to more serious drugs. In the end, he nearly overdosed on heroin.

Jerry was fully aware that he had almost lost his life, and this frightened him deeply. While he lay in a hospital bed recovering, he decided to turn his life over to God. He re-committed himself to his Catholic faith, the religion in which he had been raised, and began to attend daily Mass. But the drugs had taken a toll on Jerry's intellectual abilities; he left Northwestern and never attended any other university. He got a low-level clerical position at the telephone company. Because of his brooding and melancholy disposition, Jerry was often hard to be around.

Yet there were times when he was quite happy and would smile his great smile, be light-hearted, conversational and given over to laughter. I once ran into Jerry on the Howard El line headed to Rogers Park. He sat down next to me, opened up a small paper bag, and took out a beautiful rosary made of polished rosewood beads. Jerry had been in the Loop and visited St. Peter's Church, where he had purchased the rosary along with a tall devotional candle. "Here, would you like to have that?" he asked as he placed the rosary beads into my hand. I was stunned. It was a beautiful gift, and he had given it so spontaneously. My hand closed around the heavy beads. As I pulled the beads across my fingertips their touch was smooth and comforting and my eyes savored their reddish color. I was happy to be in possession of such a fine rosary and thanked Jerry for it. He gave me a warm smile full of satisfaction.

Jerry, Anna and I set out at 2 a.m. on a Monday morning, toting plastic bags that hid our black spray paint and strips of contact paper. We went about our task quickly and efficiently. As soon as we were finished at one El stop, we took the train to the next, until we finally reached the subway portion of the line. At that time of night on a Monday, the platforms were nearly deserted. Each station had three or four of the Albany ads. I quickly peeled off the backing on two strips of contact paper and handed them to Jerry. He jumped down into the trench, nimbly leapt over the rails, and slapped one contact strip over the abortion center's name and the other over its phone number. He then leapt back over the third rail and hoisted himself up to the platform. We ran to the next ad and the process was repeated. If anyone saw us, they paid no attention to what we were doing. I returned home at six in the morning, utterly exhausted. I slept for an hour, awoke, ate a light breakfast of cold cereal and instant coffee, gathered my books, and trudged off to my eight o'clock Old Testament class at Loyola.

At about this time, Joe Scheidler was on an El train on his way to his new job as head of Friends for Life, whose office was located in the heart of the Loop on North Michigan Avenue. Joe had been fired as executive director of the Illinois Right to Life Committee following the sit-in at Concord Medical Services. It seems that the board of directors, which had hired Joe to develop and implement pro-life educational presentations, was unhappy with Joe's more radical activities.

The train carried him and a hundred of others into the bowels of the city. Joe sank into a seat he shared with a stranger, preoccupied by his own thoughts. He was weary and discouraged. Joe felt keenly the injustice of abortion and was impatient to see justice for the unborn. He was all too aware of the Albany abortion clinic ads. The first time he saw them, just a few days before I did, he felt frustration like an icy weight sink into the pit of his stomach. He hated the ads and had written a letter of complaint to the Chicago Transit Authority. To him the signs were evidence of the world's moral decay—that places where human beings were put to death, openly, even flagrantly, advertised their services and nobody seemed to care.

Joe sighed as the train approached the Washington Avenue stop. He stood up, waited for the doors to open, and stepped onto the platform. Directly before him was an Albany ad with two large, strategically-placed strips pasted over it. He looked up and down the platform and was astonished to find that all of the Albany signs had been defaced. It was a wonderful surprise. He was soon struck by the fact that someone had crossed over the third rail to accomplish the deed.

When Joe arrived at the Friends for Life office, he immediately sat down and recorded a new message for his telephone action-line, a communication system that kept Chicago pro-lifers informed about current issues and events. He reported that "the Albany ads have been covered over by an anonymous mountain goat committed to putting an end to Albany abortuary's attempt to kill even more unborn babies."

No one tried to clean the paint off the signs and certainly no one was crazy enough or dedicated enough to jump down into the El train pit, cross the third rail, and tear off the contact paper. So the Albany ads remained blotted out for several weeks until finally they were torn down and replaced with signs for *Newsweek* magazine or the latest Ford pickup.

This was not the last time, however, that Albany would advertise on the El trains. Undaunted by the defacement of the posters, the very same ad was back up several months later, and once again Jerry, Anna, and I made a midnight run with spray paint and contact paper. Sometimes we missed defacing an ad, perhaps because someone was standing too close and might question what we were doing or try to stop us. One such ad remained on the Loyola platform—the platform I most often stood on to wait for a train. On a Friday afternoon in April, 1979, even though it was broad daylight, I decided to simply tear down the ad. On the return trip from the Loop I got off the train, walked over to the faded blue poster, and looked up and down the platform. A few people were scattered about, standing perhaps twenty to thirty feet away. I bargained with myself. I would count to fifty. If a train did not come down the line by the time I reached the end, I would tear down the ad.

I counted to fifty. No train arrived.

Tearing down a poster advertisement is not easily accomplished. I tried to find a corner that was beginning to curl away from the board. I grabbed onto a loose end and began peeling away the blue sign. Gradually small bits and pieces of it filled the palm of my hand.

"What *are* you doing?" said a loud, nasally voice that belonged to someone who was definitely angry.

I looked up. Standing next to me was Arthur Bloom, chairman of Loyola University's theatre department. I was well acquainted with him, and he with me, as I was currently playing the part of Pitti-Sing in Gilbert and Sullivan's *The Mikado*. Although I no longer dreamt of seeing my name in lights, I had decided for fun to audition for Loyola's spring musical and landed the part—a performance was scheduled for that very night. Bloom was the director.

I am not sure what caused Bloom to confront me, but I do not think he was aware that the ad was for an abortion clinic and that I was tearing it down because I was pro-life. I think he shouted at me because he saw someone—someone he knew, no less—destroying a piece of advertising. I could have simply told him I was just fooling around, shrugged my shoulders, apologized for my actions, and dashed off hoping he would not think anymore about it. Instead I decided to answer his question.

"This is an ad for an abortion clinic. They kill unborn children there."

"I don't care what it is," Bloom retorted. "You can't destroy that—it's not your property."

"Dr. Bloom, what if this wasn't an ad for an abortion clinic? Let's say it was a sign put up by the Nazis to promote the killing of Jews. Wouldn't you want someone to tear it down?" I knew Arthur bloom was Jewish and hoped my argument would make an impression on him. And it did, but not in the way I had hoped. Like many pro-lifers, I believed that I could change the minds of the Blooms of the world with an analogy between abortion and an instance of mass killing that the vast majority of people recognized as an atrocity. But Bloom simply continued to insist that since I had not paid for the ad I had no right to tear it down. "It's not your property," he said again.

"Just because it's not my property doesn't mean it's wrong to destroy it if it's going to be used to hurt someone. I mean, what if someone was going to shoot another person and I took the gun away and threw it into Lake Michigan? Would that be wrong?"

"This is a legal business!" Bloom was adamant.

At this point I could see that if what truly mattered was the legality of the business, Bloom could not be convinced by my argument about the gun. He certainly could not be persuaded that peeling off an abortion clinic ad was a good and worthy act. We were having a disagreement on the meaning of property, or maybe Bloom just thought abortions were okay. But I continued to argue my point with him, amazed that he would not at least admit that it was justified to destroy a weapon about to be used against an innocent person.

"How can you say that? Should you just stand by and let the person be killed?"

Bloom's train had already approached the platform and was slowing to a screeching halt. The doors opened, he got on, and our conversation ended as the train departed. The platform was now nearly deserted. Since it had cost me quite a bit to tear down the ad, I was going to finish the job. In another moment I had several large hunks of blue sign in my hand. I proceeded down the stairs and, as I walked to my apartment, I thrust the pieces of the poster into a city garbage bin. I sighed deeply, relieved the episode was over.

That evening I showed up for *The Mikado*'s makeup call. I was certain to see Arthur Bloom again, since he would often come into the dressing room to give last-minute notes to us on how to correct or improve our performances. I was applying white powder to my face to transform myself into Gilbert and Sullivan's comic-stereotyped vision of a Japanese lady when, through the reflection in the mirror, I saw Bloom come into the room. The dressing area was full of the usual pre-performance chatter and activity. Without the slightest hesitation Bloom came right over to me, placed his hands on my shoulders and said, "You're doing swell, Pitti-Sing honey. Keep it up."

I was startled by Bloom's display of affection and encouragement and did not know quite what to make of it. In twenty minutes I completed my makeup and put on my costume, ready for *The Mikado*'s overture to begin. I exited the dressing room just as Bloom was once again entering it. We ran right into each other. He hugged me, gave me a quick kiss on my white powdered cheek and said, with a happy voice and a wide smile, "Be marvelous, doll."

I had spent nearly every night for the last three months with Arthur Bloom and he had never treated me in such a fashion. Perhaps my arguments finally resonated with him. Maybe he thought it was wrong to criticize me so harshly up there on the platform. But it was also possible that the kiss, the hug, and the words of encouragement were Arthur Bloom's way of ensuring that I would not throw the performance.

*   *   *

In the early 1980s another Chicago abortion clinic called Biogenetics advertised on the benches of Chicago Transit Authority
bus stops. The name, Biogenetics, sounded like something out of
a Michael Crichton novel, and Chicago pro-lifers called it Bio-
genecide. Biogenetics was another of the abortion clinics featured
in the 1978 *Chicago Sun-Times* "Abortion Profiteers" series. The
November 13 edition identified Kenneth Yellin and Clifford Josefik as the owners and operators of the clinic. They were two of the
five Michigan Avenue "profiteers" whose photos were spread across
that morning's paper. Zekman and Warrick wrote:

> They pay high rents for fancy addresses, but cut corners on
> patient care. They ignore laws, but slip through cracks in
> the system with savvy defenses. They stay in the business by
> staying one step ahead of the law. For the profiteers abortion
> is big business. It's where big bucks are made. In the days to
> come, this paper will expose the dangerous and sometimes
> illegal medical practices uncovered in clinics owned and
> operated by these men—men who make their profits from
> women's pains. . . .
>
> Kenneth Yellin . . . switched from selling luxury cars to
> selling economy abortions when abortions were legalized in
> 1973. In 1974, a court ordered him to stop pretending he was
> a doctor.
>
> Clifford Josefik [was] Yellin's fast-talking partner at
> Biogenetics Ltd. 520 Michigan. What the people want
> Josefik sells: pollution control, condominiums, land, trucks,
> and abortions.

Yellin used to pass himself off as one Dr. York. He was indicted
for this and for "performing illegal abortions, reckless conduct and
theft by deception"—that is, to sell abortions, Yellin sometimes told
women that they were pregnant when they were not. The "Abortion Profiteers" reported that many of the abortionists featured in
the series deceived women in this way, but somehow Yellin was not

convicted on most of these charges. The strongest case against him was that he had performed an abortion beyond the twelfth week of pregnancy, which was illegal in Illinois at that time. Prosecutors, however, could not prove that the woman was beyond the twelfth week so the state's attorney dropped the charge, along with most of the other charges pending against Yellin. Biogenetics medical director Dr. Carlos Baldoceda sold women menstrual extractions, a "just in case" procedure offered to women whose pregnancy tests were negative. The "Abortion Profiteers" exposé stated:

> Except for the fact that it costs less, a menstrual extraction is essentially the same as an early abortion but it is not as thorough or as effective in ending pregnancy. And because such extractions usually are done on women whose periods are only a week or two late, the embryo is so tiny that it may be missed by the suction device. But the risks and discomfort of suctioning menstrual blood from the womb are as great as with an abortion, the experts say.

The *Sun-Times* described Yellin's partner, Josefik, as someone strictly interested in making money. To this end, Biogenetics required its clients who were on public aid to pay cash for the abortions, then turned around and billed Medicaid for the very same procedures. In 1976, the Illinois Legislative Advisory Committee on Public Aid finally charged the abortion center with abusing the Medicaid system.

At about 10:30 on the night of June 8, 1979, I rode with Donna Rozewski and her boyfriend, Jerry McCarthy, to the northwest side of Chicago and painted out as many of the Biogenetics bus stop ads as we could find. Most of the ads were at stops where there was little traffic or very poor lighting. Just like in the El train stations, we worked quickly and efficiently, moving from one stop to the next. We noticed that many of the ads seemed to be strategically located at bus stops near high schools.

An hour later we came to the last bus stop on the list. As we approached the corner our hearts began to race. Several street lamps and the lights of a nearby gas station made the intersection seem like the middle of a baseball stadium ready for a night game. And there were people everywhere, not to mention motorists pulling up to the stoplight. We drove down a side street, parked, and discussed what to do.

"Don't worry about the lights!" Donna said. "Who cares if people see us? It's the police we don't want."

I was so impressed by Donna's boldness that I was not going to argue against her. She was usually more cautious in such matters, but she was determined not to allow the ad to solicit customers. It was decided that I would stay in the car while Donna and Jerry painted out the bench. It was the feast of the Sacred Heart, and so we uttered a fervent prayer to Jesus under that title.

Jerry passed me his keys and I got into the driver's seat while Donna and Jerry walked the one-hundred feet or so to the corner. Donna carried the paint pan, now full of fresh orange paint, and Jerry held the roller. I sat in the car with the motor running, nervous, tense and praying. My eyes never left the rearview mirror, but I could not see the corner. About a minute later I heard the sound of running footsteps. The car doors flew open, and Jerry and Donna threw themselves into the backseat. "Go, go, go!" Jerry shouted. I stepped on the gas and sped away down the side street. Jerry and Donna were elated.

"I don't believe it, Monica. A miracle just happened! Police were right there on the corner in a squad. Right there while we were painting the bench—they looked right past us. Didn't even see us! I just don't believe it." Donna shouted into my ear. "Oh God, thank you," she said ecstatically as she slumped back into the seat.

Five months later, on Saturday, November 3, just as women began to arrive at Biogenetics for their abortions, someone shot and killed Kenneth Yellin on Lower Michigan Avenue while he was on his way to the clinic to attend to the day's business. There had been rumors that Biogenetics had ties to the Syndicate and Yellin's death appeared to be a gangland-style execution. The November 4 *Sun-Times* reported Yellin's death with a bold front page headline:

"Michigan Avenue Abortionist Slain." A huge photo showed Yellin's contorted body lying in the street. Quoting a police officer, a November 18 *Chicago Tribune* headline stated: "Creepy Kenny died in the gutter where he belonged." The story described the abortionist's pathetic end: "Kennth Yellin died on lower Michigan Avenue with his head covered with garbage."

Talking women out of abortions, getting arrested at clinic sit-ins, and now blotting out abortion clinic ads—it seems I had become a radical. The killing of the unborn swept me away. One Saturday afternoon I was actually overcome with this sense of being different. I had just returned to my Rogers Park apartment after sidewalk-counseling at Albany. It had been a hard morning. Out on the sidewalk Donna and I had spoken to a woman for over twenty minutes and she agreed with everything we said. She agreed the unborn baby was human, and that the baby had a right to live. She even agreed that abortion was a sin, but in the end she went into the clinic.

Now as I stood alone in my kitchen, I played back the conversation in my head. As I prepared myself a simple lunch I continued to think about the loss of the child. I opened the door to the refrigerator to retrieve a carton of milk. In the midst of reaching into the refrigerator my hand stopped. I was gripped by a realization. I thought, *I'm not living in a normal world anymore.* Standing there, suspended in time with one arm in the fridge, I realized that "normal" could not apply to a world in which the murder of the unborn was protected by law, and that I could no longer consider myself a normal person. I knew that I could not live my life in the expected way: get an education, get a job, get married, buy a house. I felt I could not deal with those things. No, I had to be seized by a radical act. I had to drop everything—forget about milk and lunch. Babies are being murdered. They are being murdered down the street, in my own town. I know about it and I have to give up my life and do something about it!

To be pro-life is to be enveloped by a desperate, agonizing moment in history. As awareness of injustice grips you, you cannot free yourself and it is a suffering. Here was terrible loneliness. I felt alienated from the world, from my culture, my society. I even felt alienated from my own country. Words like "liberty and justice for all" didn't seem real to me. I had a sense of painful separation. I had thrown in my lot with an unwanted people—and felt rejected with them. The unborn and I were one in the night of their abandonment. I felt the burden of being aware that a whole segment of the human family was denied their right to live.

This awareness made it hard to just be free and enjoy life. The world was not a normal place anymore. So, when in the spring of 1980, my sister Laura invited me to accompany her on a trip overseas, my first knee-jerk thought was, *But I need to be at the abortion clinic.* But I ultimately decided to go—shaking off the irrational guilt of a vacationing activist.

We visited England first and it took me a while to learn to relax. We then moved on to Italy, where, despite evidence of Catholicism everywhere, in the 1980s there was evidence of a creeping secularism. Italy, like the rest of Europe, was becoming more disengaged from its Christian past. Italy had not yet legalized abortion, but there were many in that country, particularly the Italian feminists, who in the early 1980s agitated for change.

My grandmother, Albina Milano, was born in Florence but came to America when she was seventeen. She had a sister, Caterina, who lived in Florence with her two daughters. Because of my family ties to the city, I loved visiting this place of antiquity and beauty, the town of Leonardo, Michaelangelo and the Medicis. Despite its beautiful history, Florence was not exempt from the abortion movement in Italy, which was employing a public-relations tactic used to great effect by the movement in the United States: abortion needed to be legal so women could be safe.

My sister and I checked into an inexpensive pensione—the kind of place where guests shared rooms with strangers, sacrificing privacy to save a few lira. Our roommates were Joyce—a middle-aged, very immature and chatty woman—and her unpleasantly sullen daughter Lonny. While Lonny hardly ever spoke, Joyce made up for her daughter's silence. She talked incessantly. After four days Laura and I checked out of the pensione to stay with relatives who lived just outside Florence. I confess I had a sense of relief that we would never see Joyce and Lonny again.

Laura and I decided to sightsee separately for the morning and then later meet at the Academia to see the statue of David and other Michaelangelo sculptures. On my way to our rendezvous, I crossed over the cobblestones of the Piazza de Republico. On the wall of a building was a line of posters, most of them promoting Italian political parties. On this wall was another poster, one with which I was also now familiar. When I first saw it, a similar sense of anger and dread passed through me as it had on the day I first saw the Albany ads on the Howard El line.

The poster featured black-and-white photos, superimposed against a bright purple background. Three women were walking toward the viewer. Around the neck of each hung a placard which read "Rosa, morta aborto clandestino, Elizabetha, morta aborto clandestino, Giola, morta aborto clandestino." The poster promoted the legalization of abortion because women were dying from the Italian version of the back-alley abortion.

I was on a much-needed vacation, a trip that took me away from the stresses of pro-life work, but I decided that I would do this one thing for the unborn while in Europe. I started to tear the sign down. I pulled at its edges; a few pieces started to give way, and I ripped them off. A young woman who held a dish towel in her hand came out from a small cappuccino bar a few doors away from the poster. She yelled loudly, "No! No! Polizia! Polizia!" From her gestures it appeared that she was not calling for the police but warning me about them. I said in my broken Italian, "Abortion non bueno." She responded, "Si." I assumed she was agreeing with me, but she continued to say "Polizia." She even came over and took hold of my arm to lead me away from potential trouble. I pulled my arm back and said again, as I pointed to what was left of the sign, "Abortion non bueno. Abortion muerte. This sign is coming down." I turned to finish what I had begun and the lady from the coffee shop went back inside, shaking her head in frustration. I once again began to peel the sign off the wall. In seconds I loosened two large strips of the purple ad and held them in my hand. The poster was essentially destroyed.

From somewhere behind my left ear I heard a familiar voice.

"Hm. So you're tearing down a poster."

I looked over my shoulder. Joyce was standing there next to me with her daughter Lonny, who eyed me suspiciously. Joyce glanced at the pieces of poster in my hand and then shifted her gaze to what remained of the poster on the wall.

She looked perplexed. Lonny, however, glared at me with eyes filled with anger and distrust. I thought the daughter was definitely the brighter of the two women. Unlike the episode with Dr. Bloom, I decided this time I would not take the trouble to explain myself.

"Yes," I said, smiling pleasantly as I jammed the purple cardboard shards into a nearby trash bin. "And now I am going to the Academia to see Michaelangelo's David," I stated, as if tearing down a pro-abortion poster was just another item on my list of things to see and do in Florence. Although my heart beat wildly, I smiled at the mother and daughter and swiftly made my escape in the direction of the museum.

*   *   *

After I returned from Italy, Jerry Zealy and I struck up a closer friendship. I even went out on dates with him once or twice, although I had made it clear that it would have to be strictly platonic as I was not interested in romance or getting married. Jerry did not take me seriously and constantly tried to put his arm around me, hug me, kiss me, or hold my hand. I felt I had to put a stop to the dates, which were not very enjoyable in any case. Jerry was often in a sullen mood or would use our time together to complain about his job or express his intense anger about racial discrimination.

For the next two or three years, I saw Jerry only from time to time. We both lived in Rogers Park, so we occasionally ran into each other. On one such evening I was in the Loyola El train station when he came walking through very quickly. He seemed agitated. I asked him if he was okay. He told me that he had just resigned as president of the Legion of Mary chapter at St. Ignatius. He had just come from a meeting where he had gotten up and left. I nodded sympathetically, then we said goodbye and went our separate ways.

I saw him again sometime later as I was leaving St. Jerome's parish, another old Catholic Church on the far north side of Chicago. It was a Sunday afternoon after Mass. I was walking down the very long aisle of the church as he was walking up, neatly dressed in a suit. Jerry was a reader at Mass and was probably arriving for the next liturgy. He had gained some weight and had a shorter haircut than usual. His eyes caught mine. They were unusually intense. I said hello to him. With a grim expression he nodded his head at me as a form of greeting, but he was silent. He seemed unhappy.

I later learned from mutual friends that Jerry had been fired from the job that he hated so much. Then I heard that Jerry was leaving town. He had decided to go back to his boyhood home in Tennessee and live with his father and his sisters. Jerry had been gone about a month when a former roommate of mine called and told me the news. A strange numbness seemed to radiate from the phone in my hand. It spread throughout my body and settled into that hollow place in one's heart that, when filled to the brim with pain, cannot absorb any more.

The evening winter sunset bathed my apartment in a soft yellow glow. I stared into space and thought, *How could he do it?* He believed in God, he prayed the rosary and attended daily Mass and believed in the sanctity of human life. Why wasn't his religion enough? Could it be that pro-lifers are as broken, vulnerable and human as anyone else?

It was on a gray and bitter cold February day when Joe Scheidler's "mountain goat," who had leapt the third rail to save the unborn, leapt over the rail of a Tennessee bridge and plunged his own life into the dark waters of the river below.

CHAPTER FIVE

GREEN EYES OF HATE

A simple child
That lightly draws its breath
and feels life in every limb,
What should it know of death?
—William Wordsworth

E VERY woman who passed us on the street that morning was wearing white. Sometimes only a few would stroll by, and at other times clusters of them jammed the sidewalk headed south. On this Saturday morning, May 10, during Mother's Day weekend of 1980, Grant Park was to host a massive rally sponsored by the National Organization for Women to advocate passage of the Equal Rights Amendment (ERA), a bill designed to enshrine in law that women would not be discriminated against on the basis of gender. The intent was noble, but many in the pro-life movement feared that the language of the bill would cement abortion as a constitutional right. In the early 1980s the American Civil Liberties Union filed a series of cases in Hawaii, Massachusetts, Pennsylvania and Connecticut arguing that since abortion is a medical procedure performed only on women, it is "sex discrimination," within the meaning of the states' ERAs, to deny tax funding of abortions. The rally organizers told participants to wear white, and many of the women, and some men too, sported the green-and-white buttons of the ERA.

Donna and I stood outside the Michigan Avenue Medical Center. The street was so congested and noisy that it was nearly impossible to do any sidewalk counseling. Donna had brought a handmade poster with her. Its big and colorful block letters proclaimed: "Human Life is Sacred." She propped the sign against the tall building that housed the abortion clinic. Those on their way to the ERA rally found the poster extremely provocative. Its anti-abortion message drew jeers and snide remarks from the men and women who walked past us. Some women were openly hostile and, with their right fists clenched high in the air, shouted at us: "Freedom to choose! We have a right to do what we want with our own bodies!"

Two women walked by and one commented to the other, "Of course human life is sacred."

Donna felt compelled to talk with the women. "Unfortunately, a lot of women who support the ERA also support abortion."

This, of course, infuriated the two women. Donna was swept into a terrible argument right there on the sidewalk. The woman who had just affirmed the sanctity of life now shot back, "When we didn't have abortion women had to go to back-alley butchers. Are you going to take care of all the unwanted children? You don't have a right to tell a woman what to do with her life!"

Burning with frustration, I yelled back at her, "You just said one minute ago that human life is sacred! Now you're saying it's okay to kill unborn children! If the woman doesn't want the child then all of a sudden the baby's not sacred anymore?"

The woman and her friend looked at me in disgust and proceeded on their way to the rally. I now felt too angry and frustrated to sidewalk-counsel effectively, but just then a young couple approached the door of the building. I asked the woman, "Are you going to the clinic upstairs? "Yes," she said briskly, "and I don't have time to talk to you."

Donna approached the door just as the couple was about to enter and handed the woman a small pamphlet on abortion called

"Did You Know?" It detailed fetal development and showed a photo of a healthy unborn baby at thirteen weeks as well as a photo of the remains of a baby aborted by the suction method at ten weeks.

"Look, there are a lot of complications to abortion that the clinic isn't going to tell you about," she said.

"Get out of my face!" she snapped, and brushed past Donna into the building. Her boyfriend followed. Then the woman paused, backed out of the doorway, crumpled the pamphlet, and threw it back at Donna. "Here, take this with you!" she said. As she headed for the elevator she continued to shout, "What I'm here for ain't none of your business!"

"Yes, it is my business," Donna called back. "You're about to kill my brother or sister!"

The woman snickered as she entered the elevator. "Oh, yeah."

Another small batch of women dressed in white strolled past us. A very young and quite pretty woman shouted defiantly, "Hey, I've had two abortions!"

"Well, I'm sorry to hear that," was my lame and weary response.

The woman and her friend stopped walking.

"God gave women the right to have an abortion," she said.

"Abortion denies the God-given right to life—so He certainly did not give you the right to kill your babies."

"Oh sure—can you see me runnin' around with two babies tucked under my arms?" She bowed her arms as though lifting two children around their middles. "A woman has a right to decide her life, to fulfill herself, to assert herself in the life she wants for herself."

"But you're denying a whole other person the right to exist!" I said. "You think that in order to decide your life you have to kill someone else?"

The woman ignored my question. "What are you doing about the death penalty, huh? If you're so gung-ho about other people's lives, what are you doing about that?"

"Oh, come on," I said. "Don't try to turn me into a hypocrite. Just because I'm trying to change one injustice doesn't mean I somehow have to take on all of them. We're doing all we can to help women who are pregnant and in need. Did it ever occur to you that we are saving unborn women as well as men? We've even offered to take pregnant mothers into our own homes."

"Whatever." The women shook their heads at us and continued on their way to the rally.

Five minutes later Joseph Scheidler came up with a group of about seventy people holding pro-life placards and picket signs. He was leading a Mother's Day march as a counter-protest to the NOW demonstration.

"Abortion is murder, abortionists are murderers, and anyone who gets an abortion is involved with murder!" Joe shouted, never one to be subtle. His words sounded crude and harsh, blasting through his megaphone, and they naturally provoked a lot of resentment from the passersby. Some looked at each other with expressions of disgust. Many people shook their heads. A woman dressed in white knocked the megaphone away from Joe's mouth with a violent, angry gesture. Joe put the megaphone back to his mouth and said, "You just assaulted me! You're going to be arrested for that!" I told Joe to just let her go. Getting back at her was no way to bring her around to our position. But even so I felt exceedingly frustrated at the way those who passed the pro-life protestors responded to us. They thought we were crazy and ridiculous and that the pro-life stance was ridiculous too.

Before long the pro-life marchers continued on their way and the crowds began to dissipate. Now the sidewalk was quiet and I was grateful for the reprieve. A few minutes passed in silence before I noticed a young man who looked to be in his mid-twenties standing on the sidewalk near the entrance to the building. He was well-dressed and nice-looking. I thought he had come out of the 30 South Michigan door. He stood a few feet away and stared at me while sipping a soft drink through a straw. Because I thought he had possibly come down from the abortion clinic, I wanted to talk to him. I smiled and said, "Hi." An odd look spread across his face while he stared intensely into my eyes. I did not know quite what to make of him. "What's the matter?" I asked.

The expression lingered as he spoke. "You dare smile and say hello to me when you are guilty of condemning women to their deaths?" Every syllable was laced with hatred and contempt. No one had ever spoken to me in such a fashion. I will never forget his look. His eyes were green and full of hate.

"What do you mean?" I asked incredulously. "We aren't sending anyone to their deaths."

"What have you ever done to help women before they become pregnant?"

I knew that whatever I said would not satisfy him. But I tried anyway.

"I don't understand. There's a basic sexual ethic and I believe in promoting that."

"Isn't it true that you so-called right-to-life people are trying to enact legislation to restrict contraception?"

"No," I said, "that's not true at all. The pro-life movement is not trying to make contraception illegal except those methods which are actually abortifacients—that abort life already conceived."

"Then you're against the IUD."

"It's an abortifacient."

"You *are* ridiculous," he said. Then he walked away.

I was about ready to cry. I turned to Donna. "Come on, let's get out of here," I said. "I have to get out of here."

Donna and I began to walk slowly to St. Peter's church on Madison Street—the same church where Jerry purchased the rosary he had given to me. I clutched the beads in my pocket as we walked. The church, operated by Franciscan friars, had Masses every hour as well as all-day confessions. The man's words continued to beat harshly in my ears: "You are guilty of condemning women to their deaths." I turned to Donna.

"He accused us of being women-killers!" I started to cry. "Here we are trying to protect human life and he thinks we're women-killers!" Donna pursed her lips and nodded her head.

As we continued toward St. Peter's, the world's resentment and misunderstanding was all very real to me, and it weighed me down. I poured out my hurt and frustration to Donna. I was agitated and passersby looked at me as I spoke in a loud voice.

"We are expected to solve all of the world's problems before we can be against abortion," I said. "They ask us, 'What are you doing about war? What are you doing about capital punishment? What are you doing about all of the unwanted children? What are you doing to help women before they get pregnant?'"

As we crossed Clark Street, I continued my monologue before Donna—my audience of one.

"Anyone who asks a pro-lifer 'What are you doing about war?' doesn't even know what they're asking! Such people think we should be ending wars. How can wars be ended? If we can't even convince a single abortion-bound woman to accept the life and humanity of her child, how can we be expected to prevent violence between nations? If a woman cannot love and respect her own helpless unborn child, what hope do we have for political reconciliation? It's ridiculous for those who are pro-abortion to make pro-life people out to be hypocrites with such a question. They have failed to understand the basis for peace!"

When Donna and I arrived at St. Peter's I was exhausted. The noon Mass had already begun. We slipped into a back pew. In a side chapel to our right was a full-sized replica of Michelangelo's *Pieta*. A line of people stood in the side aisle waiting to go to confession. The priest was just about to read the gospel for the day. The serenity of the church slowly began to envelop me. The words of the Mass were calm and soothing, so different from the conflict and hostile words spoken outside the clinic that morning.

"The Lord be with you," the priest began.

"And also with you," the people replied.

"A reading from the holy gospel according to John."

"Glory to you, O Lord."

The priest continued:

If you find that the world hates you, know it has hated me before you. If you belonged to the world, it would love you as its own; the reason it hates you is that you do not belong to the world. But I have chosen you out of the world. Remember what I told you: no slave is greater than his master. They will harry you as they harried me. They will respect your words as much as they respected mine. All this they will do to you because of my name, for they know nothing of him who sent me.

Donna and I looked at each other. The gospel spilled into my soul and overwhelmed me. I was dazed: "If you find that the world hates you, know that it has hated me before you. If you were of the world it would love you as its own." The pragmatic, utilitarian ethic of power over others is a thing of this world. The ethic that smashes the mystery and beauty of human life in those countless crushed and broken bodies is a thing of this world. The ethic that says it is justified to kill another person if he gets in your way is a thing of this world. I thought, *I reject this world, and so the world should reject me.*

To be pro-life is not glamorous. Indeed, many pro-lifers are simple, unsophisticated folks, like the ones humble enough to line up in St. Peter's for confession, folks who are willing to admit that truth does not begin and end with them, and who know in their very being that abortion strikes at something sacred. As I knelt in the church that day, prompted by a liberating spirit, I learned: expect rejection—and do not think another second about it.

CHAPTER SIX

THE NUN'S STORY

"We believe that the decision to have an abortion could be a good moral decision. We believe that women need to be seen as making good moral decisions for their own lives."
—Sr. Barbara Ferraro, in a speech delivered at
Marquette University, November. 2, 1987

IN THE early 1980s, Donna and I continued our sidewalk-counseling partnership. In the fall of 1982, we spent our Saturday mornings at the Albany clinic on Irving Park Road, the sister clinic to the Elston facility, whose ads I helped deface on the Howard El line.

On October 16, 1982, four teenage girls and a man in his twenties paced slowly on the sidewalk in front of the Albany Medical Center. They prayed quietly, gently intoning the words of the rosary as the beads dangled from their hands. Donna and I took up our posts near the door to the clinic. A man dressed in shabby clothes and a long black overcoat many sizes too big walked across the street and slipped into the line of those praying the rosary. His long hair and beard were unkempt and dirty, and a pair of broken glasses sat on his face. One of the temples was missing.

It began to rain and drops fell cold against our faces. Donna and I took shelter in a small niche that used to be the doorway to a pharmacy. A few minutes passed. Then a large woman with short blond hair came out of the clinic. Her blue lab coat indicated that she was a member of the Albany staff. She watched the six people praying the rosary, then started to laugh.

"Gee, how'd you get the hippie to pray with you?" She chuckled and shook her head. Donna was annoyed.

"Oh, you think prayer is so funny, do you?" she said.

The woman peered at us through her large plastic-rimmed glasses. "No, I don't think prayer is a funny subject," she responded, suddenly very serious.

"But you're belittling these people. You aren't showing them any respect," I said. "They're human beings."

"Now that's an intelligent observation," the woman replied. Then she walked the few feet to where Donna and I stood in the old doorway. She took a few moments to size us up. Her next words were spoken in a very precise and direct manner.

"I can tell by looking at the two of you that you have never experienced an orgasm in your life and that you are not sexually active."

Donna and I looked at each other for a moment, then burst out laughing. I was amused, and a bit stunned, that anyone would say such a thing, especially to people they did not even know. The absurdity of the situation bore down on me: a complete stranger on the street, in the rain, in front of an abortion clinic, commenting on our sex lives, or the lack thereof.

Later as I pondered her remark I began to understand its meaning. The woman assumed that since Donna and I were committed pro-lifers, we were not sexually active. The clinic worker believed that our view of the world, that our experience of life, made it impossible for us to understand, much less support, a woman's need to choose abortion. Little did the clinic worker know that Donna had had an abortion and understood "the need" very well. She continued: "Because you don't believe in contraception, you are restricting a woman's freedom to fulfill herself."

"Is a woman just an object for sex?" replied Donna. "Is that the only way a woman can be fulfilled?"

"No, but women have always been treated as second-class citizens. They are still being treated that way."

Donna tried to pick apart the clinic worker's view of women's

status, but it was a correct observation. Women have indeed suffered discrimination, but in the heat of our debate Donna was over-
eager to disagree with her. Then Donna decided to give an example
of an area in which women have excelled—though no radical feminist would dare concur.

"Look at the Catholic Church, and you'll see how women have
fulfilled themselves. Look at the opportunities that women have
had in the Church. Half of the religious orders have been founded
by women! And women have basically been in charge of parochial
education for hundreds of years!" Her voice rose slightly as she tried
to drive her point home.

"Yes, I know very well about the Church," the clinic worker
responded. "I'm a Roman Catholic nun myself."

Donna and I looked at each other again, but this time we did
not laugh. Everything in me wanted to deny that there could be
truth in this woman's statement. But there was something about
her that made me think she was being honest. If she could tell by
looking at us that Donna and I were not sexually active, we could
tell that she could very well be a nun.

Much had changed in the Church since the Second Vatican
Council. Many women religious no longer wore a habit; still this
woman did not dress like the other clinic workers. Her clothes were
conservative, her hair was close-cropped, and she had a reserved,
rather genteel bearing. She was certainly confident and spoke well.
If she was not actually a nun, it was possible that she had renounced
her vows, or spent some time in a novitiate.

But Donna shook her head. "You may think you're a nun, but
you're not."

"I sure am. I am a Roman Catholic nun. My name is Sister
Mary."

"What is your order?" I asked.

"The School Sisters of St. Francis."

"Where is it?" asked Donna.

"Kenosha, Wisconsin."

The School Sisters of St. Francis is indeed a religious order of

sisters with its motherhouse located in Milwaukee. In the wake of
Vatican II, the School Sisters, as well as several other communi-
ties of women religious, experimented with the structure of con-
vent life. Sisters were permitted to live apart from the community,
and under the inspiration of the Holy Spirit, they were encouraged
to try new apostolates, even take on secular jobs. I confess a certain skepticism that the Spirit led Sr. Mary to work in an abortion
clinic. I thought it unlikely that her community was aware of the
nature of her "ministry."

However, nuns who support legalized abortion are not unheard
of. In 1987, two religious sisters, Patricia Hussey and Barbara Ferraro, members of Sisters of Notre Dame de Namur, took to the
lecture circuit, mostly giving speeches on college campuses (including Catholic ones) to promote women's liberation and that abortion was necessary for such liberation. It was essentially a revolution
against Catholic sexual ethics—a feminist quest for the "will to
power." Albany's "Sister Mary" was, in many ways, the pre-cursor
to Sister Donna Quinn, a Sinsinawa Dominican nun, who twenty-
five years later escorted women into a Hinsdale, Illinois, abortion
clinic. Quinn was already well-known for her outspoken support
of legalized abortion. With twenty-three other religious sisters,
that included Hussey and Ferraro, she signed a full-page ad in the
October 7, 1985, edition of the *New York Times* opposing Catholic teaching on abortion by stating that a diversity of legitimate
opinions existed within the Church on the abortion issue—even
opinions such as Quinn's that supported the legalized killing of
the unborn. Since the mid-1970s Quinn had gained a reputation
for her dissent from Catholic teaching, not only on abortion, but
on contraception, homosexuality and the male priesthood as well.

In 2009 pro-lifers who sidewalk counseled at the ACU abortion
clinic in the wealthy Chicago suburb, recognized Sister Donna, an
elderly, petite woman with close cropped hair, as she helped escort
women into the building. The discovery led to a public scandal. Since
Quinn was directly aiding and abetting the killing of the unborn,
many Catholics, citing the *Code of Canon Law*, called for the nun's

excommunication. At first, Quinn's religious superior, Sr. Patricia Mulcahey, seemed to defend, or at least excuse, Quinn's involvement with the clinic. In an email sent to *LifeSite News*, an online, pro-life, news outlet, she said that Quinn "sees her volunteer activity as accompanying women who are verbally abused by protestors." But Quinn's religious community, perhaps feeling pressure from Church officials, soon publicly affirmed in a press release that the Sinsinawa Dominicans, faithful to Catholic teaching, supported the "dignity and value of every human life from conception to natural death," and declared abortion to be "an act of violence that destroys the life of the unborn." Quinn's superiors directed her to quit her "ministry." Upon doing so, however, Quinn felt the need to state: "I wish to make it clear that this is my decision. Respect for women's moral agency is of critical importance to me." She looked forward to "dialogue with our congregation on these matters as a way of informing my actions as well as educating the community."

When Donna and I stood outside Albany this Saturday in 1982, we found it impossible to believe that the woman who now confronted us was a nun. Donna challenged her again. "Maybe you were a nun and left the order . . . but there's no way you're a nun now."

"No, I am a nun, right now, with vows of poverty, chastity, and obedience," she insisted.

"Then how come you're working in an abortion clinic?" Sister Mary took a step closer. She was a large woman, and she drew herself up to her full height, intimidating us with her size, her light blue eyes narrowing. She seemed to enjoy looming over us.

"Because, my dear, we must preserve the freedom to choose."

"Do you believe that human life is sacred?" I asked.

"Yes."

"Then how can you work in an abortion clinic? How can you work in a place like that—in a place where people are killed?"

"Because I respect people's right to choose."

"But you are helping a woman to decide to kill her own child."

"I am helping that woman make the decision she feels is best for her."

"But you believe human life is sacred."

"Yes, I do. But not everyone believes that."

"Why don't you help these women come to terms with reality?" Donna joined in. "Help the woman see that she is aborting a person. The unborn are human—it's a biological fact."

"No it's not," replied Sister Mary.

Donna and I were not surprised at all that our nun chose to deny the scientific evidence of the humanity of the fetus, but Sister Mary's defense of abortion went way beyond whether the fetus was a human being or not, as she continued:

"But that's not the issue here. Even if it could be shown, beyond any doubt, that the fetus is as human as you or I, abortion would still be a woman's right."

"What on earth are you talking about?" I asked. "How can you say such a thing? Even *Roe versus Wade* said that if the unborn child is a person the whole case collapses."

"Well, I'm not only talking about legal rights—I'm talking about the ultimate right of each person to self-determination, the liberty to choose, and so it's a question of human dignity."

Now I began to understand. When Sister Mary declared, "We have to preserve the freedom to choose," this was not solely political or even feminist jargon. Sister Mary did not mean simply the freedom of a woman to choose abortion. She was referring to freedom in a much broader sense—the freedom to choose what to do for oneself, unconstrained by others or society at large. According to this ethic, the greatest human good is freedom of choice, and the greatest evil is the force that keeps someone from acting upon his or her choice. Thus, when choices are restricted, freedom is compromised. All that matters is the exercise of sheer human will. Human dignity and autonomy cannot be had without it. It seemed the sister was better acquainted with Jean Paul Sartre than St. Francis of Assisi.

"Sorry," Donna interjected, "But I don't see how killing an innocent person makes me free."

"Personhood depends on at least some rudimentary ability to

think—and fetuses, at least in the early stages of development, lack this quality," she explained. "Though I suppose it is possible that even an atheist might conclude that the fetus is human—it depends on one's personal philosophy."

"Whether you're a believer or an atheist, the fact is, people are dying in that abortion clinic right now," Donna argued, her voice rising sharply. She pointed to the clinic. "You're helping these women choose to kill."

"Don't shout. I'm respecting their right to choose."

"But the result of their choosing is a dead human person!"

"Don't shout" Sister Mary said again. "Don't you understand that no one can restrict a person's freedom to choose? A person's right to choose?"

I tried to get at the heart of the issue by a more direct route.

"Sister Mary, are you a person?"

"Now *that's* a very intelligent question."

"Are you?"

She sighed. "Yes, it is reasonable to say that I am."

"Do I have the right to kill you?"

"No."

"Okay, but according to your own logic, don't you have to respect my choice to kill you?"

"Why would I have to?"

"Because if no one can restrict a person's freedom to choose, then on what basis can you restrict my right to kill you?"

"I have the freedom to choose to tell you not to kill me, and I can choose to defend myself."

"But you're saying that there's nothing wrong with *my* choice to kill you, right? You might stop me, if you choose, so I might not actually kill you, but you can't say that there is anything wrong with my own personal choice, right?"

Sister Mary explained: "Your choice would be wrong if you didn't act for some good."

"No, No," Donna objected. "You're saying that the end can justify the means and that might makes right."

"Not at all," our nun responded, shaking her head. "Look, in the case of abortion, ethics are not clear. It's wrong for you to dictate the choices people make—it's wrong for you to restrict their freedom—if you do that you trample on their rights."

"But what about persons that can't choose like you? It's not just the unborn. What about the mentally handicapped? What about the elderly? Some of them can't make their own decisions anymore. Are they less of a person than you?"

"You know," I continued, "What you're talking about here isn't freedom. It's *license*. There's a difference. By your way of thinking, any tyrant could do anything he wanted to his people. The Communist *gulags* would be perfectly justified."

I then decided to switch topics. "Are you chaste?"

"Yes. I practice my vow of chastity."

"Then why do you look down on us for not being sexually active?"

"Because I *choose* to be chaste."

We assured Sister Mary that our choice not to have sex outside of marriage was our completely free choice. In Sister Mary's way of thinking, we could not be free if we were forced into chastity by circumstances or even compelled to refrain from sex for fear of offending God or the Church.

"Let me tell you about the saddest thing I've ever encountered," Sister Mary continued. "A woman called this clinic totally frantic that she had to have an abortion. She had to have it before one o'clock on a particular day. The woman asked if she could come through the back door. 'What?' I said. 'Listen, this is the seventies. Women don't have to come through the back door to have abortions anymore.' Well, it turned out that this woman was active in the right-to-life movement and was going to have this abortion before she got on a plane that afternoon to go to the National Right to Life convention! So even your own folks will betray the cause when they see the need for abortion."

Sister Mary was a master at psyching out the opposition. Donna and I did not know whether to believe her or not. We were still trying to figure out if she was a real nun. It was possible that she had just made up her story to crush our morale, and, true or not, she was getting close to her goal.

Suddenly another worker appeared at the door and called Sister Mary back into the clinic. There was a note of urgency in her voice. Donna and I were damp from standing in the rain, but we decided to stay at the clinic a bit longer. A few minutes later, Sister Mary came back out.

"Well, it's your lucky day," she said. "A girl left."

"And did you help this girl make the decision that was best for her?" I asked sarcastically.

Our nun looked away from us, fixing her gaze on some point across the street behind us. "The girl's one of you pro-lifers. She's in with the Scheidler bunch. We wouldn't do 'er."

I shook my head and smiled, no longer shocked by her story. I felt confident that this liberated nun *was* only spinning tales after all.

She spoke again. "We do your people all the time here!" Then she leered at the rosary in Donna's hand. "And sixty-eight percent of the women having abortions are Catholic! Those are the statistics!"

Sister Mary went back to the abortion clinic. Donna and I continued to huddle in the niche and wait for the next client.

A couple from India approached the clinic door. Donna and I engaged them in conversation, and the four of us spoke for a few minutes, standing only a few feet from the clinic's entrance. "I am out of work," explained the man through a thick Indian accent. "We have four children already. We are not here for abortion, only for the Pill." His wife looked away from us shyly and eyed the door to the building.

Sister Mary pushed open the door, held it wide, and ushered the couple into the waiting room. After they were inside, Sister Mary yelled: "You two were blocking the door! Don't you people know that you've got to keep moving? You can't stand in one place!"

"We have every right to stand on this sidewalk and speak to people and you know it!" Donna shot back.

From the perspective of the abortion clinic staff, it was important that those who tried to talk women out of abortions be forced to keep moving. They knew that if we had to parade around in a circle we would not be able to approach their customers. "Fine, I'm calling the police," Sr. Mary threatened. Then she withdrew.

The small group praying the rosary had already disbanded. "Let's go," Donna said. "It's raining, my feet hurt, and, look, a bus is coming that we can catch."

"No, I want to stay. If we leave now, the clinic workers will think their threat chased us off. I'm not going. If we go, it'll look like we are guilty of doing something wrong when we're not. Besides, we're not picketers. We're not demonstrating against abortion. We're trying to help women and we didn't block their dumb door!"

Sister Mary's threat became a reality. Three squad cars pulled up to the curb. A policewoman, two policemen, a plainclothes officer, and a Sergeant Walsh got out. Donna and I were huddled in the niche again to avoid the rain. The sergeant walked over to us, accompanied by one of the male officers.

"Are you from Right-to-Life?" the sergeant snapped.

"Yes."

"You have to keep moving, and don't block the door," he said gruffly.

"We didn't—"

"Listen, lady, we both saw you. Don't even try to deny it."

Donna and I were befuddled and frustrated by the officers' anger. Why were they so mad? What had we done to provoke them? It is possible that the sergeant saw us standing by the door as we spoke to the Indian couple. But he would not permit us to explain what we were doing and that we were not blocking the door. We made several attempts to explain ourselves, but the police did not want to listen.

"Just keep moving and don't block their door. I don't want to hear what you have to say, just don't block the door."

"We don't have to keep moving," Donna insisted.

"I know the law better than you do, lady. If I arrest you, you can argue the law in front of a judge. What are you doing out here so late anyway? You're not usually here this late."

Sister Mary had emerged from the clinic to observe the confrontation. She stood with another woman, a clinic customer, who was waiting for a friend to pick her up.

"Look," Sergeant Walsh said. "I'm with you people. I'm a Catholic. I'm probably a better Catholic than you'll ever be, but I'll arrest you if this clinic complains again. Now don't block the door and that's all!"

To my surprise, Walsh walked over to Sister Mary. "I'm not with you at all. But I have to protect you. I'll uphold the law," he told her.

I found it interesting that he needed to identify himself as a Catholic when Donna and I had not told him our religious affiliation. I began to understand that Walsh's anger was simply a reflection of his torn conscience. Ultimately Walsh, and officers like him, were angry at the law that allowed abortion and imposed on them the duty to protect its practice.

Walsh turned away brusquely and walked back to his squad car. He peeled away quickly. The other officer began to walk back to his squad car as the others began to leave. I left Donna in the niche and hurried to catch up to him.

"Why wouldn't you let us say anything in our defense?" I yelled at him.

"Do what we say!" he shouted back.

"But why are you all so angry?"

"I'm not angry!" he shouted.

"You just don't have any idea what we're trying to do here," I said as I turned away from him and began to walk back to Donna. To my surprise the officer followed me.

"I'm standing out here in the rain getting wet!" he shouted, as if he couldn't believe he could be doing something so ridiculous. "Now just don't block that door!"

"Fine! We aren't going to!"

The police left and Sister Mary and the other woman went back into the clinic. Donna and I were cold, wet, exhausted and frustrated. The rain continued to pour. Now that the sidewalk was clear, I could hear the sound of raindrops as they hit the wet and shiny pavement. Suddenly, to my surprise, I saw that one of the young policemen had returned. He pulled his squad car up to the curb in front of the clinic. He had remained in his vehicle when Walsh was speaking to us.

"You do understand about not blocking the door," he said with concern and kindness in his voice.

"We understand very well, officer," I told him.

A few moments after he left, the officer with whom Donna and I had quarreled pulled his squad car up to the corner at the side street at the end of the block. He glanced our way. I decided to make a friendly gesture to show him that we had no hard feelings. I waved to him. He waved back. Then for a moment he paused. He looked straight ahead through his rain-spattered windshield and then slowly pulled away.

Another Irving Park Road bus was slowly approaching. It stopped across the street. Rain began to pour even harder as Donna and I raced against the light and caught the bus just as it was about to pull away. Tired and wet we sank into a seat. Perhaps too bewildered by that morning's confrontation, neither of us spoke. Our debate with Sr. Mary pounded in my ears. This nun, this ex-nun, this run-a-way from the novitiate—whatever she was—had taught me a bitter lesson about abortion. She opened up a philosophy of choice and an argument for abortion that I had not imagined. I had come to believe that the controversy about abortion hinged on whether or not the unborn child was a person. Even the *Roe v. Wade* decision itself had acknowledged that if it could be shown that the fetus was a person according to the meaning of the 14th Amendment then "the appellant's case, of course, collapses, for the fetus' right to life would then be guaranteed specifically by the Amendment." Perhaps for many, maybe even the majority of those involved in the abortion war, this continues to be the central issue. But I suddenly felt overwhelmed. Abortion was, after all, about something even bigger than "simply" the right to life. Sr. Mary had revealed to me a whole new dimension to the abortion debate, born perhaps from a Nietzschian world—a world with no God of any kind and no moral standard. The prime value was human liberty and its exercise without restraint, and so, for Sister Mary abortion was a sacrament—Albany her shrine.

CHAPTER SEVEN

THIS POOR YOUNGLING

"From this day forward I shall no longer tinker with the machinery of death."
>   —Supreme Court Justice Harry Blackmun,
>   author of *Roe v. Wade*,
>   commenting on capital punishment.

SIDEWALK-COUNSELING, sit-ins, arrests, and court dates occupied the bulk of my pro-life activity in the mid-1980s. By 1985, I had taken on a minor leadership role, having organized sit-ins with Joe Scheidler at Biogenetics, Concord and the Albany clinic. But in addition to my growing radicalism, I also served on the board of directors of the Illinois Right to Life Committee. In 1985, after attending a year's worth of meetings, I was offered the position of executive director. In May of 1985, then, I stepped into the position from which, ironically, Joe Scheidler had been fired in 1978, the year he and I first met. The IRLC board knew that, like Joe, I was a committed activist, but my superiors on the board and I came to an agreement that when I led or participated in sit-ins, I would not do so as the director of the IRLC.

In any case, there was little time for any conflict to develop, as my new position would only be a short-term summer stint, as I planned to leave Chicago in August. I had graduated four years earlier from Loyola with a Master's Degree in Theology, and had taught religion since then at Madonna High School for Girls on

Chicago's west side. Soon I would head north to Milwaukee to begin work on my doctorate at Marquette University. While my new position afforded me a measure of authority, it would not be until I moved to Milwaukee that I would really come into my own as an activist leader.

Illinois Right to Life still maintained its small, cluttered three-office suite in the Monadnock Building in the heart of downtown Chicago. On the morning of Tuesday, July 30, I took my usual El train to work. A man sitting in front of me was reading the *Chicago Sun-Times*. As I glanced over his shoulder, a headline caught my eye: "Abortion ban for retarded girl lifted." I settled back into my seat and gazed out the window at a beautiful summer day.

After getting off the train, I saw a *Chicago Sun-Times* newspaper machine at the corner of Jackson and Clark, dropped in my quarter, and retrieved a paper from the box. One of my duties as executive director of the IRLC was to keep the action hotline updated with current pro-life news and events, and I thought this article might supply some fresh material. When I arrived at the office, I said hello to the secretary, Gertrude, and went to my office. I sipped a cup of coffee and started to read the article.

The article reported that, on the previous day, the Illinois Appellate Court had ruled that a mother could obtain an abortion for her pregnant eighteen-year-old daughter, who the *Sun-Times* described as "severely retarded." This ruling overturned the decision of circuit court Judge Richard Dowdle, who had said that the girl's mother could not seek an abortion because there was no evidence that the "procedure was necessary to protect the girl's life or health." The American Civil Liberties Union Reproductive Rights Project, a division of the ACLU that sought to protect and advance access to legalized abortion, represented the mother in appealing Judge Dowdle's decision.

According to the *Sun-Times*, the girl had become pregnant by a neighborhood youth, who likely had taken advantage of the mentally handicapped girl's vulnerability. The girl's mother wanted her daughter's baby aborted because "[if a] girl with the mental capacity of a five-year-old can't take care of herself, how can she be expected to care for a child?"

The ACLU had recruited two doctors to testify in favor of aborting the baby, who was now nearly four months gestational age. Dr. Jerry L. Warren, a psychologist, and Dr. Marvin Roser, an obstetrician, both spoke of the girl's pregnancy only in the bleakest terms. Dr. Roser, however, never actually examined the teen, but told the court that the girl did not understand what it means to be pregnant, would not be able to cooperate with the birth process, and that the delivery would cause her psychological and physical harm. Warren even stated, ironically, that the baby should be aborted because the girl would not take physical precautions "in order to avoid injury to herself or the fetus."

The three appellate court judges who heard the case did not seem to pay very much attention to the "expert" medical testimony. They empowered the mother to abort her daughter's baby because, as their written opinion stated:

"Plainly, there is no legal requirement that a medical necessity exist before a guardian can consent to an abortion." In effect, their decision was abortion-on-demand for the mentally handicapped at the discretion of the legal guardian. The ACLU was completely correct in viewing the case as setting a precedent. The legal right to an abortion had not yet been extended to a guardian of a mentally handicapped person, and the ACLU saw this case as an opportunity to facilitate just that. Attorneys Colleen Connell and Benjamin Wolf of ACLU's Reproductive Rights Project represented the mother. The *Sun-Times* reported they saw their successful overturning of Judge Dowdle's decision as a declaration that "the disabled have constitutional rights to reproductive freedom."

In four days the appellate court was to issue a writ of mandate to Judge Dowdle ordering him to allow the mother to arrange for the abortion. The unborn child had a court-appointed guardian, an attorney named Thomas Chuhak, and if he filed an appeal to the Illinois Supreme Court before the end of the four days the writ would be automatically stayed, and the abortion delayed pending the Illinois Supreme Court hearing. An appeal would give us a window of opportunity, and therefore hope that the baby's life would be spared.

I was determined to do what I could to protect this child. I threw the *Sun-Times* down on the desk, looked up Chuhak's number in the Yellow Pages, and placed the call. Chuhak himself answered. I introduced myself to him and told him that I was the executive director of the Illinois Right to Life Committee.

"I certainly hope you plan to appeal the decision before the writ of mandate is issued," I said, coming to the point. "Why is the court only giving you four days? Is that enough time to file the appeal?"

"Well, yes, we do plan to appeal, but I can't do anything until the court issues its written opinion. That might not be 'til this afternoon or tomorrow," Chuhak answered. I told him I hoped the baby's life would be saved. He responded, "I plan to do my best on this case."

As I spoke to him, I was struck by the idea that I really should talk with the girl's mother myself. I asked Chuhak if he would give me her name and address, but he refused, saying that would violate legal ethics. In my briefcase I had the names, address, and phone number of a couple who was looking to adopt a child. I said that even I would happily adopt the girl's baby, but Chuhak refused to pass on any names or information to the girl's mother. He told me that he was not allowed to have any contact with the plaintiff. Undoubtedly this had something to do with legal ethics too. Chuhak suggested I talk to Connell and Wolf at the ACLU.

When I hung up the phone, I had a slightly uneasy feeling about Chuhak. He sounded sincere enough on the unborn baby's behalf, but there was a certain hesitancy in his voice and a distracted vagueness in his tone that made me a little uncomfortable.

After I spoke with Chuhak I immediately called Colleen Connell at the ACLU. When Connell came to the phone I introduced myself and told her I wanted to adopt the girl's baby. Connell's tone was hard-edged and terse, her obvious disdain thinly veiled behind a cool and authoritative professionalism.

She refused to give my name to the mother and said adoption had already been discussed with her. I tried to reason with Connell.

"Do you really want this baby to die?" I finally asked her.

She hung up the phone.

I immediately dialed the ACLU number again. This time I asked for Benjamin Wolf.

"I have right in front of me the name of a couple who I know would be willing to adopt this child."

"I'm sorry, I will not pass on any names to our client."

"Well, why not?" I asked, still trying to be pleasant.

"It's not in the best interest of my client."

"Wouldn't it be better to have the baby adopted than aborted?"

"You know, if you were really sincere about adoption, you would be concerned about babies already living," Wolf said.

"Please don't be medieval," I replied. "This unborn baby's as alive as any other child."

"No, it's not. It's not yet a person with rights. And as I said, there are plenty of children already born, children with special needs that no one wants to adopt," Wolf said.

"Yes, that's true, but those children are not in danger of being attacked. There's a certain urgency about the child in question here."

"I've said all I'm going to say to you," Wolf responded, then hung up.

The phone receiver was attached to my ear for the rest of the day. I talked to Maura Quinlin, a lawyer with Americans United for Life whose office was directly across the street from the IRLC. I asked her to call Chuhak and give him any advice he might need to assure that his appeal was filed on time. Maura was very eager to help. I also called Greg Morrow, an outgoing, distinguished-looking man in his fifties and a seasoned sidewalk counselor who spent many Saturday mornings at Concord talking women out of abortions.

Greg's son's mother-in-law, Mary Boyle, who had a mentally handicapped child, was very familiar with schools for special-needs children in Chicago. Chuhak had told me that the pregnant girl attended school during the day, and I asked Mary if she would make some calls to find out if there were any pregnant girls in the system. She, too, was eager to help.

That afternoon I called Joe Scheidler. He was not in his office at the Pro-Life Action League, which he founded after Friends for Life closed its doors in 1982. I spoke with his wife, Ann, who told me that she and Joe would be happy to adopt the baby themselves, and she gave me the name of another couple who had been trying to adopt.

Even after I left the office for the day and went back home, I continued to make calls. Thus far Mary Boyle had not found the girl but said she would continue to try. I called Patrick Crotty, an attorney who had defended me when I was arrested for a sit-in at Biogenetics in Chicago four years earlier. He agreed to accompany me to the ACLU offices the next morning. We intended to present Connell and Wolf with the names of the couples who wanted to adopt the girl's baby. Finally I flopped into my bed exhausted, a prayer for God's help fading on my lips.

On the morning of Wednesday, July 31, Patrick met me on the street outside of the ACLU. This was not the first time I had been at the Chicago ACLU's high-rise suite. I was there four years earlier, two days before Christmas, with Joe Scheidler and about six other people. Joe used to go around to the ACLU, Planned Parenthood and City Hall carrying a crèche and singing Christmas carols. Joe did it partly for fun and partly in protest. The ACLU had been litigating cases for years to ban nativity scenes on government property and Christmas carols in public schools. Our small troupe crowded in at the door of the office. Joe stood at the front holding his small cardboard crèche and we stood behind him holding our sheet music. As we launched into our chorus of "Joy to the World," the staff smiled at us and laughed, apparently enjoying the unexpected break from their work.

The atmosphere at the Planned Parenthood offices was considerably less jovial. We decided to sing the "Coventry Carol," a strange and haunting lament for Herod's slaughter of the Beth-lehem infants. David Levine, the executive director of Chicago Planned Parenthood, three staff members and a young woman seated in a waiting room chair made up our audience.

Our roving little choir contained some very good voices. Joe Scheidler himself was a trained baritone, and our rendition of the Carol was quite beautiful—and effective. The message of the song was not lost on the workers. Levine listened to the song with a frown on his face.

> O sisters too, how may we do
> For to preserve this day
> This poor Youngling for whom we do sing
> Bye, bye, lully, lullay?
> Herod the king, in his raging,
> Charged he hath this day
> His men of might, in his own sight
> All children young to slay.
> Then woe is me, poor Child, for Thee!
> And every mourn and say,
> For thy parting neither say nor sing
> Bye, bye, lully, lullay.

As we neared the end of the song I cast a glance at the young woman in the waiting room. She was staring at us, tears in her eyes. I wondered if perhaps she was pregnant and at Planned Parenthood to seek advice on abortion. Perhaps she already had an abortion. She was the only one in the office who did not appear to resent our song.

On this hot July morning, Patrick Crotty and I probably would have been better received at the ACLU if we had sung a few Christmas carols. The secretary would not let us see either Connell or Wolf, claiming they were both too busy writing briefs that they were already behind in completing.

"But we only need a few minutes of their time," I insisted.

The secretary continued to cordially refuse us. All I could do was hand her the list of names of prospective adoptive parents, which she promised to pass on to the attorneys. Patrick took out a business card from his wallet and gave it to the secretary and asked her to have Mr. Wolf call him.

As I walked the short distance back to my office, I deliberated about what to do next. I poured my third cup of coffee and slumped into the desk chair. That morning's *Sun-Times* still lay on my desk, unread. I picked it up and began to flip through it, glancing at headlines here and there. The headline on page three gave me a jolt: "Pro-life leader offers to take baby as abortion alternative." The story was about Joe and Ann Scheidler's offer to adopt the girl's baby. Joe was quoted, "I just wanted the grandmother to know there is someone willing and eager to adopt the baby if the pregnancy is allowed to continue." I was elated. There was every possibility that the girl's mother—the baby's grandmother—would see the article.

I decided it was time to get back in touch with Thomas Chuhak. It was silly and fruitless to try to work with ACLU attorneys. Chuhak knew the girl and the mother and could easily get in touch with them. At this point I could not have cared less about legal ethics—an innocent human being's death was about to be sanctioned, and we were bothering about professional protocol. From my perspective, if Chuhak was the guardian for the unborn baby, his job was to advocate for the life of the child. I saw no reason why he could not pass the names of potential adoptive parents to the girl's mother or permit a third party to do so. I dialed his number.

"Hi, this is Monica again, from Illinois Right to Life."

That was as far as I got. Chuhak cut me off immediately. "The written opinion just came down," he said hurriedly. "I can't talk to you right now. I have to be somewhere right away."

"Okay," I said firmly, "but there's something very important I want to discuss with you."

"I'll be out the rest of the day, Chuhak responded. "Call me in the morning."

"Okay, I will," I said, and hung up the phone. I had the distinctly uncomfortable feeling that Chuhak did not want to speak with me. I hoped that wherever he was rushing off to so suddenly had to do with filing an appeal to stay the deadly mandate.

That evening Benjamin Wolf spoke as a guest on a WIND radio talk show. It was a call-in show, and both Joe Scheidler and I got on the air. Joe reiterated his offer to adopt the girl's baby, and I said that there were other couples who would adopt the child as well.

"We are dealing with two lives," I said. "We should work to do what is best for the girl and her baby without deliberately harming either."

"Isn't it preposterous for a mentally-retarded girl to have a baby?" the host of the program argued.

"It's only impossible if you have no hope," I responded. "Why should this situation be a cause for despair? The ACLU acts like there is absolutely nobody in the whole world who could possibly be a mother and father to this child. I don't see how discriminating against the girl or her baby can be an act of justice."

Thursday, the first day of August, was supposed to be my day off. I did not go into the office, but I spent nearly the entire day on the telephone anyway. I had been consumed for three days by the effort to save this baby from abortion, and I was now a bundle of frayed nerves. It was difficult to eat and difficult to sleep. Each moment was a battle between hope and anxiety, but my determination had not weakened.

I spent hours trying to talk to Chuhak, but every time I called his office, he was on another line, in a meeting or out to lunch. I called Maura Quinlin and asked her to call Chuhak. Perhaps, since she was an attorney herself, Chuhak would feel better speaking to her. I wanted to know if he had filed the appeal. Maura assured me she would call him. Twenty minutes later my phone rang. Maura was on the other end of the line, boiling with indignation and anger.

Maura recounted to me her conversation with Chuhak, and told me that he was not going to appeal the decision now, but rather wait until he had more time to prepare and after emotions had cooled down. Perhaps Chuhak believed that strategy might have provided a better chance of winning the case, but by that time the baby would be dead.

"Please go see Judge Dowdle," I begged Maura, "and ask him to make you the *guardian ad litem*." Judge Dowdle had appointed Chuhak in the first place. If he would permit Maura to replace him, she could file an emergency petition to the Illinois Supreme Court to request a stay of the mandate.

Maura went to see Judge Dowdle that afternoon at his office in the Daley Center in downtown Chicago. When she arrived, Wolf and Connell were already there. They had been notified of the meeting—this too had something to do with legal ethics. Maura told Dowdle that an appeal needed to be filed immediately in order to save the baby. Maura said she was willing to do that and take over the guardianship, but Dowdle would not remove Chuhak as guardian. After the meeting ended, Wolf and Connell caught up to Maura in the hallway.

"I hope you're prepared to be sued," Connell threatened.

"Sued?" Maura asked. "For what?"

"Yes, sued—for court costs, because your little meeting with Dowdle took us away from our work."

"Gee, I didn't know ACLU attorneys were so petty," said Maura as she turned and walked away.

I decided to visit Judge Dowdle myself. I was going to make one final plea that Chuhak be replaced as guardian. Patrick Crotty agreed to go with me the next morning, which was the fourth day—the day the mandate would be given to Dowdle to grant permission for the girl's abortion. I went to bed that night pleading to another Judge: "God, do something, please. I don't know what, just do something so the baby won't die."

I awoke the next morning with my heart already racing. Pat was supposed to call and tell me when to be at Dowdle's office, but it was now ten o'clock and the phone had not rung. I could not wait another moment. I got into my rusted 1977 Toyota Celica and dashed downtown. Unbelievably, in the middle of a Chicago business day, I found a parking space just outside the Daley Center. I ran into the building and raced to the elevators. As I rode up to the eighteenth floor I caught my breath and wiped the sweat from my forehead. Finally, the doors slid open and I ran to Dowdle's court. The room was completely empty except for a tall, dark-haired young woman who was sorting papers near the judge's bench. I walked toward her.

"Hi. I wonder if you could tell me if Judge Dowdle issued the appellate court mandate concerning the abortion for the mentally handicapped girl?"

The woman glanced up at me once, then looked back down at her papers and continued shuffling through them as she spoke.

"I didn't want anything to do with that. I was supposed to process the mandate, but I wouldn't."

I was delighted to hear that this woman, Dowdle's court clerk, had taken a stand, but I was afraid that the mandate had already been given.

"I commend you for your stand. I wish a lot of others would do the same."

I asked the woman her name. She told me it was Alice.

"Well, Alice, do you know if the mandate's been issued?"

"I don't know. I had nothin' to do with it," she said in disgust. "Go ask the other clerk, Lisa. She processed it. She's here somewhere."

I left Dowdle's court and walked toward the suite of judge's offices. When another young woman came out of the door carrying papers in her hand, we nearly bumped into one another.

"Can I help you?" she asked.

"I'm from the Illinois Right to Life Committee, and I'm very interested in the case involving the mentally handicapped girl who's pregnant."

"Oh, yes. I got the mandate for that case this morning."

I had found Lisa.

"Do you know if the ACLU lawyers were here this morning?"

"Oh yes, they were already here," said the clerk.

I was surprised at how extremely friendly and open the clerk was with me. Unlike most clerks I had encountered, she was not terse or in a hurry. However, it was now apparent that the mandate had been issued. My attempts to save the baby were growing bleaker every second.

Lisa shuffled the documents in her hands.

"These are the papers for the case," she said, holding them out in front of me.

I hadn't even asked to see them. I didn't know what sort of papers they were. I might have been staring at the top page of the mandate itself. But I didn't care what they were. This was an utterly unexpected chance—I could never have predicted that a court clerk would be standing in front of me with the very documents I needed to see. I was searching for one thing only: information that would lead me to the mother.

Lisa let me feast my eyes. Before long I spotted the mother's name and address. In seconds I had it all committed to memory.

I don't know why Lisa let me see those papers. I thought the case was under a court seal. I accepted it all as an instance of grace.

I decided I still wanted to talk to Dowdle to find out exactly what had happened. I also wanted Chuhak, who was going to argue the appeal whether the baby was dead or alive, removed from the case. Dowdle was out to lunch. I sat on a bench in the hall and waited for him. Dowdle returned a short while later and his secretary admitted me into his office.

Dowdle sat behind a desk cluttered with papers and notes. He was a tall, lanky man with large hands and a deep voice. He was in his early sixties. I sat down in a chair in front of his desk and told him who I was and why I had come.

"Did you already hand down the mandate for the abortion?" I asked him.

"I issued it this morning," he said. There was an unmistakable look of dismay on his face.

"It's too late then," I said.

"Look, I'm against abortion. It's against my religion. I'm against the *Roe* decision and I'm against this appellate court decision. But I'm sworn to uphold the law. I'm disgusted with the appellate court's decision." I was staring at a man who truly regretted that he had to issue a mandate that would probably result in the death of an unborn child. It was as though abortion was a kind of a machine with pulleys and gears all twisting in every direction and this poor soul had become trapped in the mesh.

I told him that Chuhak had not filed the appeal on time to save the baby and asked if he would make me the guardian for the unborn child, but he refused.

"You know, I think the baby's already dead," he said. "I think the abortion was prearranged at some clinic, with a doctor standing by as soon as the mandate was issued. Besides, no matter what you might think about Chuhak, he still has the skill to argue a good appeal."

I shook my head, dismayed. I got up from my chair, thanked Dowdle for his time, and left the office. For now I was done with attorneys, clerks and judges.

I immediately went to the phone booth in the hallway and called Greg Morrow. I told him I had the mother's name and address, and I didn't want to visit her alone. Greg agreed to come, and I picked him up at his home on the southwest side.

Margaret, the mother of the pregnant girl, lived on the South Side. Her address took us to the heart of the inner city, to a drab, run-down, ugly neighborhood. I pulled up in front of a small, two-story brick home. As Greg and I got out of the car and walked toward the house I could feel my palms grow clammy. My heart beat wildly, and a terrible nervousness gnawed at the pit of my stomach. In my hand I clutched some pro-life pamphlets. I expected that as soon as the people at home knew who we were, they would fly into an indignant rage, curse us, call the police and slam the door in our faces. I knocked on the door. Within seconds a young black man in his mid-twenties opened it.

"Hi. We're here to see Margaret," I said.

"Okay. Come on in," he said, holding the door open for us.

Greg and I stepped inside. The living room was poorly lit and the furniture and carpeting were worn and shabby. I noticed that the carpet runners on the stairs to the second floor were worn completely through in the center of each step. On the living room couch a young girl sat watching television. When Greg and I entered the room, she looked up at us with wide, brown eyes. Moments later an older woman emerged from the kitchen and came into the living room. She was in her early fifties. Her face, lined with age and worry, betrayed a difficult life. I asked if she was Margaret, hoping I didn't sound like a reporter or an agent from the IRS.

"Yes, I am," the woman answered as she eyed us both suspiciously. "What's this all about?"

"Margaret, you don't know me and I don't know you, but I want you to know that I really care about you and your daughter. Four days ago I read about you in the paper and I've been looking for you ever since. We would like to help you and your daughter."

"Help? How? Besides, the lawyers said I shouldn't talk to no one about this case."

At this point, a man who was about Margaret's age came into the room. We all exchanged greetings. He introduced himself as Thomas, Margaret's husband. Then the girl who had been sitting on the couch got up and went over to Margaret.

"Mama, I want to go outside. I want ice cream."

Her childlike speech told me that I was indeed looking at the girl who was the center of so much conflict. After reading the newspaper, the court's written opinion, and speaking to the ACLU attorneys, I half-expected the girl to be deformed and babbling. What I saw was an eighteen-year-old woman, physically healthy with the mental capacity of a young child.

"This is Dorsey," said Margaret. "She's my child from a previous marriage, but we call her Peaches."

Greg and I continued to explain: "Your daughter is the reason we're here," Greg concluded. "We were hoping to change your mind about aborting your daughter's baby."

"Well, I'll be honest with you," said Margaret. "I really don't know what we're gonna do."

Her words took me by surprise. Was this the same woman who, championed by the ACLU itself, had just come through a messy and high-profile legal battle so she could gain the right to make an abortion decision for her daughter? Greg and I had arrived at a critical moment. Margaret was wavering between getting the abortion and allowing the pregnancy to continue. She was open to guidance. Greg and I showed her the pamphlets we had brought that described fetal development and abortion procedures, as well as photos of aborted babies. Both Margaret and Thomas were visibly horrified at the pictures.

"I didn't know it was like that!" Margaret said. "But, you know, I'm afraid Peaches can't handle havin' the baby."

Greg and I offered Margaret the name of a pro-life obstetrician who, after examining Peaches at no cost, would determine what sort of delivery she needed to minimize the health risks. Margaret explained that she still thought of herself as a religious person, and both she and her husband agreed that the situation called for real trust in God. Only with His power and mercy could this pregnancy be brought to term.

We talked with Margaret and her husband for over two hours. Afterwards, Greg and I walked with Peaches to the corner grocer and bought her an ice cream. Peaches was extremely gentle and affectionate. It was easy to see how a neighborhood boy could have exploited her. Her mental disability was a result of oxygen loss at birth. She had a twin brother, born first, who was completely healthy. By the end of the evening, Margaret assured us that Peaches' pregnancy would continue. I went home relieved, happy, and astounded that the baby's life was saved after so much effort had been spent toward ending it.

In the following months, Greg and I often visited Margaret's family. Even though we were often tempted, Greg and I never told the media or the ACLU that Peaches' baby was not going to be killed. We wanted the pregnancy to continue quietly, without any interference.

Five months after Judge Dowdle issued the mandate, Peaches delivered a healthy, five-pound baby boy. She named him Marky. Confounding the "experts," Peaches was not traumatized by the caesarean section. Margaret and Thomas decided to raise the baby themselves rather than place him for adoption.

Greg and I visited Peaches a week after Marky was born. As we stepped into Margaret's living room I felt a deep sense of satisfaction—even accomplishment. Soon I would be leaving Chicago— a city that had been my training ground in pro-life work. I was glad that my activist experience there was ending with the joy of Peaches' baby.

Peaches was dressed in a bathrobe and was sitting comfortably in a cushioned chair. She gave us a smile when we said hello. Little Marky was asleep in a bassinet next to her. Margaret came into the room with a smile on her lined and careworn face. We asked how Peaches was doing.

"Sometimes she's irritable because of the incision, but I think she's doing pretty well," said Margaret. "We're happy it all worked out."

"He's a beautiful baby," said Greg.

"Yeah, he is," Margaret agreed, another smile breaking across her face.

I wondered if Connell and Wolf knew about the baby. Margaret said she did not think so. She had had no contact with them for several weeks. Apparently the ACLU attorneys were only interested in using Peaches' pregnancy to litigate a case to advance the cause of reproductive rights. They would never stand in this living room to offer encouragement to Peaches and her mother and be drawn into the wonder and beauty of this child. As I gazed at the baby, I felt embedded in the hand of God. I felt Him there. God and I looked together at Peaches and her child. The tiny newborn was enveloped in peaceful sleep—unaware that the world had judged he should never have been born.

PART II

THE EDGE OF THE WORLD

CHAPTER EIGHT

BREAD AND ROSES

As we come marching, marching, we battle too for men,
For they are women's children, and we mother them again.
Our lives shall not be sweated from birth until life closes;
Hearts starve as well as bodies; give us bread, but give us roses.
Bread and Roses.

—Lyrics by James Oppenheim,
for a song written for the
1910 women's Lowell,
Massachusetts textile strike.

I GATHERED Hector into my arms, placed the cat in the passenger seat of my Celica and, while a friend drove a rental van containing all my worldly possessions, we made the two-hour trek northward to Milwaukee, home of the Brewers, bratwurst and the Pabst and Miller breweries. The Schlitz Brewing Company, "the beer that made Milwaukee famous," had closed operations only a few years before I arrived.

As we sped northward up I-94 I knew that I was not headed toward Milwaukee only to study for a Ph.D. I was now a seasoned activist who had already gained something of a reputation for leadership. Between 1978 and 1985 I had spent hundreds of hours sidewalk counseling at Chicago abortion clinics. I had planned and participated in a half-dozen sit-ins. I had been arrested at Biogenetics, the Michigan Avenue Medical Center, the Concord

Medical Center, the Albany Medical Center on Elston Avenue and its sister clinic on Irving Park Road. In 1984, I organized a small sit-in group and called it Citizens for a Pro-Life Society. While my move to Milwaukee was necessitated by doctoral studies, a whole new episode fighting abortion was about to begin, an episode that would take me into dark places I never could have envisioned.

I was already familiar with Milwaukee. Over the last couple of years I had visited the city to give workshops on picketing and sidewalk-counseling to pro-life activists. Sandy Schultz, a homemaker in her late twenties and a devout Lutheran, was the leader of a group of demonstrators who picketed the Milwaukee clinics. Her group was called the Milwaukee Pro-Life Coalition, and their activities accounted for the majority of the pro-life presence at the city's clinics. In an effort to increase the coalition's members and effectiveness, Sandy invited me and others to come up and share our insights on how to save unborn babies.

Accordingly, in June, 1984, Joe Scheidler and I were guests at an activist conference sponsored by the coalition. Jerry Horn, who lived in Appleton, Wisconsin, was also invited. He and his good friend Norm Stone were "on-fire-for-the-Lord" evangelical Christians, though Jerry would eventually convert to Catholicism in 1997. In 1984, he and Norm were a constant thorn in the side of the Fox Valley Reproductive Health Center, an abortion clinic near Appleton. They were arrested that year for entering the clinic to hand out pamphlets and to talk to women in the waiting room. By the standards of the time, this was considered an enormously bold action. Norm and Jerry were the first pro-lifers in the state to be arrested for their activism.

Joe, Jerry and I gave our workshops to about thirty pro-lifers in a sectioned-off corner of the lobby at the Wisconsin Hotel in downtown Milwaukee. The rather run-down edifice was located just around the block from the Bread and Roses Women's Health Center near Third and Wisconsin, which we had picketed just that morning.

After the luncheon, Joe, Jerry, and I decided on the spur of the

moment to pay Bread and Roses a personal visit. Our intention was
to go into the clinic's waiting room and pass out pro-life literature
to any women waiting to get an abortion. Joe, who had done this
many times in Chicago, referred to it as a "clinic blitz."

We entered the building and took the elevator to the seventh
floor. When the elevators opened, we crossed a small hallway to
the double glass doors of Bread and Roses. Joe pushed one of the
doors open. Suddenly a young black man dressed in medical whites
sprang to his feet and dashed out from behind the reception desk
toward the door. Apparently he had recognized us from that morning's picket, or perhaps he simply could tell we were not prospective
clients. "You get out of here!" he yelled as he frantically tried to
push the door shut against us. He managed to shove it closed, and
placed his weight against it. Joe and Jerry tried to push it back open,
but the worker had turned the bolt from the inside and locked it.

Jerry yelled through the glass. "Why don't you take our literature and show it to the women?"

I saw through the glass a stout, bespectacled woman in a long
skirt standing behind the reception desk talking on the phone and
looking in our direction. We got back into the elevator, took it to
the ground floor, and walked out of the building. I was impressed
by the clinic worker's almost crazed dedication to keeping us out.
He acted as if the clinic was a fortress under siege, which he was
sworn to protect at all costs. He certainly did not behave as if it was
a business open to the public. In any case, it certainly was not open
to us.

The three of us walked down the street and were met by two
police officers. They had responded to the clinic's distress call.

"You were just at the abortion clinic, weren't you?" one officer
asked.

"Yes, to give women information the clinic won't give them," I
said. "But we didn't get in."

The police whipped out their citation pads and on the spot
issued us tickets for disorderly conduct. We had the option of
returning to Milwaukee two weeks later to have our case reviewed

by a city attorney. Joe, Jerry and I were very unhappy that we would have to travel some distance for a hearing, but it seemed we had no choice if we were going to try to explain ourselves.

On a warm, sunny day at the end of June, Joe wedged his large body into my Celica, and we drove back up to Milwaukee. We met Jerry at the Milwaukee City Attorney's Office. The large bespectacled woman from Bread and Roses was there, accompanied by a young man in a dark blue suit, the attorney for the abortion clinic. We were called into a little office by a young black man, a city attorney. The woman, who identified herself as the clinic director, spoke first.

"These three people tried to enter my clinic. They wouldn't leave and were yelling in the hall."

"We consider this a serious incident," the clinic attorney said sternly.

The city attorney wanted to hear our side of the story.

"The three of us wanted to go into the abortion clinic to give information to women in the waiting room. We intended to go in, pass out the literature and leave, but when we got to the door one of the workers held it closed and then locked it so we couldn't get in and we finally left," I explained.

"They wanted to disrupt our business," said the director.

The city attorney seemed ill at ease. He hesitated for a moment "Well," he said finally, "I am not going to charge the tickets at this time. I'm going to hold them open for six months. If there are no other arrests during that time, the tickets will be dismissed. But I am requiring that you not have contact with this clinic."

"Meaning what?" asked Joe.

"Meaning that you don't go in, that you don't enter it."

I immediately felt a deep ache of conscience. I could not comply with the stipulation, and I certainly did not want to give him the impression that I would comply with something that compromised my defense of unborn children. Even though I was still living in Chicago and it was very unlikely that I would feel a need to enter Bread and Roses anytime soon—or in the distant future, for

that matter—I felt I had to speak up. I did not want to anger the
city attorney and risk that he would change his mind about leaving
the tickets open. Nonetheless, I found myself saying, "I don't agree
with your requirement. This is an abortion clinic. Unborn children
are dying there, and I can't say I won't ever go in there to save a
life."

The city attorney now seemed even more ill at ease.

"Um, do you intend to go in there?" he asked.

"No, I don't, but I can't promise that I won't."

"Okay. I understand that's how you feel. The tickets will stay
open for six months."

The Bread and Roses attorney was angry.

"So you're not charging them?" he asked indignantly.

"No, I'm not."

The city attorney seemed reluctant to charge us all along. Perhaps he was sympathetic to our pro-life efforts, or perhaps he simply felt the incident too insignificant. He may not have wanted
to bring the case to trial without a neutral witness or police officer. Whatever his reason, Joe, Jerry and I left his office relieved
and satisfied. This situation would be very different ten years later
when pro-lifers would be charged, brought to trial, and convicted
on the word of a clinic worker or escort. In the late 1980s, after tens
of thousands of pro-lifers were arrested in Operation Rescue sit-
ins, the legal system became less tolerant and more hostile toward
right-to-life activists. But on this day we were not criminals, but
simply social activists for whom a city attorney seemed to have a
measure of respect.

*   *   *

In January of 1986, a meeting took place at Sandy Schultz's modest
Milwaukee bungalow. Eight people assembled in her small living
room to discuss the possibility of doing a sit-in at a Milwaukee
clinic. Even though abortion-on-demand had been legal for thirteen years, no pro-life sit-ins had yet been organized in the city.

Sandy and other local leaders associated with Lutherans for Life were glad that I had moved to Wisconsin, and they hoped I could use the experience I gained in Chicago to launch sit-ins in their area. I was extremely eager to see a sit-in take place, and I committed myself to organizing one.

Recruiting enough people to make the sit-in effective was a difficult task. Most recruitment was done by word of mouth at various pro-life meetings, at pickets, and by calling people Sandy and other activists recommended. After two months of preparation twelve people had volunteered to go into a clinic and block the doors to the procedure rooms. Most were associated in one way or another with Lutherans for Life, and one, Fr. Thaddeus Bryl, was a Catholic priest from the Milwaukee archdiocese. My friend Christine LeBlanc, a graduate student at Marquette, agreed to participate, and opened her small east side apartment for a final meeting and rehearsal.

I proposed that we call our group Citizens for a Pro-Life Society, the same name we used for the Chicago sit-in group, but some of the Milwaukee recruits thought the name was too lengthy for media purposes. So we shortened the name to the more simple— and rather bland—Citizens for Life.

We decided to conduct our sit-in at Bread and Roses, the clinic in the heart of downtown Milwaukee across from the swank Grand Avenue Mall. I had learned a lot about Bread and Roses since moving to Milwaukee. The clinic was now managed by two young women, Mary Voght and Palmyra Lanza. The woman who had managed the clinic when Joe, Jerry, and I tried to enter two years earlier was no longer there. The center's ad in the Yellow Pages described Bread and Roses as a clinic that provided "professional health care for women by women," and it prided itself on offering a full range of gynecological services. The first service listed in the ad, in heavy bold type, was "abortion offered through the eighteenth week of pregnancy." About a year later, when Bread and Roses lost its lease and was forced to move to another building, its Yellow Page ad told patients that it offered abortions through the twenty-first week, or fifth month, of pregnancy.

While women managed Bread and Roses and other tasks were performed by hired female help, male doctors performed the abortions. One was Polish-born Aleksander Jakubowski; the other was Emilio Lontok, who came to the States from the Philippines. In the spring of 1987, a Bread and Roses newsletter called *Irregular Periodical* ran a profile on Jakubowski. It reported that he had studied medicine in Gdansk, Poland, in 1956; the same year abortion was legalized in that country. It went on:

> Performing abortions was thus a routine part of his training in obstetrics and gynecology. Although Poland is 99 percent Catholic, when the government instituted population control measures for economic reasons there was little public response. "There was no picketing, no protesting," Dr. Jakubowski, 49, recalled. "Nobody was poking their noses into other people's business as the antiabortionists do here. . . ." Married and the father of three daughters, ages 27, 18, and 16, Dr. Jakubowski believes that education about sexuality should begin early. "As soon as my daughters were ready, they were invited to come into my office and grab the [birth control] samples."

In May of 1984, the pristine reputation of Bread and Roses was shattered by a news report that twenty-five of the fetal children killed in the clinic had been found in a garbage dumpster. A driver for Bay Shore Clinical Laboratories had picked up the fetal remains and, while driving, became ill from the odor emitted from the containers she had just loaded into the van. She stopped the van and dumped the containers into a dumpster in a parking lot at the Mill Medical Center, on Milwaukee's far north side. The next day a group of children, ages four through eleven, rummaged through the dumpster, discovered the containers, opened them, and actually handled the torn body parts of the unborn children. Police were called to the scene. A May 15, 1984, *Milwaukee Journal* article reported: "When asked what was in the gray plastic containers they were playing with, the children replied, 'Little people.'"

The fetal remains were traced back to Bread and Roses, and news that aborted fetuses had been discovered in a trash dumpster spread all over the Midwest. The incident benefited pro-life efforts; while the general public was quite aware that abortions occurred, the Bread and Roses incident brought to light that recognizable human beings were actually being killed and, in this case, disposed of in the trash. The twenty-five bodies went to the coroner's office for examination. Later, Milwaukee County Supervisor William O'Donnell, turned the bodies over to Dan Zeidler, executive director of Wisconsin Citizens Concerned for Life, who arranged a burial for them at Holy Cross Cemetery. The remains were buried in a human cemetery only because they had found their way into the hands of pro-lifers. Their simple granite gravestone bears the inscription "Holy Innocents—Little People."

Bread and Roses tried to be more than just an average abortion clinic. It was a clinic with a mission; for its directors, abortion was almost a sacred rite of self-determination born out of radical feminism. When a woman got a breast exam or a pap smear there, she was given the impression that she was participating in something much more significant than a medical procedure. She was committing an act of "reproductive choice"—the backbone of women's liberation. The very name of the clinic was taken from the lyrics of a suffragette song written for the famous Lowell, Massachusetts strike of female textile mill workers.

However, when the clinic was purchased by Aleksander Jakubowski in 1986, feminist ideology took a backseat to profit. He also opened a sister facility in Madison which promoted itself as concerned primarily with the needs of women, in keeping with Bread and Roses' original feminist ideology. But an exposé in the October 1988 edition of the Madison-based journal, *Feminist Voices*, forever damaged Bread and Roses' progressive image. Several of Bread and Roses' former employees described how women were moved rapidly through the abortion process so that Jakubowski could maximize the number of abortions performed. Twilight sleep, a form of anesthesia, was pushed on women even when they didn't want it, suction cannulas were recycled, group counseling rather than individual counseling was the norm, and Jakubowski's manner was described as "not particularly caring or concerned about anything more than getting the procedure done without any problems."

In order to plan the sit-in, I needed to see the Bread and Roses abortion clinic myself; specifically, I needed to see where the procedure rooms were located. I went to the clinic on a Thursday afternoon at three o'clock. Bread and Roses scheduled abortions in the morning, but I took pro-life literature with me in case women were there. I felt apprehensive—what if I had to try to talk a woman out of an abortion on the premises? If I got thrown out or arrested, our sit-in might be compromised, but I could not in good faith just let an abortion-bound woman sit in the waiting room without trying to talk to her.

I took the elevator up to the seventh floor. When the doors opened, I was confronted once again by the same glass doors that had been shut against us a year and a half earlier. But today all I had to do was open the door and walk in. All was eerily quiet. Directly to my left sat a young receptionist behind the same small desk at which our zealous clinic defender had sat a year and a half earlier. Across from her, on the other end of the room, a large woman wearing a white lab coat sat idly with her hands in her lap. On my right was an open door that led to a long narrow hallway that curved near the end. I could see several doors off the hallway, which led, I guessed, to the procedure rooms.

I turned to the receptionist.

"Could I wait for a friend in the waiting room?"

"Sure."

She pointed down another long hallway that led in the opposite direction from the procedure rooms. This hall was lined with three administrative offices. I passed a young short-haired woman who was seated at a desk in one of the offices looking at some papers. She, as I later found out, was Mary Voght. I entered the waiting room. It was carpeted, had a comfortable couch and soft chairs and, to my surprise, was totally empty. Across the hall from the waiting room was another small room filled with beanbag chairs. Perhaps this was what passed for Bread and Roses' recovery room, or perhaps it was a room where children could wait for their mothers. I thought this made for a rather clumsy setup. A woman would have to walk the entire length of the clinic to get from the waiting room to the procedure room.

I was keenly aware of being completely alone in the waiting room of an abortion clinic. The room, in its silence and isolation, seemed to bear the shadows and the memory of all the women who had awaited their abortions in apprehension, sorrow and fear.

I never expected to have this room all to myself, and I took full advantage of the opportunity to look around. Wherever I looked I was confronted by literature proclaiming a woman's right to abortion and the necessity of keeping abortion legal. Large framed posters from the National Abortion Rights Action League and Planned Parenthood hung on the waiting room walls. Newsletters from the Religious Coalition for Abortion Rights were spread out on the coffee table. *Conscience*, the newsletter of Catholics for a Free Choice, was there, probably to ease the guilt of the clinic's Catholic customers.

I placed my pro-life literature on the coffee tables and magazine racks and stuffed pro-life pamphlets inside the magazines themselves. I looked around the room once more. A small wheeled table with coffee pots and cups on it sat in one corner. A small wooden plaque on a wall near the door caught my eye. I walked over for a closer look. On it was engraved "This clinic has been designated a nuclear-free zone." The irony of the statement was not lost on me. I felt I was standing in a world gone mad.

*   *   *

On Saturday March 8, 1986, I arose at 5:50 in the morning with a nervous ache in my stomach. It was still dark outside. I knew in another couple of hours I would be blocking that odd, curving hallway to the procedure rooms at Bread and Roses. Too anxious to eat, I managed to down half a glass of milk and half a banana. I stepped out into the frosty silent morning, drove into downtown Milwaukee, left my car at the Grand Avenue Mall, and tried to ignore the nervousness gnawing at my gut as I walked the short distance to our prearranged meeting place, the Burger King on Wisconsin Avenue. I pushed open the glass door and immediately spied a number of my pro-life friends seated at two tables toward the back of the restaurant.

When everyone was assembled I gave some final instructions on our strategy for entering the building. At 7:30 a.m. we slurped down the last few sips of coffee, got up from our tables, and walked quietly toward the clinic, only three doors away. We divided our-selves into small groups of twos and threes and staggered our approach, one group entering the building every one to five min-utes. A single security guard sat at a small counter just inside the building's very cramped foyer. Anyone who entered had to sign in. Some of the pro-lifers were paired together, and the guard prob-ably assumed that such couples were headed to the abortion clinic anyway.

The first seven to enter the building took the elevator to the fifth floor and waited silently for the others to arrive. The second batch arrived on the fifth floor to find the first group huddled anx-iously in the hallway. They crowded into the elevator with us. As the elevator lifted us to the seventh floor my heart raced wildly—my stomach twisted itself into knots. I noticed I was breathing heavily.

Chris LeBlanc, Carol Robbins, the mother of seven children, and Claude and Mary Lou Gagnon, a well-dressed and elegant-looking middle-aged couple were at the front of the elevator. Each carried a pair of handcuffs. As soon as the elevator opened, all four exploded into the hall, quickly pushed open one of the doors, and rushed down the corridor where the procedure rooms were located. They quickly entered one of the rooms. Hurriedly the foursome looked around the room to locate items to which they could attach themselves. Carol handcuffed herself to a leg of the cart that held the suction machine. Chris handcuffed herself to the inside door-knob of the room while the Gagnon's clasped their cuffs to the room's small radiator.

The rest of us followed immediately, gathering two rows deep at the mouth of the hallway. Three young men, Tim Regner, Jay Lucsak and Edmund Miller, remained in the hallway outside the clinic, locking their arms firmly to block the glass doors.

Ellen Gagnon, Claude and Mary Lou's daughter, entered the clinic with us. Young and very pretty, she was accompanied by her five-year-old daughter Sarah, born when Ellen was an unmarried seventeen-year-old. Holding her daughter's hand, Ellen quickly disappeared down the long hallway that led to the waiting room. Several chairs were already occupied by women scheduled for abortions that morning. Ellen tried to distribute literature to the women. A few took her pamphlets. She hoped to share her experi-ence—that she too was once frightened with an unplanned preg-nancy—and to show them the beautiful daughter she had been tempted to abort. Ellen was not the only unwed mother in our company. Standing next to me was pretty and petite Anne Haines, the mother of a three-year-old boy named Jesse.

The entire Bread and Roses staff was caught off guard. They seemed stunned, but when they finally realized what was tak-ing place, their puzzlement quickly dissolved into rage. The large woman I had seen sitting idly when I had checked out the clinic now sprang into action. With the help of two other employees, she shoved against us to break our human wall. When that didn't work, they tried to pull us away from the door, screaming obscenities and yelling at us to get out of the clinic.

Standing at the head of the group, I opened up a "Life or Death" pamphlet, naively hoping that the pictures of the aborted babies might make an impression on the clinic staff, but one of them reached over and tore it from my hands, ripping it to shreds. Some of our group began to recite the Lord's Prayer:

. . . hallowed be thy name
Thy kingdom come,
Thy will be done
on earth, as it is in Heaven. . . .

There was a boom box-type radio on a shelf in the reception area. A staff member ran over to it and turned it up to full volume. We found our own voices drowned out by Mick Jagger and the Rolling Stones:

. . . but it's all right now—
in fact it's a gas
but it's all right
I'm Jumpin' Jack Flash
it's a gas gas gas. . . .

The receptionist emerged from the elevator, reporting for work, and walked the few steps to the clinic door only to be confronted by the trio of young men who blocked it. She screamed for them to move aside. When they continued to block her way, she proceeded to hit Jay Luczak several times about his face and head to get him to move. She shouted, "Get the f--- out of my way" and shrieked, "You have no right to be here!" In the end she managed to squeeze past Jay and into the clinic.

The elevator doors opened again. This time a man wearing a long grey coat emerged. He was bald and in his late forties. I had never seen him before and was not sure who he was, until someone in our group yelled, "That's Jakubowski!"

Aleksander Jakubowski was tall and broad, and he managed to push himself past the three men barricading the doorway. Once inside, he tried to push through our wall toward the procedure rooms, wedging himself in between Father Thaddeus Bryl and the door jamb. Robert Braun, who would prove to be one of the most steadfast and fearless pro-life activists in Milwaukee, quickly stepped in front of Fr. Bryl, plugging the space against Jakubowski. I too moved over to keep Jakubowski from getting through. I felt very small, dwarfed by this large man whose body pressed against mine as he tried to shove his way past. Without ever saying a word, the abortionist gave up trying to get through our human shield. He turned around and left the clinic to await the assistance of the police. I was relieved and a bit surprised that our little band had been able to keep him out.

A reporter from the *Milwaukee Journal* was permitted inside the clinic. He asked our names, where we were from, and what churches we attended. The church question was odd; I did not think a civil rights or antiwar demonstrator would have been queried on the matter of church affiliation. I suspected that the reporter was playing up the religious angle to stereotype the pro-life movement, but even so I told him that I was a Roman Catholic.

Within about twenty minutes, five police officers arrived. They stood in the hallway for a few minutes talking to Edmund, Jay and Tim. An officer ordered them to step aside. They did not respond, and they did not move. Consequently, the police led them away from the door. They offered no resistance and one of the officers began to write out their municipal citations for disorderly conduct as the trio stood under the watchful eye of two policemen. The two remaining officers entered the clinic and planted themselves in front of us. Palmyra Lanza, the clinic's co-director, walked up to them. "I want these people out of here!" she demanded. Sergeant Robert Moe, a heavyset, blue-eyed veteran of the force, stepped closer to our group. He had a kind expression on his face.

"Okay, folks, you've made your point. You can continue your protest downstairs on the street."

"This is not a protest of abortion," I explained. "This is a defense of the unborn scheduled to die here today."

"But you've already made your point," he said again. "If you leave now, there will be no arrests."

"If we leave now, who will defend the babies?" asked Fr. Bryl in his soft voice.

"This is your final chance. If you leave immediately you will not be arrested," Sergeant Moe stated. At this point one member of our human wall opted to go. We knew that he would participate up to the point of arrest, and we shifted ourselves slightly so he could walk out. Now there were only five of us left.

"Anybody else?" asked Sergeant Moe. He did not seem particularly eager to arrest anyone.

Moe spoke briefly with Palmyra Lanza. Then, with Moe at her side, she strode over to the group and told each one of us, "My name is Palmyra Lanza, the director of this clinic. You're trespassing, and you have to leave."

The five of us stood with our arms locked and said nothing.

"Then I am informing you that you are under arrest," said Moe gently. His quiet voice seemed to betray a certain sympathy with us.

We continued to stand silently. Moe waited for a few more policemen to arrive. Then the arrests began. Some of us walked, but others went limp, collapsing to the floor in an act of passive resistance. The police officers had to pick them up and carry them bodily out of the clinic. When the doorway was partially cleared, three policemen entered the hallway that led to the procedure rooms. After a moment they came back out to inform Sergeant Moe that they needed some heavy bolt cutters. Moe put in a call on his radio. Once the bolt cutters arrived, the cuffs were easily snapped apart, and the foursome were loaded into the police van, each still wearing a portion of a cuff like a bracelet. Mary Lou Gagnon refused to walk, and she was placed in a wheeled desk chair and transported down the hall, into the elevator, and out onto the sidewalk below, where the police lifted her small body into the police van.

Two policemen lifted me up and placed me in a wheelchair. I went completely limp and kept slipping out of the chair. "What's the matter?" one of the officers asked the other. "Is there something wrong with her legs?" Finally they just picked me up, carried me into the elevator, hauled me out into the street, and deposited me into the police van.

Altogether nine of us were arrested and taken to the First District Police Station on State Street. The men and women were placed into separate holding cells where freshly-arrested people await their fate: either being bonded out to await trial or taken to a different, more permanent jail.

The female cell was a fifteen-by-fifteen cement-block room with a white ceiling and a gray floor. There were no windows. There was a dirty toilet in one corner, partially hidden by a short protruding wall which afforded some semblance of privacy to anyone desperate enough to use it. Cement benches lined the walls of the cubicle.

After we had been in the holding cell for an hour, Sergeant Moe entered toting a clipboard in front of him.

"Well, ladies," he began in a cordial tone, "you're going to be charged with Criminal Trespass to a Medical Facility. Here's how the charge reads." He looked down at his clipboard: "Whoever intentionally enters a medical facility without the consent of some person lawfully upon the premises, under circumstances tending to create or provoke a breach of the peace, is guilty of a Class B misdemeanor."

Looking up at us, Moe peered over his bifocals. "So there you have it, ladies. This is a state charge and your bond is set at five hundred dollars."

"What!" I gasped. "Five hundred dollars. That's ridiculous. Why so much?"

"Is that five hundred dollars each?" asked Mary Lou Gagnon, incredulous.

"Yes," said Moe, who for the first time glanced sternly at us. "I gave you all plenty of warning."

We could easily have been released on our own recognizance, but for some reason the captain on duty wanted the maximum bond. A few of us could pay it, but most did not have the ready cash. Friends on the outside set to work collecting the money. An anonymous Milwaukee businessman posted twenty-five hundred dollars for those who needed it. We later learned that our anonymous benefactor was Jerry Hiller, owner of Milwaukee's beautiful vintage Astor Hotel. He was a devout Lutheran, a member of Lutherans for Life, and a close friend of Sandy Schultz.

Our mug shots and fingerprints were taken, and by five o'clock in the evening everyone had been released, except for Robert Braun, who had refused bail. We had managed to remain inside Bread and Roses for over an hour and, with Ellen in the waiting room, the women there were given every opportunity to change their minds. I had not yet spoken to Ellen about how things had gone for her; she had left the clinic before the sit-in was over.

The media interest in our sit-in was something none of us expected. I thought perhaps an article would appear somewhere in the local paper and that there would be some local coverage of the story on television and radio. It turned out to be a media frenzy. That Saturday's *Milwaukee Journal* carried the front-page headline "12 Arrested in Protest" with a large picture of clinic personnel trying to pull us away from the door. We appeared passive while the staff members looked extremely aggressive. The story was balanced and full of details and quotes that accurately expressed the purpose of the sit-in. The reporter even mentioned the earlier Bread and Roses scandal over the finding of "fetuses" in a trash bin two years earlier. The reporter did not fail to mention that "[t]he 13 [pro-lifers] were from Catholic, Assembly of God and fundamentalist churches in Southern Wisconsin."

The sit-in was Saturday's top story on all three major network affiliates and was also given a great deal of space on the front page of the *Milwaukee Journal's* Metro section in the Sunday paper, complete with several photos; one featured Carol Robbins handcuffed to the suction-machine cart. However, this time the headlines were less complimentary. The early edition stated, "Abortion protestors bring militancy to clinic here," and the later edition stated "Abortion protestors get rougher." Despite all our efforts to conduct ourselves in a nonviolent and passive manner, the paper depicted us as physically aggressive. Mary Voght was quoted as saying, "Bread and Roses might pursue battery charges against several of the protestors, based on allegations that protestors shoved clinic staff members and patients." Of course, no such charges were ever filed. The reporter did mention that one staff member, the receptionist, "attempting to gain access to the office began hitting one of the men, shouting: 'How dare you do this. Get out of my way.' The man, who only identified himself as Jay, of Milwaukee, protected his head from the blows, moved aside and the woman entered the clinic."

After eleven years of picketing and sidewalk-counseling in Milwaukee, our sit-in dramatically heightened the social and moral war between pro-lifers and abortion providers in the city. Clinic personnel, abortionists, and the women who sought their services could no longer be assured that anti-abortion protesters would just stay on the sidewalk and behave for fear of the law. Pro-lifers had done something different. Perhaps this was why the media was so interested in the sit-in. The practice of abortion itself had been disrupted. Clinics were now fearful that the sit-in would become a regular feature of anti-abortionist efforts in Milwaukee.

Ellen Gagnon, with her little daughter Sarah, tried her best to persuade women in the waiting room. But it did not appear that our sit-in saved any babies. In addition to the dozen or so picketers outside, Sandy Schultz and another sidewalk-counselor were out on the street. If a woman was dissuaded from keeping her appointment that morning, we would never know it.

Those of us who participated in the Bread and Roses sit-in expected it to create public controversy, but it created a stir within pro-life circles as well. In particular, many Evangelical Christians were disturbed and confused over the issue of Christians violating government statutes, activity that they believed was contrary to the duty of obedience to lawful civil authority. Our sit-in took place a full two years before the appearance of Operation Rescue, when thinking within the ranks of Evangelicals had evolved on this subject. In addition, many pro-lifers were concerned that blocking doors to an abortion clinic was an ineffective means of saving the unborn. Therefore, a few months after the sit-in, the Milwaukee chapter of the Christian Action Council, a group with which Sandy Schultz was also active, invited me to explain the philosophical justification for the pro-life sit-in. I wrote in their summer 1986 newsletter:

One failure of the pro-life movement is that while we say and believe the preborn are human, we often fail to act as though they really are human—human beings whose very lives are destroyed with unspeakable violence. The sit-in is a response to the preborn child who is about to face the abortionist's knife. Those who sit-in perform a concrete witness to the mothers, the fathers, the abortionists and the community by demonstrating that preborn children slated for death are worthy of defense.

The sit-in shows the mother in particular that her child has value. . . . Many ask, "What does a sit-in accomplish?" "How many babies are saved?" "Isn't it all just a waste of time?" First of all, some babies have been saved because of sit-ins. However, those who are only concerned about the net number of babies saved pose the wrong question. When the parents of a preborn child schedule an abortion, in effect, their baby has become abandoned. To block the door to the abortion chamber may be the only act of love performed for that child in his life. Even if killed by the abortion, the child did not leave this world unloved. Someone performed an act of sacrifice for him. Therefore, don't ask only how many babies have been saved, ask first how many babies have been loved.

Not only did our Bread and Roses sit-in alter the social landscape of the abortion conflict, but the experience would forever alter my own personal social landscape as well. Immediately following the sit-in, Edmund Miller and I became very close friends. In the weeks following the sit-in we saw one another nearly every day, and soon partnered with each other doing sidewalk counseling on the streets of Milwaukee. Forged together in the front-lines of abortion activism, we delighted in each other's company—a bond that would eventually lead to something more than friendship.

CHAPTER NINE

GHOSTS AND ZEROS

"Agitate. Agitate. Agitate"
—Frederick Douglass, when asked
how one should overcome
the system of slavery.

MILWAUKEE Circuit Court Judge Patricia McMahon, while a law student in the 1970s, had participated in a protest at The Grill, the male-only section of Heinemann's restaurant in Milwaukee. She and a few other women entered The Grill, sat down, and insisted on being served. They were not served, but they weren't thrown out either. They filed a federal lawsuit charging the restaurant with discrimination and prevailed, forcing the restaurant to open its doors to female customers. Even though McMahon had not been arrested, she was certainly risking arrest. Thus those of us charged with Criminal Trespass to a Medical Facility were scheduled to be tried before a judge who understood the need to challenge prevailing law—if not actually violate the law—for the sake of a higher good.

The trial for the sit-in began one year after we blocked access to the clinic's procedure rooms; March, 1987, therefore, was peppered with several pretrial hearings before McMahon. Our attorneys, Michael Bowen and Gene Pigatti, told us that McMahon was a "liberal's liberal," but, despite her political leanings, they believed she would be a good and fair judge. In previous cases,

McMahon had reportedly proven herself a staunch defender of the First Amendment. However, McMahon disclosed during a pretrial hearing that her law clerk had previously served as Elinor Yeo's attorney. Yeo, an ordained minister of the United Church of Christ, was the manager of the Milwaukee Women's Health Organization, an abortion clinic located at Twelfth and State. Eight pro-lifers, including Edmund Miller, Robert Braun, and me, had staged a sit-in there in May of 1986, just two months after the sit-in at Bread and Roses. McMahon gave us the chance to substitute another judge in her place, though she emphasized that she could be fair and impartial. Father Bryl stirred in his seat. He had a deep misgiving that McMahon would not be fair, and he adamantly believed that we should substitute another judge. But our attorneys were equally adamant that we stay with McMahon, and we did.

At another pretrial hearing, Gene and Michael presented arguments that the law of Criminal Trespass to a Medical Facility was unconstitutional on the grounds that it unfairly singled out certain types of persons, namely pro-lifers, for stiffer penalties. While pro-lifers might be arrested, tried, and convicted under the law, those involved in labor-related disputes, for instance, were exempt. Judge McMahon rejected our arguments and ruled that the law was constitutional because its language appeared "facially neutral." Anyone trespassing upon a medical facility, except for those protesting unjust wages, with an intent to provoke a breach of the peace would be in violation of the law, not just abortion protestors. Moreover, while the law was passed by the Wisconsin legislature because of a rising concern over pro-life clinic blockades, the law, as written, did apply to all medical facilities, not just those providing abortions.

Failing to win our motion against the law of Criminal Trespass to a Medical Facility, we petitioned the court to grant us the "defense of necessity." Similar to Carmen Speranza's strategy in the 1978 Concord Clinic case, our attorneys argued that our actions were justified because they amounted to a defense of human life. I held out little hope that McMahon would grant the defense. When Carmen had petitioned the Cook County Circuit Court, the defense of necessity within the context of abortion, was still a reasonable and legally viable proposal. During the mid-1970s, when pro-lifers first began to stage sit-ins at abortion clinics, activists were extremely optimistic about prevailing in court. They could defend the humanity of the unborn on the legal system's own terms and demonstrate the fallacy of *Roe v. Wade*. This was our great hope that February day in 1978 when we gathered in the conference room of the Illinois Right to Life Committee to plan the Concord sit-in. The necessity defense was a *de facto* ratification of the pro-life position.

But the optimism of pro-life activists was dashed. The pro-lifers acquitted by the necessity defense became the exception to the rule. After a few initial successes, mostly in Virginia, the majority of pro-lifers who blocked the doors to abortion clinics were routinely denied the necessity defense and jailed. Cook County circuit court judges refused to allow this defense. Carmen appealed the lower court's decision in the Concord case specifically arguing that our actions were needed to protect innocent human lives from imminent danger. On December 31, 1980, in our case, *Illinois v. Kriska*, the Illinois Appellate Court ruled against us.

The State, armed with Concord's *amicus* brief, presented to the court an argument that none of us who blocked the hall to Concord's procedure rooms ever expected—an argument we found cold and chilling. Lawyers for Concord stated that the United States Supreme Court, in *Roe v. Wade*, did not recognize the fetus as a person and therefore ruled, with some regulation by the state, that a woman had an absolute right to an abortion. Concord lawyers argued:

> As behavior protected by the Constitution and regulated by statute in every state, abortion cannot be defined as "public or private injury." As we have shown, the defendants' contention that the fetus suffers great injury has no meaning for this Court, nor does it qualify as the requisite "injury" to justify the assertion of the defense of necessity. . . . [T]he fetus has

no rights, nor does the State or any individual have an interest in protecting the continuation of fetal development. During this period, the mother's individual rights are absolute. . . .

The only rights involved in an abortion performed . . . are the rights of the mother. . . . [As] defendants stated in their memorandum, their actions "were calculated to save the lives of these unborn children." Defendants' acts were intended to protect nonexistent rights and prevent the exercise of rights guaranteed by the Constitution.

According to the laws of the United States, when unborn children are killed in abortion no injury takes place, no rights are infringed, suffering and injustice do not occur. The loss of unborn children in elective abortion not only has "no meaning for the Court," but it has "no meaning" for anyone else either, neither to the state nor to the individual.

Without a defense of necessity there was nothing to prevent the mere technicalities of our trespass case to be proven. Although those arrested in the Concord sit-in were given the light sentence of six months court supervision, the trial we hoped for on behalf of the unborn never happened.

After so much initial optimism, losing the Illinois appeal was a huge blow. Soon after, I picked up a book that helped me make some sense of just how *Roe v. Wade* perceives the status of the unborn child. In his book, *A Private Choice*, former federal judge John T. Noonan of the U.S. Ninth Circuit Court of Appeals explained:

In both the first phase of pregnancy and the second the Constitution gave no recognition of any kind to the unborn. The Constitution did not appear to perceive the unborn's existence, except as that existence had to be contended to make the performance of an operation destroying the unborn comprehensible. Wearing the glasses of the Constitution, Mr. Justice Blackmun spoke only of "a theory of life" when he spoke of the states' contention that the rights of the child should be recognized. The child became less than a being; on the way to becoming a ghost it became a ghost—a theory whose tenuous and debatable character suggested that no living reality was present at all. To express the matter mathematically, the child became a zero when weighed against the liberty of a carrier.

Even though we knew that a defense of necessity was unlikely, we felt that we needed to ask McMahon for it anyway—after all, this was a different state, different legal precedent, a different judge; and we simply lived in hope that justice might prevail. But once McMahon denied our petition we again faced the horrifically artificial judicial world in which truth and morality are determined by legal positivism, the world in which something is real only because the law says it is real, not because it *is* real. As far as the law is concerned, unborn children do not exist, and those who block the doors to an abortion clinic do not defend anyone.

Judge McMahon explained in her written decision why she denied us the necessity defense, arguing that that prevention of death or harm to another person "is an objective, not a subjective determination." In other words, when the court claims the unborn to be non-persons, that's an objective view—while our view, that they are indeed persons is purely subjective and thus of no consequence. "Abortion is legal," she wrote, thus "it is unreasonable to believe that one must commit an act of criminal trespass to protest an activity that is legal and constitutionally protected." Of course, it was not the law that denied the personhood of the unborn and dismissed their existence that was unreasonable. As far as the law was concerned, we were unreasonable for believing the unborn did exist, that they were about to be put to death, and that they needed someone to intervene on their behalf.

I walked out of the courtroom frustrated and angry with McMahon's decision. As I stood in the hallway a reporter for the *Milwaukee Sentinel* approached me.

"So how do you feel about McMahon's ruling?" he asked, pen and reporter's pad in hand.

I told him: "Pro-life defendants should just plead insanity. We must be insane to block doors to an abortion center, get arrested and go to jail for absolutely no good reason!"

E. Michael McCann, the Catholic and pro-life Milwaukee district attorney, withdrew his office from the prosecution of our case. McCann cited his anti-abortion views and his doubts about the constitutionality of the Criminal Trespass to a Medical Facility law with which we had been charged. A special prosecutor, the young, smart and ambitious Jeffery Kremers, was assigned to our case. Kremers, tall and lean, dressed in the finest suits, carried himself with an aloof, superior air, and was passionately committed to "a woman's right to choose." The first time I saw him was at a pretrial conference scheduled several months before the trial actually began.

He sauntered into the room, tossed a stack of file folders on the conference table, then turned and addressed us with a gruff, "What do you people think you're doing?" He seemed to be personally offended that we had blocked access to an abortion clinic. He asked us if our group had a leader. I raised my hand. He scowled at me and wrote something down on his legal pad, his reddish eyebrows knit. His blue eyes blazed with contempt as he questioned each defendant.

Now that Judge McMahon had denied us a defense of necessity, she seemed intent on purging the trial of its abortion-related elements. After all, the abortions that occurred at the Bread and Roses clinic were legally insignificant. On the first day of the trial, April 6, 1986, Kremers told the jury in his opening statement that this was a simple trespass case and, without a defense of necessity, we were forced to argue our case on mere technicalities. We tried nonetheless to present to the jury the humanity of the unborn. This meant we had to risk talking about abortion honestly. With nine defendants, seven of them acting as their own attorneys, McMahon had some difficulty controlling every aspect of what went on in court and what we said in front of the jury during testimony.

McMahon began her purge by instructing Gene Pigatti and Michael Bowen to stop using "language colored by opinion." By this she meant words like "abortion," "abortionist," "abortion clinics," "abortion mill," "killing," "murder" and "suction machine." She ordered lawyers and defendants to use "neutral speech" so as not to bias the jury. For example, Bread and Roses was to be called a "facility," not an "abortion clinic," and the "suction machine" became simply "equipment."

I found this completely insane. Little did McMahon know that during the days I stood before her in court and listened while she denied the reality of abortion, I spent my nights digging silver duct-taped boxes out of the dumpster behind the Michigan Avenue Medical Center—boxes filled with the remains of the aborted unborn. The retrievals of the aborted babies had begun. These children were not shredded by something that was now being referred to as "facility equipment." The workers at 30 South Michigan had tried to deny their very existence by dumping them in a trash container, and now McMahon was doing the same thing with her judicial authority. Every day I saw the grisly remains of unborn children whom our judge attempted to keep hidden in neutral, "inoffensive" language—reducing them to "ghosts and zeros."

On the first day of the trial Father Bryl took the stand.*
THE WITNESS: My name is Reverend Thaddeus J. Bryl, B-R-Y-L. . . .

Ladies and gentlemen of the jury, I'm going to give you my account of what happened, what I wanted to accomplish, why I was there. I attended none of the planning meetings. I knew about this rescue mission to go on, and I thought it would be a good thing for me to be there. It was years that I, so to speak, protested in front of an abortion mill in prayer. I and the others would be in front of an abortion mill every Saturday morning for years in prayer. And, of course, I still do it. Prayer is what we know changes things.

What our prayer has accomplished, I have no way of knowing here on this earth, but certainly I will know at one

_____
* This testimony is taken directly from the original court transcript.

time or another. When I heard about the rescue mission which was planned for the 8th of March, 1986, I thought it would be a very good thing for me to be part of that, to see if I had the courage of my convictions, to see if I could be as defenseless as those little ones we tried to defend.

At this point, Judge McMahon suddenly stopped Fr. Bryl's testimony and sent the jury out of the courtroom.

THE COURT: Your testimony, Father Bryl, should be what you did, what you said, on March 8, 1986, and you may state briefly why you did it, but not every statement that you make should contain that comment [regarding your beliefs about abortion]. This is all irrelevant, and the court is limiting you to a brief statement of why. Do you understand that?

DEFENDANT BRYL: I do now, thank you. Okay, thank you.

THE COURT: Thank you. And you agree to comply with that ruling?

DEFENDANT BRYL: Yes.

THE COURT: I know you probably don't agree with it, but that's the ruling of the Court.

DEFENDANT BRYL: No, I agree with it. But I don't know how far I could go.

THE COURT: Do you understand now that you just state what happened on March 8, 1986, what did you do, what did they do, and avoid what I would say is language that's colored by opinion, and I think that's what things like abortion mills should not be used. This is the Bread and Roses facility when you talk about the facility, the Bread and Roses clinic. Okay? . . .

MR. KREMERS: Judge, I'd like to just make one statement on the record. I am getting a little tired of every time a defendant in this case gets admonished for doing something, they will say, Well, now I understand. I don't think any of these defendants are unintelligent in any sense of the word. They, in fact, have shown right to the contrary by their statements and their questions that they have asked, and I just want to put my position on this on the record.

MR. PIGATTI: No need for a response, Your Honor.

MR. BOWEN: I would limit my response to Mr. Kremers' comment to the observation that in my judgment it was uncalled for.

THE COURT: Well, I am concerned—The Court has made numerous rulings, and all the parties have been here when those rulings have been made, and I expect to have compliance with those rulings, and there are sanctions for noncompliance, and those sanctions will be used. I think that the Court has adequately explained that, has made numerous offers for further explanations if anyone didn't understand them.

Later that day, Anne Haines took the stand. Gene Pigatti asked her why she was at Bread and Roses on March 8, 1986.

A: Well, basically, I was very fearful of being arrested and taken away from my child since I'm the sole supporter of Jesse, and I knew that this action could result in that, so it took a lot of praying and talking to people about it before I could decide to do something like that.

Q: You ultimately, though, did decide to join in this demonstration.

A: Yes, I did.

Q: Okay. And, since you didn't reach that decision 'til the day before, it is fair that you did not participate in any of the planning sessions that we've heard about?

A: No, I didn't. I guess I didn't go to them because I was trying to look for excuses not to go, but the more I thought about it, and with the background I had knowing about nonviolent direct action, I had a 16-week course on it at school, and in my philosophy major it's addressed a lot, too, so I felt aptly prepared to do an action.

Q: Okay. So on March 8, 1986, why did you go to the Bread and Roses facility?

A: I think there's several reasons I went. I guess simply the first reason was that I had seen a nine-hour documentary on the Jewish holocaust, and I had realized that people in Auschwitz let the killing happen, and I realized as a citizen of the United States I was doing the same thing, and I couldn't turn my back on that. I knew I had to go in there, make myself vulnerable like the women—I knew what it was like to be in a crisis pregnancy situation, and that is the most vulnerable thing you can imagine, and I had to show them that I was willing to do that, and I had to stand there in solidarity with the unborn children that day, who were the ultimate victims of vulnerability.

We were all surprised that McMahon permitted Anne to say as much as she did. After her testimony, McMahon dismissed the jury for the day, but she did not dismiss the rest of us.

THE COURT: Maybe because it's late in the day, but I am losing my patience, I think particularly with this witness, who is represented by counsel. There was repeated statements and testimony that reflected her opinion as to this facility, her opinion as to why she was present, her opinion on any number of things, and I would ask counsel, before we proceed tomorrow, to talk with the witness and defendant about that. I think it was improper.

Both McMahon and Kremers were angry that the nine of us would not behave the way they wanted. They wanted a sanitized trial on criminal trespass. We wanted a trial that would do justice to the unborn. They wanted us to act as though the unborn did not exist and in conscience we resisted the fiction. The tension between McMahon, the defendants, and our attorneys did not go unnoticed by the media. The next day's headlines read "Judge 'losing patience' with defendants in clinic trespassing trial" and "Judge rebukes lawyer for abortion protestor."

In this, Milwaukee's first trial of pro-lifers, we were still able to talk about abortion and the unborn to some extent since McMahon was not totally prepared to handle wayward defendants. But she had also been assigned to Edmund and Robert Braun's trial for the sit-in at the Milwaukee Women's Health Organization, Elinor Yeo's clinic. Their case was heard one year after the Bread and Roses trial, and by then McMahon had become even more restrictive and heavy-handed. She prevented their trial from straying into the truth about abortion by simply banning any and all words about abortion and the unborn before they could be spoken. When I was called to testify, she told me, "You may not use the words 'unborn children,' and 'abortion clinic.' Furthermore you will not be permitted to use the words 'fetus,' 'embryo,' 'killing,' or 'murder.'" I told McMahon I could not comply with her rule. As a consequence she told me that I would not be permitted to testify.

* * *

Our trial for the Bread and Roses sit-in lasted six days. Since I was not formally represented by an attorney I opted to give my own closing statement to the jury. I strode up to the men and women who would decide our fate. The only real hope we had of an acquittal was to convince the jury, or at least two members, that a system of right and wrong existed beyond the cold facticity of the law. We had to appeal to them on the level of conscience. The barriers set up by the court to keep this a simple case of trespassing made that task very difficult. We hoped that a juror's conscience would be stirred to acquit us because we tried to defend life. Of the seven of us acting as our own attorneys, only Chris LeBlanc and I opted to give a closing statement. Chris spoke first.

> . . . . When we go into the clinic, our actions have to reinforce what our counselors are doing with those women. Our counselors are saying, yes, we know you are vulnerable, and we care about that. We are trying to be very sensitive and make this a very personable demonstration. . . . The counselors are offering alternatives to abortion. They are saying please, trust

us that we will help you. Although we are total strangers, we want to help you.

Now what can we do as demonstrators to show that we are trustworthy and credible, and that our love for them is a real concern, not just empty words? We can do it by our actions. When we talk about vulnerability, about linking our arms so our arms can't defend ourselves, to show we are interdependent with one another, we are standing with solidarity with the unborn, who are even more dependent than we are. . . . When we handcuff ourselves to doorknobs or radiators, whatever, we are saying yes, we understand that you may feel chained to this child. Wherever you go you can't escape that pregnancy. You may feel bound to it. We understand that. That's why we are doing this, to show we understand it. It's not from a position of power that we are making this appeal to you. It's not a demand, but rather, it's an appeal. We are appealing to your conscience. We are appealing to your sense of trust. We are saying, please, trust us. We are willing to take a risk to help you.

At this point Kremers objected, saying that comments about the unborn were not relevant to this case. Chris speedily finished her remarks and sat down. I got up and approached the jury.

. . . Mr. Kremers has alluded to a violation of peace and order. I submit to you that our actions were to secure real peace. . . . You are . . . going to decide an issue of justice . . . and a court of law is designed to promote the truth, not what I think. It is not what I have a subjective view about, but what really is. Everyone who takes the stand takes an oath to tell the truth, the whole truth, and nothing but the truth, so help you God. Mr. Kremers has asked you, as jurors, to find the truth. Judge McMahon has also told you that this is about the truth. And it just reminds me so vividly of a case in which issues of truth were of ultimate value and importance. And the man who stood accused said he came to witness to the truth, and that anyone . . . who was committed to the truth heard his voice. Let us not give the response the civil magistrate gave so long

ago, Qudi est Veritas? Truth . . . well, what does that mean?" It
means something. And right now that issue is in your hands to
decide. Mr. Kremers said that if we did this why don't we just
take responsibility for it. I am willing to take responsibility for
it, but I'm not here for myself. . . . I am here for others—others
who are hidden, who can't speak for themselves.

My response was undoubtedly too cryptic for the jury to catch
my meaning: that real truth existed beyond this court and that it
was by this standard of truth that we should be judged. I knew if I
just blurted out what I really wanted to say I would be immediately
silenced by the court. Kremers, however, understood my message.
He got up to address the jury again.

> Some of you may be thinking, "but we want to hear the
> answers to those questions. We want to talk about this. We
> want them to be able to say whatever they want to say. We
> don't want to know about these rules of law, objections, and
> all the stuff you told us about." I'm not sure you really do,
> because I don't think that any of you really want to get into
> a debate or a vote on the issue that they want you to. You
> weren't picked for that purpose. You haven't been given the
> full story on that. You haven't heard both sides of the issue.
> That's not the charge here. That shouldn't be the basis of your
> decision. . . . And you owe it to yourselves and to the people in
> this community to give a verdict that's based on the law, not
> based on your religion, or based on your compassion, or based
> on your sympathy. That may sound cold and calculating, but it
> gives us a society that is based on the law and not individuals.

Since there were so many defendants, the seven who acted as
their own attorneys sat at a long table set up behind the usual table
for attorneys and their clients. During the trial I placed a very small
three-inch crucifix on the table in front me. Television cameras
from the local stations had been in court all week, and one night,
as I watched a news story about our trial, the camera focused on my
small crucifix. I was startled by the close-up image of Christ's body
lying flat on the table. It was a tiny body—and so similar to the

bodies of the unborn children we were retrieving from the trash.

Late on the night of April 13, after deliberating for seven hours, the jury filed back into McMahon's courtroom one last time. McMahon asked Gene and Michael if they wanted the jury polled, which meant that each juror would speak his or her verdict aloud. I looked at each juror as the word "guilty" was spoken twelve times. Each word felt like the blow of a hammer.

Jeff Kremers left the court with a smile. I think he was not only happy, but relieved. During the lengthy deliberation, I saw him sitting on a bench in the hall outside the courtroom, and his glance caught mine. He looked anxious, nervous, even vulnerable, just as we were. I did not expect to see him that way. I think that despite his efforts to stifle the truth about abortion, Kremers was, nonetheless, afraid the jury would acquit us, and the case might turn out to be about abortion after all.

In the very same week that we were convicted, a jury in Massachusetts exonerated Amy Carter, the daughter of ex-president Jimmy Carter, Abbie Hoffman, and their co-defendants, for their protest of CIA recruitment at the University of Massachusetts. The April 16, 1987, *New York Times* reported that Judge Richard F. Connons gave Carter's defense team "virtually anything it wanted, including the necessity defense," which the *Times* described as "a law that exonerates people that commit crimes if they reasonably believe that their actions will prevent other crimes that pose the 'clear and immediate threat' of greater harm." But in the eyes of the law, abortion was not a crime and did not pose a clear and immediate threat of greater harm to anyone than did our clinic trespass.

Kremers had triumphed. He presented to the jury an ancient human fear: that if the law, which is believed to provide ultimate order in society, is disregarded, anarchy will prevail. So a jury not "given the full story" must enforce even unjust laws for the sake of an order—even an Order that permits the killing of innocent human beings and punishes those who try to protect them. Any defendant in such a situation learns that the law without "the full story" is a hard and brutal thing.

CHAPTER TEN

"THE FETUS INCIDENT"

"Tell them it's surgery and surgery is bloody."
—Chris Gouda of Planned Parenthood of
Milwaukee on how to discuss abortion with
a child who has seen a photo of an aborted
baby, *Milwaukee Journal*, May 30, 1999

THE morning sun beat down upon us and the small remains of the aborted babies began to shrivel in the heat. I occasionally bathed the torn body parts in formalin solution as I stood behind one of the long tables we had set up on the wide sidewalk in front of the Michigan Avenue Medical Center. It was an unusually warm spring day, May 6, 1987. We had laid out nearly six hundred bodies of unborn children we had dug out of the trash behind the 30 South Michigan clinic. This was our "on the street" press conference organized by Joe Scheidler, meant to expose to the public the victims of abortion. It must still rank as one of the most unusual press conferences in journalistic history.

Most of the bodies remained in their plastic Whirl Paks, neatly stacked together in homemade infant-sized coffins. These were made by Peter Krump, who put his carpentry skills to work and constructed the small white wooden boxes. We took several of the torn bodies out of their plastic containers and assembled them in trays for the media and passersby to observe on the busy avenue.

A few moments after the tables were set up and the bodies

displayed, two Filipino workers from the abortion clinic came down to see what was happening. They looked at the trays of bodies and the children's coffins filled with the familiar Whirl Paks. They glanced at the enormous spectacle laid out in front of their clinic for all to see before dashing quickly back into the building. No other workers came out during the remainder of the press conference. The clinic workers and Dr. Florendo never expected that the unborn they had buried in the trash in the back alley might one day reemerge on their front doorstep.

Dozens of reporters arrived. So did the police, who confronted Joe about the tables set up on the street. Many who walked to and fro upon Michigan Avenue stopped at the tables to peer at the bodies. I was impressed by their spontaneous expressions of horror. Most of those who looked at the crushed bodies were dumbfounded at the obvious humanity of the fetal babies and aghast at the evidence of violence written upon the torn flesh and severed limbs. One man who came by shook his head and muttered, "This ain't nothin' but murder." A group of three African American women paused to gaze at the bodies. One began to cry. "That's a baby! A real baby!" said another, completely amazed. Many looked at the bodies, shook their heads sympathetically, and kept on walking.

There was something pure in these reactions. These people were not prepared for what they saw. They were on the street that morning walking to work, or going shopping, or to the library or the museum, but wherever they were going they did not expect to see what we had laid out for them. The aborted babies, who were never meant to be seen, now intruded into the lives of these strangers. The passersby had no psychological preparation, no time to set up any mental barriers against the obvious tragedy of the torn bodies, no opportunity to theorize about abortion or put it into a ready-made political category. They had not read any editorials or commentaries just before arriving on the scene that might somehow mitigate the reality that these were real human beings who had suffered a form of violence. For me it was a privileged moment to see a kind of spontaneous enlightenment erupt in the souls of others. I knew that those who saw the fetal children would never think of abortion in the same way again.

Joe addressed the gathering crowd: "These are the real victims of abortion, killed right here, at this abortion clinic." Joe gestured toward the door. "We took these bodies, these children, out of the trash dumpster in the alley right behind this clinic. It's obvious these babies were murdered, murdered violently, and then just tossed into the trash with coffee grounds and cigarette butts. We want the world to see these victims, to see their humanity, and be moved to work to stop the holocaust," he shouted above the noise of the traffic.

About twenty minutes into the press conference, the police ordered Joe to take down the tables. They said we needed a city permit to erect them. Now we had to hold the coffins and the trays in our hands as we stood on the street. This made the event appear more like a picket than a press conference. After another hour we gently placed the bodies of the aborted babies back into their coffins. We loaded them into Peter Krump's van, then he and I transported them to a funeral home on the south side of Chicago.

We were disappointed with the media coverage. What we had hoped would happen did not. Despite over five hundred bodies of aborted babies laid out before them, the media chose not to show the victims themselves. The reporters took photographs of the coffins, but not what they contained. The television camera crews filmed us, but never the broken bodies that we held in our hands.

Over the years pro-lifers would complain to the media that they deliberately refuse to show images of aborted children to the public. The typical response is that the remains are too shocking, too grotesque for the six o'clock news, too offensive to viewer sensibilities. Pro-lifers have never been satisfied with that answer. Even as late as the 1980s, major television networks and affiliates still showed footage and still shots of war and crime victims, and even today it is not unknown for major news outlets to include such images, albeit with a warning of the "graphic nature" of the content. Film can be edited and pictures can be cropped. But the media has never been willing to show to the public images of aborted babies, however benign or "tastefully presented."*

Jack Houston, a *Chicago Tribune* reporter who was present at the conference, sought out Colleen Connell who still headed-up the Reproductive Rights Project of the ACLU. He asked for her opinion of the event. She stated:

---

* A notable exception is the display of photos of aborted babies printed in the online edition of the *New York Times*, Oct. 10, 2009—photos taken by the author, of babies retrieved from trash dumpsters behind two Michigan abortion clinics. The photos were featured as part of a news story by *Times* reporter Damien Cave, following the fatal shooting of pro-lifer, James Pouillon, in Owosso, Michigan, September 11, 2009. Pouillon was killed by Harlan Drake, a resident of Owosso, who objected to the graphic sign of an aborted baby Pouillon held during his one-man abortion protest.

It is interesting to note that the July 29, 2010 *Time* magazine cover featured a graphic, disturbing image of an Afghan woman—with her nose missing—having had it and her ears sliced off by the Taliban. In response to some readers' complaints, *Time* editor, Richard Stengel printed a defense of the photo. He agreed that the picture was "shocking and disturbing." He acknowledged that children would certainly be exposed to the image but stated that "bad things happen to people, and it is part of our job to confront and explain them. In the end, I felt that the image is a window into the reality of what is happening." He referred to the leak of classified documents that sparked debate about the Afghan war and stated: "Our story and the haunting cover image . . . are meant to contribute to that debate . . . what you see in these pictures . . . is something you cannot find in those 91,000 documents: a combination of emotional truth and insight. . . ." After reading Stengel's editorial, many pro-lifers felt his words could very well apply to the showing of images of aborted unborn children—something the secular media continues to refuse to do.

Photographer Todd Maisel, defended his graphic images of the 9/11 terrorist attack, in particular his photo of a man's severed hand—a photo printed in the *New York Daily News*: "Some people thought it was wrong, but that's what happened that day. It was a horror. I saw body parts all over the place. The horror of that day must not be diminished" (*American Photo* magazine, Sept./Oct. 2011).

Basically, the parade in front of the 30 S. Michigan clinic was nothing but a shameless effort to exploit the human emotions that are invoked anytime people see blood. I think what's deliberately obscured by the organizers of that march is the real issue of whether a woman has a constitutional right to control her own reproductive functions. . . . And what the protestors have done today is an attempt to manipulate public opinion by showing the byproducts that we'd really see as the consequence of any surgery.

Houston asked Connell if she saw any difference between the byproducts of "any surgery" and those of abortion. Her reply, unsurprisingly, was simply, "No."

Columnist Linda Gorov of the *Chicago Sun-Times* was also there on the sidewalk that morning. Her critique of our display appeared the day after the conference. "Sometimes concern about a problem takes an even uglier form than the problem," she wrote. "No one ever said abortion was pretty. But neither was the League's little media display." Yet Gorov expressed some ambiguity over the fetal remains:

All the anti-abortion pickets in the world cannot convey the loss you feel when you look at a ten-week old fetus in the bright sunlight. You can be for abortion or against abortion. It doesn't matter. You look and you look away and you feel lousy for a long time afterward.

Gorov concluded her piece with this observation:

"They're killing babies upstairs," Monica Migliorino, director of Citizens for Life of Milwaukee, said as she waded into the crowd.

Migliorino had more to say, even if you didn't want to hear it.

A woman in her late twenties strolled by. Her belly was big, big enough to catch everyone's eye. The woman didn't stop. You can understand why.

But Migliorino wanted to use her as the perfect pro-life example. She chased the pregnant lady up Michigan Avenue, demanding her opinion.

"I'm pregnant. I'm very happy with it. But it's my choice," the woman replied, visibly shaken.

She was moving faster now, one hand holding her stomach.

"She would kill that child," Migliorino shouted as heads turned.

The woman was almost running now. She was running faster than seemed safe for someone so far along. She turned the corner quickly and escaped. Migliorino, the pro-lifer, should be ashamed.

She of all people should know you can't guard the life of one child and endanger the next. You can't care about the fetus on the sidewalk but not a fetus in the womb.

Unless all a fetus is to you is a visual aid.

I was outraged by the story. Gorov had incorrectly reported several aspects of the incident and portrayed me as a hypocrite. I immediately wrote a letter of my own to the editor of the *Sun-Times* and called the paper to demand that they print it. An editor in the letters department assured me it would appear. I felt at least somewhat vindicated. Topped with the headline "The fetus incident," this version of my letter was published six days after Gorov's article.

Week after week for two months pro-lifers retrieved the remains of aborted fetuses from a trash dumpster behind the Michigan Avenue Medical Center at 30 S. Michigan. The experience has been physically and spiritually debilitating for all involved. I was thus saddened and dismayed to read Linda Gorov's sarcastic and derogatory account (May 7) of the press conference in which the fetuses were displayed.

Particularly distressing was her totally mistaken report of an incident between myself and a pregnant woman in which Ms. Gorov accused me of endangering the woman's unborn child—an accusation that has absolutely no basis in fact. Ms. Gorov left out whole portions of the incident that would provide readers with a true and accurate understanding.

First of all, I did not seek to use the woman as "the perfect pro-life example." I couldn't. The woman was not pro-life. The woman had woven her way through over 500 victims of abortion shouting for all to hear, "It's my choice! It's my choice" I looked up to see that the woman shouting this slogan was actually pregnant herself.

I held in my own hand the aborted fetus killed by the ethics of choice. I caught up to the woman, wondering if she would be honest enough to look at the face of abortion. Among other things, Ms. Gorov did not report that the woman stated to me that fetuses were not human beings. I asked her, "Do you say that if you did not want the child in your womb right now you would abort him?" The woman exclaimed "Yes. It's my choice! It's my choice!" She touched her abdomen, using her own baby as a visual aid for her pro-abortion attitude. I said to her, "You would actually kill your own child?"

The ethics of choice this woman espoused is that very same deadly instrument that caused nearly 600 fetuses to be thrown out. I had real concern for this woman who apparently did not recognize the inherent value of her own child.

I am very relieved that this woman wants her child. If she did not, it is entirely possible that the fetus I held in my hand that morning could have been hers.

The *Sun-Times* had edited my letter. The paper left out that the woman did not run from me—she and I walked together—and that she did not have to "escape" since it was I who left her. At no time was the woman in any physical distress. But far more important was the *Sun-Times'* subtle change of my language. I had used the very impersonal word "fetuses" when referring to the unborn. Or had I? I immediately looked at my original copy of the letter. I had used the terms "aborted babies," "aborted children," "preborn baby," "500 babies," etc.—never "fetus." The *Sun-Times* had deliberately censored my words.

Frustrated and angry I called the editorial department for an explanation. I was put in touch with a member of the editorial staff. He was very kind and supportive and in complete agreement with my complaint. He told me that prior to the letter's publication the editorial staff had a meeting in which my letter was discussed. One editor stated that "to call fetuses 'children' or 'babies' was as inaccurate as saying that the Pope was not Catholic." I told the staff member I wanted an apology. On May 18, the *Sun-Times* printed this clarification:

> A letter published May 13 from Monica M. Migliorino . . . employed "fetus" in place of other terms, such as "pre-born child" or "aborted baby," that appeared in the original letter. This newspaper's practice calls for the clinically objective "fetus" in news stories and features, but we regret the substitution in this case. We reserve the right to edit all letters, usually trimming for space and changing for accuracy, taste and clarity. But we recognize the right of writers on behalf of specific movements to use their own standard rhetoric to convey a moral message or political statement.

The *Sun-Times'* preference for "neutral language" mirrored the trend throughout the vast majority of the media. However, as "clinically objective" as the term "fetus" may be, it is also a term that distances the unborn from the rest of humanity. It is depersonalizing, and when applied to the unborn, helps facilitate their deaths. It is far easier to kill something that is not in relation to you. The advocates of legal abortion deliberately utilize the term to cast the unborn out of relation to the rest of the human family. The language facilitates an alienation of the woman to her unborn child. It places the child in isolation from her and from all other members of the human family.

Abortion is about empowering women. In order for this to happen they must become autonomous in a deadly kind of way. Instead of drawing others into human communion, the abortion ethic demands that the woman first be alienated from those over whom she seeks to have power. Once the unborn are cast out of relation to her, they are cast out of relation to the entire human community. Once cast out of relation to us, members of this now-subhuman class may be annihilated with impunity.

Those who are inclined to acknowledge the humanity of the fetus, even if unconsciously, refer to the fetus as an "unborn baby" or "child." This language of recognition is not a pro-life contrivance; it flows from the inherent human bond between ourselves and the intrauterine person. The language discloses this bond and affirms it. Language that "humanizes" fetuses reveals the truth about them and us. They, along with us, are members of the human family. When we want to reject the unborn, we first reject them from the human family by naming them as something less than, or other than, human.

* * *

On the warm spring night of Saturday, April 25, 1987, Edmund and I took our last box of aborted babies out of the trash behind the Michigan Avenue Medical Center. We had come down from Milwaukee to Chicago to attend the Pro-Life Action League's benefit dinner the next evening. I was to be honored with the David Droessler Award* for "outstanding performance in the pro-life cause."

When the dinner was over, Edmund and I began our trek back to Milwaukee. As we left Chicago we passed by the St. Nicholas Albanian Greek Orthodox Church. In this church a miraculous

---

* Droessler was a building contractor from Hazel Green, Wisconsin. The father of nine children, he was very active in pro-life work. In October of 1984, he flew a plane from Timmerman Field in Milwaukee to take Fran O'Meara, founder of the Milwaukee Pregnancy Help Line, to a northern Wisconsin town where she was scheduled to deliver a speech. On the flight they met with bad weather. The plane crashed, and both Droessler and O'Meara were killed.

icon of the Virgin was kept; news reports described an oily liquid that formed at the bottom of the painted eyes and flowed down the painting onto the shoulders of the infant Jesus held in her lap. St. Nicholas became a pilgrimage center as thousands flocked to Chicago's west side to see the icon for themselves.

Edmund and I decided to stop there and ask a priest to bless the aborted babies with the oil from the icon. We thought it best to leave the box in the car until we explained our request. We entered a door that brought us into the church hall where we found a priest wearing a long, black cassock and the traditional Eastern-rite pectoral cross. He sat across the hall talking to a nun in a long grey habit. As we approached, the nun finished speaking with him, took his hand, and kissed it. Then she walked quickly out of the room. The priest turned his attention to the two young strangers before him.

"Father, we have a favor to ask of you," I said.

"Certainly, certainly. What is it?" he asked, looking at us kindly.

"Well," Edmund explained, "we have in our car a small box. Last night we went to an alley behind an abortion clinic in Chicago and we took it out of the trash. It contains the remains of aborted babies."

A look of horror spread across the priest's face and he made the sign of the cross several times over his chest. "God have mercy," he said. His eyes were open wide. "Did you call the police? They should know about this. They should be told."

I was touched by his compassionate naiveté. "The clinic isn't doing anything illegal," I said. "I mean, it's legal to kill the babies and there's no law in Illinois against just throwing them away."

"Well, what can I do?" he asked.

"Will you bless the babies' bodies with the oil coming from the icon?" Edmund asked.

He explained to us that the priests of the church had discerned that the Virgin wanted her tears to be used to anoint people for healing purposes—"and, well, it's a little late for that in this case."

Edmund and I were disappointed. "Then could you please just

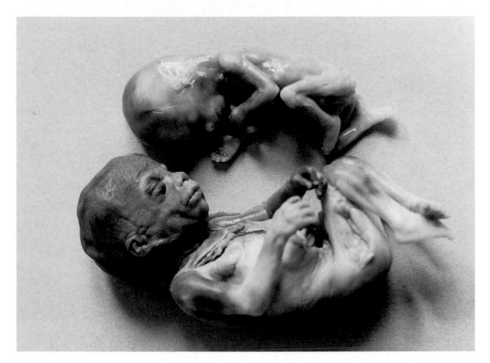

Above: Unborn babies named Patrick and Sarah, 24 and 21 weeks, killed by prostaglandin abortion method at the University of Wisconsin Hospital, buried March 17, 2000 at Resurrection Cemetery, Romeoville, IL.

Below: Baby aborted at the Michigan Avenue Medical Center, suction abortion, 16 weeks. Retrieved from clinic trash dumpster April 1987. Buried May 11, 1987 in St. Mary's Cemetery, Evergreen Park, IL. Note very visible life-line in palm of hand.

Above: Hand and foot of 7-month-old unborn baby. Aborted using the D & E method. Retrieved in 1988 from the Vital Med loading dock, Northbrook, IL.

Below: Foot of unborn baby, 16 weeks, killed by suction abortion at Reginald Sharpe's Women's Advisory abortion clinic, Livonia, MI, April 2008. Retrieved from clinic dumpster April 2008. Buried June 29, 2008 at Assumption Grotto parish cemetery, Detroit, MI. John Quinn, then auxiliary bishop of Detroit, presided over the funeral rites.

Above: Hand of unborn baby, 7 weeks with uterine matter, killed by suction abortion method, January 2010 at Woman's Choice abortion clinic, Lansing, MI. Retrieved from the trash by Chris Vencklase, February 26, 2010 with 16 other bodies. Baby buried November 20, 2010 at St. Joseph's Cemetery, Lansing, MI. Funeral rites presided over by Diocese of Lansing bishop Earl Boyea.

Below: Unborn baby, 18 weeks, killed by saline abortion method at the University of Wisconsin Hospital, buried March 17, 2000 at Resurrection Cemetery, Romeoville, IL. Also featured in the *New York Times LensBlog*.

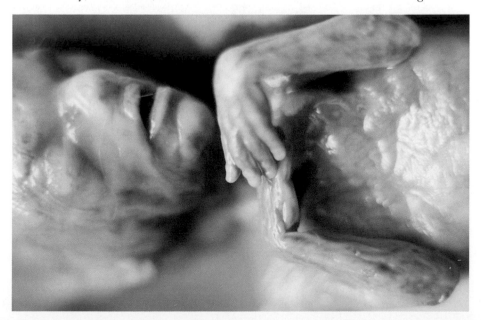

Above: "Baby Face." 21 week-old black baby, aborted March 14, 1987 at the Michigan Avenue Medical Center, Chicago, IL. Buried June 21, 1987 in St. Mary's Cemetery, Evergreen Park, IL. Photo displayed in court before Judge Patricia McMahon.

Below: Leg of unborn baby with veins visible—14 weeks. Killed by suction abortion by Dr. Marks at the Raleigh Women's Health Organization, retrieved from the Vital Med Loading dock, 1988. Buried in Chapel Hill, NC.

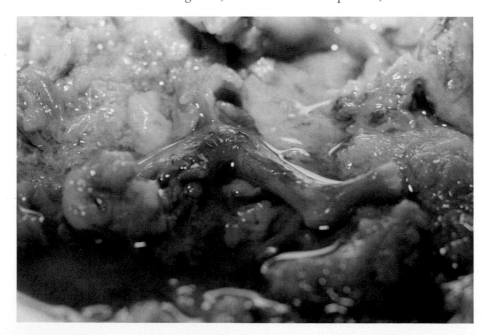

Top: September 10, 1988. Coffins containing the remains of 1,200 aborted babies retrieved from the Vital Med loading dock, Northbrook, IL are taken out of Trinity Evangelical Lutheran Church in Milwaukee at end of funeral service. Author (wearing blue suit) processes out of the church behind last coffin.

Center: The funeral rite concluded, a young girl pays her respects to the remains of aborted babies retrieved from the Vital Med loading dock, Northbrook, IL, just before their remains are placed into the ground at Holy Cross Catholic Cemetery, Milwaukee, WI.

Below: At Holy Cross Catholic Cemetery, Edmund Miller (beard and glasses) helps lower coffins into the ground that contain the remains of 1,200 aborted babies he aided in retrieving from the Vital Med loading dock.

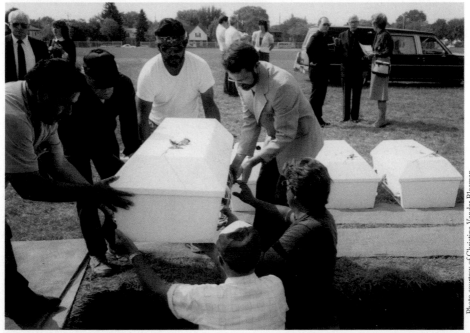

Photo that appeared August 6, 1988 on the front page of the *Tallahassee Democrat* of the Rose Lawn Cemetery burial of 721 aborted babies retrieved from the Vital Med Laboratory.

Above: Grave marker for 1,200 aborted babies retrieved from the Vital Med loading dock and buried September 10, 1988 at Holy Cross Catholic Cemetery, Milwaukee, WI.

Below: Grave marker at St. Mary's Cemetery, Evergreen Park, IL, for unborn babies retrieved from the dumpster behind the Michigan Avenue Medical Center.

Above: April 25, 1991. Pro-lifer chained to the axle of Bread and Roses' Aleksander Jakubowski's Mercedes Benz at Wendy's Interstate 94 rescue organized by the Missionaries to the Preborn, Milwaukee, WI.

Below: The Wendy's overpass rescue—pro-lifers and Illinois State troopers gather near the east entrance to the Wendy's Interstate 94 overpass restaurant. Bread and Roses' abortionist Aleksander Jakubowski stands on other side of the car in blue blazer.

Above: June 21, 1993. Citizens for Life's "driveway rescue." Pro-lifers sit at the end of the driveway of abortionist Neville Sender's Fox Point, WI home, preventing him from driving to the Summit Women's Health Organization to conduct abortion procedures. Sender watches the scene from behind his car, standing to the left of police officer.

Below: June 21, 1993. Abortionist Neville Sender lectures members of Citizens for Life who block the end of the driveway of his home in Fox Point, WI, preventing him from driving to the Summit Women's Health Organization and to conduct abortion procedures.

The crematorium at "Pet Haven" pet cemetery in Milwaukee where the bodies of aborted babies were burned.

Above: August 3, 1992. Police officer arrives on the scene and examines the interior of the fortified car at Citizens for Life "car rescue" at the Imperial Health Services abortion clinic, Milwaukee, WI. Note pro-lifer sitting on pavement through a hole cut in the floor of the car.

Below: Attempt to open the abortion clinic during Citizens for Life "car rescue."

Members of Citizens for Life block the door to the Imperial Health Center on the 11th floor of the Continental Bank Building, Milwaukee, WI. Author is standing at right in hallway niche. Special prosecutor Jeffrey Kremers charged her with three criminal counts. She was convicted and sentenced to a 9-month jail term by Milwaukee Circuit Court Judge Charles Schudson.

March 14, 1987. The loading dock in the alley behind the Michigan Avenue Medical Center, 30 South Michigan Avenue, Chicago, IL. Tim Murphy and Jerry McCarthy search the trash dumpsters for remains of unborn babies aborted at the clinic earlier that week.

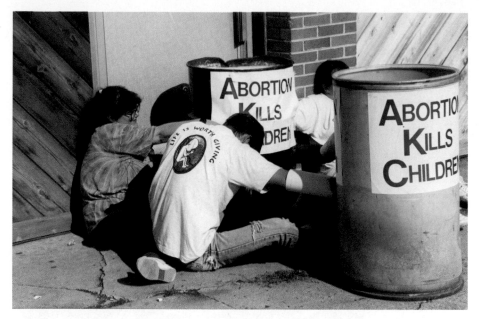

Above: August 3, 1992. Michael Schmedicke, his arms in PVC pipes secured in cement filled barrels, with other pro-lifers, blocks the back door of the Imperial Health services abortion clinic during Citizens for Life "car rescue."

Below: June 4, 1994. Police officers peer into car to observe pro-lifers chained inside at Citizens for Life "car rescue" at Affiliated Medical Services, Milwaukee, WI., the first rescue to take place in the U.S. after President Bill Clinton signed the Freedom of Access to Clinic Entrances Act law—known as FACE—on May 20, 1994.

Above: July 30, 1988. Cardinal Joseph Bernadin officiates at the funeral for 2,000 aborted babies whose bodies were retrieved from the Vital Med loading dock in Northbrook, IL. The babies were buried at Queen of Heaven Cemetery, Hillside, IL.

Below: September 10, 1988. Greg Gesch reads Psalm 94 at funeral service for 1,200 aborted babies retrieved from the Vital Med laboratory at Trinity Evangelical Lutheran Church, Milwaukee, WI.

June 4, 1994. Barb Schlosser is arrested after a pro-life sit-in at Affiliated Medical Services in Milwaukee, the first pro-life rescue to take place after President Bill Clinton signed the Freedom of Access to Clinic Entrances Act.

bless the bodies in the sanctuary with holy water near the weeping icon?"

The priest nodded. "Yes, sure, of course I can do that." Edmund went to the car and came back with the duct-taped box. We entered the small, dimly-lit church. Out on the busy street, cars whizzed by, lights blinked and shone, and people hustled down the sidewalks of a world filled with noise and distraction. As soon as we stepped into the church that world faded away. Now all was strangely quiet. The icon-covered walls and ceiling drew us to the things of heaven, all that was holy and mysterious. The small church was dimly lit— illuminated only by the tapers of many pilgrims, and their dancing flames bathed the church in an amber glow.

The priest told Edmund to place the box on a chair to the left of the sanctuary. The weeping icon was only a few feet away. The priest opened the box and the dark blood-colored, formalin-filled Whirl Paks were now exposed to the priest. He blessed them solemnly and carefully, and sprinkled holy water on them as he ended the prayer in the name of the Father, the Son and the Holy Ghost.

The brief ritual was over. The priest looked up at us.

"Thank you, Father, and God bless you," I said.

He lingered for a moment at the weeping icon and turned to leave. He glanced back at us, his own dark eyes glistening with tears. Overcome with emotion, he drifted silently back into the darkness of the sanctuary.

In the night these children lay on a filth-heap, consecrated to the trash. The next day they lay consecrated in a shrine. Between the rising and the setting of the sun, the tortured moral drama of our age was played.

CHAPTER ELEVEN

SECRET CEREMONY

*"She picked her way through the slush, afraid of falling and
hurting the baby, thinking at the same time, fleetingly, how easy
it would be to simply leave her, in a garbage Dumpster, or on the
steps of a church or anywhere."*
—Caroline Gill in *The Memory Keepers Daughter*

THE press conference on the busy sidewalk outside of 30 South
Michigan Avenue was only the first of two plans we had for
the bodies of the abortion victims. Now we shifted our focus to
arranging their burial, which was the more important of the two
events. We hoped to plan a public and well-attended ceremony. A
religious graveside ceremony would draw attention to the reality
of the violence and tragedy of legalized abortion. It would affirm
to the world, as nothing else could, that these unborn children,
killed by abortion and now laid to rest alongside the bodies of other
human beings, were indeed full members of the human race. Joe
Scheidler, and I, along with Tim Murphy, Peter Krump and Andy
Scholberg, had already approached the Archdiocese of Chicago for
their help.

Immediately following the press conference, Peter Krump and
I delivered the ten small boxes containing the fetal remains to a
funeral home on Chicago's south side. Father Roger Coughlin, of
the Chicago Archdiocesan Respect Life Office, had arranged for

the bodies to be taken there, and we intended to keep the babies at the funeral home until we were able to complete the necessary planning for a well-publicized funeral that we hoped would take place in the next three or four weeks. Everyone active in the pro-life movement in the Chicago area would have the opportunity to participate in a very rare pro-life event. We even hoped that Joseph Cardinal Bernardin, Archbishop of Chicago, might officiate at the graveside service.

Because we had time to plan the event, I took nine of the bodies back to Milwaukee with me. I was not completely satisfied with the photos Edmund and I had taken thus far and wanted to shoot some additional pictures of the abortion victims. At the time I was not completely sure what we were going to do with the photos, but soon we started using them while sidewalk counseling. In years to come they were blown up into large posters for pickets and eventually would be widely disseminated on the Internet. But all I knew at the time was that it was important to keep a record of the violence done to these human beings. I told Father Coughlin, who arrived on Michigan Avenue toward the end of the press conference, that I planned to return the bodies in time for the burial.

When I returned to Milwaukee, I contacted Donald Massaro, assistant director of the cemeteries for the Archdiocese of Chicago, to request a burial plot for the aborted babies. Massaro told me he had to check things out with the Chancery Office. I waited for several days before calling him back. When I did, Massaro informed me that no plot would be provided. I was shocked. Would the Church refuse these victims of violence a burial space? Massaro explained that he had received advice from attorneys for the archdiocese, who had discouraged him from providing the plot because of possible lawsuits. They told him that a mother of one of the aborted babies might sue the archdiocese for imposing religion on her dead child.

I wrote a letter to Cardinal Bernardin. In it, I explained how our group had retrieved the remains of the aborted babies from the trash and that the archdiocese had refused them a plot in one of its cemeteries. I asked the cardinal not only to intervene, but also to officiate at the ceremony. Apparently, Cardinal Bernardin did intervene; Father Coughlin was assigned to work with us, and he made arrangements that the babies would be buried at St. Mary's Cemetery in Evergreen Park, Illinois.

* * *

On Monday, May 11, 1987, the nine of us convicted of Criminal Trespass to a Medical Facility walked into Judge McMahon's court once again. In my hand I carried a plain manila folder. We took our seats at the back of the room where spectators usually sat and waited for our sentencing hearing to begin. Directly behind us, jammed tightly together against the back wall, stood a cluster of eager reporters, photographers and television cameras. Donning her judge's robe, McMahon entered the court room and mounted the bench.

Each defendant stood and gave a sentencing statement. When it was my turn I stood up with the closed folder in my hand and faced McMahon.

"Your honor, I think it is important for you to know that on the days I sat in this courtroom, on trial for defending the lives of unborn children, I traveled at night to an alley behind an abortion clinic. I opened up the trash dumpster in this filthy, rat-infested place and retrieved the very bodies of the victims of abortion. The truth about abortion needs to be known."

I opened up the manila folder and held it up for McMahon to see. "This is the face of abortion."

Inside the folder I had taped a large photograph I had taken of one of the babies from the 30 South Michigan dumpster, a five-month-old child killed by the dilation and evacuation method. It was the photo of the unborn child I simply referred to as Baby Face—the one whose right eye and lower jaw was missing. About the child's head, pooled in dark blood, were his torn arms, legs, a hand, a foot, and part of his rib cage. Nestled as it was in the gore, the baby's face emerged with the serene and dignified appearance of a death mask.

"I believe we would have won this case if we were permitted to discuss the real issue, if we were permitted to have the defense of necessity, the defense of others—to show the jury the reality of abortion."

I turned around and held up the photo for the reporters and cameras.

"This is not just my 'sincerely held belief,' I said, echoing Kremers' characterization of our opposition to abortion.

"Miss Migliorino, you may close that folder," McMahon said curtly from behind the bench. I turned around again and sat down, and kept the folder open in my lap.

McMahon sentenced me to two years probation and thirty days in the Milwaukee House of Correction. Most of the other defendants received only probation, except for Robert Braun, who was also ordered to do thirty days in jail but with no probation. In the state of Wisconsin, defendants have the right to refuse probation and take some other alternative sentence. I did refuse and McMahon increased my jail time from thirty days to forty-five. All sentences were deferred pending our appeal.

At the very moment that I stood before McMahon, sentenced for defending the lives of the unborn, the aborted babies from the Michigan Avenue Medical Center were being lowered into the ground. I had no idea that our babies were being buried that day. As our sentences were read out, the broken bodies were laid to rest in the very same dirty, blood-stained boxes in which they had been hastily tossed into the dumpster. The ten-minute, nearly secret ceremony was performed by Father Coughlin. The public had not been invited to attend and there was not a single reporter, not even from the archdiocesan paper, to record the story. There was no church service, no hearse and no coffins. Peter Krump was notified of the burial and he immediately called Tim Murphy. None of the others who had rescued the babies from the trash had been told that the burial was going to take place. The archdiocese deliberately kept the burial quiet to avoid any publicity.

I found out about the burial the following day from Joe Scheidler. He called me, furious. He had received a letter from Father Coughlin, dated the day of the burial. Joe read the short message to me over the phone:

> Dear Joe,
>   I trust that you will be happy to know that the bodies of the 500-600 victims of the 30 S. Michigan Avenue abortion mill have been laid to rest.

The letter then listed all those who attended the small graveside ceremony. Joe and I were anything but happy to learn a day late that our babies had been buried without our being told. I felt deprived of a final closure to the sad, gory episode and I was livid that the archdiocese had seen fit to keep it quiet. We both felt that, by keeping their brief funeral a clandestine affair, an injustice had been done to the victims of a nationally legalized slaughter.

Joe Scheidler wrote back to Father Coughlin to explain how we felt about the significance of a public burial. While the press conference on Michigan Avenue drew some public attention to abortion, it was the burial that would have been the most profound witness to the humanity of these children. Joe believed that a solemn, well-conducted ceremony would have also humanized the pro-life activists in the public mind. Joe wrote to Coughlin:

> Ann Gerber of the Lerner Home Newspapers referred to us as fanatics, sick and stupid, dangerous clowns, and pathetic nerds. Those were the nice comments.
>   But the funeral is the event that casts us in a good light and the abortionists in a sinister light. The babies are not out in public but are placed in closed caskets. They are shown reverence and respect. A number of religious leaders speak of their humanity, their tragic deaths, their unhappy mothers. A children's choir sings, and a box is filled with toys the children might have played with if they had been allowed to live. The box of toys is buried with them. All of this is moving and

constitutes a fitting tribute to these little victims of our great national crime. The funeral ceremony brings out better than the abortion-find itself the terrible loss we all experience with the death of a child. . . .

. . . most disastrous is the loss of a marvelous opportunity to make these children's short lives more meaningful. So much could have been conveyed through a public and well-publicized funeral ceremony. So many people could have been touched by the spectacle of reverence being shown to the unborn. . . .

I am only glad that I had no part in the decision to hurry up the burial of these children and to do it in secret.

The nine aborted babies I had taken back with me after the press conference still needed a final resting place. Perhaps Father Coughlin, in his haste, forgot about them, or perhaps he just thought I would make separate arrangements for them. I was irritated that these nine were forgotten in the hurry to bury the rest quickly and quietly. I made several calls over a three-day period to the Chicago archdiocese. For some reason I was referred to one of Cardinal Bernardin's chancellors, but to get to him, I had to go through his secretary. She asked what I was calling about, and I explained that I was involved in the rescue of the aborted babies from behind a Chicago clinic. I told her I still had nine bodies that were not buried and that I wished to make arrangements for them to be interred with the others.

"What are you doing with those bodies?" she asked.

I was taken aback.

"Well, we kept them back to photograph them," I said.

Before I could explain further, the voice on the other end shrieked, "What? Photograph them? That's awful! What a terrible thing to do!"

I never expected a secretary who worked for a Catholic archdiocese to react this way. She obviously did not realize the photographs were of immense value, both as a documentation of the injustice of abortion and a real-time record that could be used to save other children from a similar fate.

"Look, just let me talk to the chancellor."

But I did not fare any better with him. I asked if we could do another ceremony for these nine aborted babies. He responded, "We don't want a media circus." I got the distinct impression that the archdiocese didn't trust us. Funerals for aborted babies were still new to the pro-life movement, and the Church was hesitant to be a part of anything that might devolve into a media stunt, or worse, result in its being accused of exploiting the babies' bodies. But I was starting to fear that the archdiocese would not help me bury these nine other babies.

I wrote another letter to Cardinal Bernardin, once again asking him to intervene, but I also wanted him to realize what these aborted babies meant to us and what a burial for them would have meant to us.

> The world, which judges according to the flesh and not according to the mind of Christ and the Spirit, does not understand the grave and indeed diabolical tragedy in the fact that human beings were dismembered and literally thrown away in the trash. Furthermore, very few people realize the enormous sorrow those of us feel even now who went to this filthy, rat-infested alley to retrieve the remains of the preborn children out of the garbage. The graphic images of these mangled abandoned children have carved a scar into my eye that will remain forever.
>
> When we had these babies with us we regarded them as if they were the body of Jesus Himself just taken down from the Cross. We refused to allow them to stay in any dirty place like a garage or a shed, but found them space inside our houses. We called priests to bless them.
>
> As long as we had the bodies of these children they were a reminder to pray for true peace in the world—to pray for the mothers and fathers of these children—and to pray for the abortionist who was hired to kill them.

We had always looked forward with the greatest desire
to the burial service for these children. When we asked if the
archdiocese would provide a burial plot we never thought there
would not be a formal burial ceremony for these victims of
our American holocaust. We thought there would be a service
which we would help plan, participate in, and invite others
to attend. We believed nothing we could have done would
have been a greater witness to the world to the humanity of
these children, and the national tragedy they represent could
be mourned by all.

. . . It was a God-given privilege and a blessing that we
were able to retrieve at least these five hundred victims of
abortion from the degradation of being permanently "buried"
at a refuse dump somewhere. A planned and formal ceremony
would have been a real testimony to the Chicago community
and the world that indeed these preborn children were human
and their lives sacred.

I went on to tell Bernardin that I intended to organize a graveside memorial service sometime in June and asked that the nine
fetal babies, who had been left out of the original burial, be laid to
rest at that time.

On June 3, I received a phone call from Father Coughlin. He
was reluctant to bury the babies during the memorial service, which
I had set for June 27. He was afraid of media coverage and afraid of
possible legal difficulties and did not think that St. Mary's cemetery
permitted burials on Saturdays anyway.

The next day I called the cemetery and asked if burials on a Saturday were a problem. I was told they were not, so I sat down and
wrote Father Coughlin a letter urging him to bury the nine aborted
babies during the service. I felt it necessary to repeatedly assure him
that the ceremony we planned would be dignified and respectful,
just as any other funeral would be—and that if the media were notified it was "only to promote the sanctity of human life in the eye of
the public." I told him that the archdiocese had little to fear from
lawsuits. Other burials of aborted children had occurred around the

country and the only lawsuit concerned a case of sixteen thousand aborted babies discovered in a semi trailer owned by the state of California. The state wanted to turn them over to a Christian group for burial, but the ACLU stepped in, saying this would be a breach of the separation of church and state.

A few days later I received a letter from Cardinal Bernardin.

> I want you to know that I share the pain of this terrible tragedy. I also want to affirm the work of Father Roger Coughlin in arranging for the interment [of the five hundred aborted babies]. I feel that we can take some consolation in knowing that these aborted babies were buried with the dignity and reverence which they did not enjoy in their short lives.
>
> In your letter, it mentions that there are nine other abortion victims who were not included in the burial. Perhaps we have different approaches in dealing with this situation, but I do not feel it is appropriate to hold a public ceremony. Moreover, I do not want the Catholic cemetery to be used for a media event. However, the Church stands ready to provide a quiet, reverent burial which will respect the dignity of these babies. If you wish the Church to participate in this manner, please contact Fr. Coughlin who will make arrangements similar to the previous interment.

Because I wanted the nine to be buried with the others who were killed at the Michigan Avenue Medical Center, I agreed to the cardinal's requests. The memorial service and burial took place as planned on Saturday, June 27. Everyone who helped retrieve the babies from the dumpster attended, as well as Father Coughlin and Father Michael Pollard, director of the archdiocesan cemeteries. Almost one hundred people came to lay the infants to rest, including several members of the Ebenezer Baptist Church, a mostly African American community on Chicago's south side. The pastor, Reverend Hiram Crawford, Sr., preached at the service. Scripture was read, hymns were sung, and prayers were offered. Edmund's brother, Christopher Miller, a professional violinist, played "Amazing Grace." The nine aborted babies were placed in one of the small white children's coffins Peter Krump had crafted. At the end of an hour, the coffin was lowered into the ground. These outcast fetal children were at last laid to rest.

That evening I sat down and wrote a very lengthy letter to my friend Joe Wall, a veteran pro-life activist who lived in Philadelphia. Writing to him was a kind of therapy, as I needed to express my great frustration in the way the official Church dealt with the victims of abortion—and how they had dealt with those of us who had retrieved them from the trash. I tried to reason out why the chancery insisted on secret burials.

> I think the archdiocese refused to make the burial a public event—a vehicle for preaching against abortion, etc.— because it was afraid that it would look as if the Church was exploiting or merely using the babies' bodies, taken from the trash, in order to promote its "sectarian—narrow" beliefs that abortion is wrong. Somehow the Church did not want to be perceived as using this "abortion find" to preach against abortion. Somehow they found "exploiting" the situation repugnant. Somehow they got the weird idea that the public condemnation of these babies' deaths and being thrown into the trash was a crass exploitation of the babies. . . . Indeed I know from chancery people I've talked to, that many priests and employees down there . . . believed that us pro-lifers didn't really have any care or reverence for these babies' remains. . . .
>
> Finally, the whole thing resides in churchmen not really understanding that abortion is not an abstract issue. It's real— so real that you can actually get your hands on the bodies of the murder victims. But because abortion has not really broken the heart or gotten under the skin of the bureaucrats, they really didn't know what should have been done when the babies' bodies were right in the palm of their hands! Instead of preaching against abortion from rooftops and pulpits—and taking a leadership voice—they treated these 500 murder victims with no more real consideration than if they had died in their sleep!

Now that the burials were completed, I thought that we would be permitted to purchase a headstone for the grave and that the inscription would somehow indicate that the unborn buried beneath it were killed by abortion. But, once again, the archdiocese extended its influence even over the marker. Donald Massaro told me that no marker would be placed on the grave for at least a year, and that he would not permit any reference to the abortion deaths of the children to be part of the marker's inscription—words like *abortion*, *murder*, *slain*, *killed*, or "other terms of this nature." Furthermore, he would not permit the dates that marked the beginning and end of the retrieval, which indicated the collective time these children lived and died, to be inscribed on the stone.

It felt like Judge McMahon's courtroom all over again; a sanitized trial, a sanitized grave marker with no mention of abortion, no mention of the murder of the aborted babies. The gravestone needed to be a testimony to the special character of these babies. When a person comes across the grave, it should be plain that this grave has a unique meaning, just like the tomb of a hero or a martyr or a soldier who died for his country. It just seemed natural to me that the importance of this grave should be noted. The only significant thing that ever happened to these children was that they were crushed as a consequence of legalized abortion.

I wrote a letter to Donald Massaro, Father Coughlin, and Father Pollard literally begging that the gravestone mention that these babies had been aborted. Dick O'Connor, who took my place as executive director of the Illinois Right to Life Committee, tried for three weeks to arrange a meeting with Father Pollard, but he received no response. My letters were written late in November, 1987, over six months after the first burial occurred. I asked Father Pollard if this inscription could be placed on the gravestone:

Here lie 500 aborted children
"He will wipe every tear from their eye" (Rev. 21:4)
Feb. 28–April 25, 1987

Father Pollard continued to reject the word "aborted." I wrote back to him conceding to his wishes. It was futile to continue fighting. I suggested the following inscription:

"A voice was heard in Rama . . .
Rachel weeping for her children." (Mt. 2:18)
HOLY INNOCENTS
Preborn Children of God
Feb. 28–April 25, 1987

On January 14, 1988, Father Pollard wrote back to me. He was very happy with my final suggestion and said that a grave marker was being made. I too felt something very close to satisfaction. "Holy Innocents" referred to Herod's slaughter of the infants in Bethlehem. It was enough of an affirmation of what had happened to this small remnant.

And so that spring, a year after the aborted children were laid in the ground, a stone was set to mark their place of rest. The stone covered the grave of those slain by abortion. But the red granite could never cover our hearts against the memory of those dark and awful nights when we pulled their broken bodies out of the trash— the fruit of power that wields itself without restraint in the voids of alienation.

CHAPTER TWELVE

THE LAST WORK OF MERCY

"Foul deeds shall rise"
—Hamlet

O N FEBRUARY 18, 1988, I got into my car and drove to the far northwest side of Milwaukee. I was searching for a specific address along an isolated dirt road. To my right the road was lined with trees, and to my left the fresh snow glistened brightly on open fields. The trees, soft and feathered in their bareness, stood silently against the sunny winter sky.

I was looking for something called the HGS Corporation, which was supposed to be located somewhere on this country road. I drove slowly, searching for a sign or a mailbox, but before long I came to a sharp curve that led back to the main highway. Frustrated, I turned my car around, wondering if there even was such a thing as an HGS Corporation. I saw nothing that looked the least bit commercial or industrial, and no address was visible on the few buildings alongside the road.

But just as I was about to give up and head back, I saw a smokestack jutting up from a cluster of evergreens, its peak black with soot. Perhaps I had found what I was looking for. I slowed my car to a crawl and spied a sign near a driveway. It read "Pet Haven Cemetery and Crematory." Another sign, this one very faded and partially hidden by the branches of a huge tree, spelled out "HGS Corporation."

After children had discovered the remains of twenty-seven babies aborted at Bread and Roses, Milwaukee alderman Howard Tietz pushed an ordinance through the city council stipulating that hospitals could not dispose of either miscarried or aborted babies by placing them in trash containers. Medical facilities, including abortion clinics, had to file an end-of-the-year report with the Milwaukee Health Department that documented their "manner of disposition." In these records the HGS Corporation was cited as a location where the bodies of aborted babies were disposed. The bodies came from three Milwaukee abortion clinics. Bread and Roses had the bodies shipped directly to Pet Haven. Another Milwaukee abortion clinic, Imperial Health Center, first sent the remains of the aborted unborn to Physicians Clinical Laboratory, a Milwaukee pathology lab, and from there the bodies were shipped to Pet Haven. The third, Affiliated Medical Services, had the aborted fetal remains picked up directly by Henry and Jacquelyn Shane, who owned and operated the pet cemetery. The industrial acronym HGS was simply the initials of Henry George Shane. Later, I would discover that the Health Department had no idea that the HGS Corporation was a cemetery and crematory for animals.

I pulled into the driveway, eager to get a better look at the place. A small white farmhouse sat at the end of the driveway in a small clearing. As I parked the car, I saw a red-haired, middle-aged woman come out of a small office attached to the front end of the house. She waved at me.

"Can I help you?" she asked amiably.

"Well," I said, "This is a pet cemetery, isn't it?"

"Yes, it is," she replied.

"Do you mind if I visit?"

"Not at all," she said enthusiastically, and pointed to the back end of the property. "The cemetery's up the hill there, beyond that pile of wood."

I trudged through the snow up the small hill and came to rows of gravestones that protruded through the deep drifts. Several of them were quite large, and some bore a photo of the beloved pet buried beneath. One stone was engraved with the words "Laddie, we miss you." An ornate, pink granite tombstone with a photo of a large white rabbit read "Puff Puff—he gave his heart and asked for nothing." Another tombstone for a dog was inscribed "Rover, we've committed you into the loving arms of Jesus."

I walked along the rows of pet graves, circling around to get a closer look at the smokestack-building itself. It looked like an oversized garage, and the roof was customized to accommodate the tall metal chimney pipe. I stepped up to the building and peered through a window in the door. The room was dominated by a huge square machine studded with industrial dials and levers and temperature gauges eerily silent in the heavy winter quiet.

I turned and walked back to my car. As I passed the white farmhouse the red-haired woman stepped out and waved to me again. I decided it might be a good idea to have some written information about Pet Haven, so I asked the woman if she had a business card and pamphlets available. "Sure," she said cheerfully. "Come into the office."

I followed her into a small room. She told me her name was Jacquelyn Shane and that she, along with her husband Henry, owned and operated the Pet Haven Cemetery. The room was filled with funeral items specially designed for animals. Small caskets for cats and dogs were displayed on a low table. Funeral urns made of stained glass were arranged nearby. More traditional brass urns were also on sale, along with wreaths and artificial flowers that mourners could place at the gravesite of Fido or Felix. A painting of St. Francis of Assisi hung on one wall.

Jacquelyn gave me a brief tour of the office, showing me the urns and the caskets. She held out a small box. I peered inside. It contained a sealed plastic bag full of the ashes of a cat, ready to be picked up by its owner. She explained that many customers held funeral services for their dead pets. She opened a photo album and showed me pictures of animal wakes. I gazed at the photos of dead animals laid out in white caskets set around with flowers and candles. One picture was of an Irish Setter laid out as if in a funeral parlor—its red hair standing out against a casket lined with white satin.

"I saw your incinerator in the shed out there. Do you use that for the animals?" I asked.

"Oh yes, but it's not an incinerator," she corrected me pleasantly. "It's a crematory. A *human* crematory," she beamed. She seemed quite proud of the machine.

"Human?"

"Oh yes. It's designed for humans, but we use it for animals."

"Well, how about other types of tissue? Amputated limbs, for example. Do you burn that kind of stuff?" I asked, trying for all the world to sound as naive as possible.

"Oh no," said Jacquelyn, "Only animals. We don't burn anything human. You need a special license for that."

Jacquelyn gave me reprints of news articles published in local papers about Pet Haven and a business card. The motto on the card read: "All pets buried with complete dignity."

The Shanes took great pride in their business. They believed their pet cemetery rescued dead pets from inhumane rendering plants where their fats would be extracted for commercial purposes and the rest of their bodies destroyed. Their business sprang from a moral conviction that animals, especially pets, deserved to be buried with honor and dignity appropriate to loyal and loving creatures. The Shanes' business had been featured in a February 1985 *Milwaukee Magazine* article:

> "You'd be surprised how many people want their dog or cat buried with them," [said Henry] approaching his workshed. "And it's legal in Wisconsin to put an animal in a human cemetery, so this'll be a service we can offer next year."
>
> One such pair presently occupies a plot on the grounds, he mentions. And soon there undoubtedly will be several more. "Like I said, people get really close to their pets."
>
> [Shane] opens the shed's garage door and reveals an imposing two-year-old state-of-the-art crematory. "It's a Crawford," he says proudly. "The Cadillac of crematories. . . ."

[Shane] fires up the Crawford for demonstration purposes. The lower afterburners kick in first and the temperature is displayed digitally on the LED read-out. After about three minutes two gas pilots shoot torrid flames into a vacant chamber from above.

"We mostly do dogs," he says, watching the fire through an observation hatch. "We do a lot of cats and birds and occasionally something more unusual. . . ."

"Like I said twenty years ago," he adds confidently, "people bury people because they have to. But people bury pets because they want to."

Perhaps the Shanes believed that there was nothing really wrong with burning the bodies of aborted babies, but it was not cremation—to them, it was simply waste disposal. Apparently, they didn't believe that incineration of the remains of aborted babies with animal carcasses was a denigration of human dignity. After all, respect given to the human corpse is a way to respect the person who once lived. The Christian religion recognizes burial of the dead as the last of seven corporal works of mercy. Burial of the dead is a sign that human beings are in relation to one another, tied together by more than just nominal relationships. Authentic human living requires a recognition that human beings are interrelated on a very personal level.

Even in ancient cultures it was an abomination to refuse funeral rites to a human. Something sacred was stolen from the gods when the living refused to entomb the dead. To leave a body unburied was the worst kind of ostracism: cut off from the living, the abandoned person, left unburied, was also denied a place among the dead.

Sophocles' great heroine Antigone even sacrificed her life to bury her brother Polyneices, defying the edit of Creon of Thebes who had ordered that Polyneices' corpse be left to rot on a field of battle. Antigone "brought thirsty dust in her hands and from a shapely ewer of bronze, held high, with thrice-poured drink offering she crowned the dead." Arrested and awaiting her death sentence

Antigone faced Creon and declared that his mortal decrees could not "override the written and unfailing statutes of heaven."

*   *   *

Only a few weeks before my Pet Haven discovery, Joe Scheidler, accompanied by his friend Andy Scholberg, drove up to Milwaukee. Joe had been invited to give a speech at Marquette University. Afterward he, Andy, and I went to an International House of Pancakes down the street for coffee. As soon as we settled into a booth, Andy leaned toward me and whispered, "Monica, we've found the mother lode." I looked at him quizzically. He explained that an anonymous employee of a pathology lab called Vital Med in Northbrook, Illinois, had telephoned Conrad Wojnar, the director of three crisis pregnancy centers in the Chicago area.

Andy continued: "Whoever that employee was, she told Conrad that the bodies of aborted babies were being left out on a loading dock for garbage disposal. She said to him, 'You pro-life folks have got to do something,' and she told Conrad how to get to the bodies."

Only one year before that, I had sorted through the trash bins behind the Michigan Avenue Medical Center searching for the remains of the aborted unborn. I never thought I would do such a thing again. Yet in the very month I discovered Pet Haven's secret, I was again reclaiming the small broken bodies from their trash-bin cradles.

On the evening of February 20, 1988, just two days after my first visit to Pet Haven, Edmund and I drove down to Wilmette, Illinois to meet Tim Murphy and a few other Chicago pro-lifers. Tim drove the lead car, and the rest of us followed to a large industrial park in Northbrook. Covered by the darkness of night, we wove our way through the deserted, labyrinthine streets between buildings and empty parking lots. Finally we arrived at our destination: a large garage connected to the building that housed the pathology lab.

We parked our cars in the parking lot of a building across the street. I got out of the car and breathed in the cold night air. The laboratory building was wedged between two veins of the Illinois expressway. I-294 continued south, and the other turned east to connect motorists with the Edens expressway and downtown Chicago.

I looked into the sky. Off to the west, across the expressway, was a tower built with green-colored glass blocks. Illuminated red letters spelled out "Lake Arbor Centre." To the north I could see a large ring of white lights burning brightly against the darkness like a spaceship hovering over the earth. This, I later discovered, was only an architectural feature of the NutraSweet building, but at the time the glowing halo made the scene eerie and surreal.

Our small group walked to the entrance of the garage. A utility door had been left open, so we entered to find ourselves standing on a long concrete ramp that led down to the loading dock. On the dock were three green dumpsters. Several heavy-duty cardboard barrels were stacked along the back wall. We began to walk slowly down the ramp. I could see dozens and dozens of boxes strewn haphazardly about the dock. As we approached I felt a cold numbness stealing over me. When we reached the loading dock I knelt by a stack of boxes to examine them more closely. Pulling back the flaps of one of the boxes, I saw that it was filled to the top with the bodies of aborted babies. There were literally hundreds of them, all packed in the familiar Whirl-Paks and specimen jars. Each box on the dock was similarly filled with fetal remains. The cardboard barrels also contained Whirl-Paks, mixed in with waste and debris.

I was struck by the realization that all of these fetal children had been alive only a few short days ago. Now they lay dead and abandoned, cut from their mothers' wombs, cut from the human race: corpses of fetal bodies stacked on a loading dock inside an industrial park in boxes marked "for disposal."

As I stood on the edge of the loading dock it seemed my journey and theirs had brought us together at the edge of the world. Here the aborted had been cast adrift in a desolate sea. A dark, sad, heavy revelation suddenly took life deep inside me. Abortion wasn't just about killing—and pro-life work wasn't just about restoring to the unborn their right-to-life. In the image of those tiny human lives scattered about the loading dock I came to know the true plight of the aborted unborn: they were horribly, frighteningly alone.

We had to go to the edge of the world to bring the abandoned back—to give what remained of them their first and last human embrace. The aborted babies had been piled on the loading dock to await their final journey to an industrial incinerator company called Precision Energy Systems. The bodies had been shipped by parcel post to Vital Med from nine different clinics. The boxes that contained the fetal remains had return addresses on them. Most of the remains were from a string of clinics run by Susan Hill of the Women's Health Organization. Apparently the WHO clinics had a group contract with Vital Med.*

Each Whirl Pak or specimen jar had a number written on it. Also scribbled on the fetal containers were the words "uterine contents," "uterine tissue," or "POC," short for "products of conception." Ironically, almost every container bore the name of the baby's mother. It seemed strange that the mothers who had aborted their children in life were still bound to them in death.

We had stumbled into the middle of a terrible secret. The ugly aftermath of abortion was laid bare before us in this house of death. We could stick our hands inside the boxes and come out with fists full of broken bodies. At the edge of the world, in this desolate extremity, abortion presented human beings according to the structure of its ethic. These were not human beings in-relation to others, to their mothers and fathers who gave them life and then gave them death. These fetal humans were reduced to a simple mass of impersonal matter, their human individuality crushed out of them.

---

* We also found remains that night from two Milwaukee abortion clinics: Summit, one of the WHO clinics, and Metropolitan Medical Services. Besides Milwaukee, aborted babies had been shipped to Vital Med from clinics in Fargo, ND, Fort Wayne, IN, Raleigh, NC, Wilmington, DE, Fairfield, NJ, and Chicago and Harvey, IL.

* * *

Two weeks later, on March 8, 1988, I went back to Pet Haven with Sandy Schultz, who was now active with a local chapter of the Christian Action Council. Sandy, seven months pregnant at the time, agreed to accompany me on my visit. Together we hoped to persuade the Shanes to stop burning the remains of the aborted fetal children with the carcasses of dead animals. We thought, if we could demonstrate to them how they were helping the abortion industry, we might be able to persuade them to reconsider.

When we drove onto the property, the couple was standing outside their office. This time Jacquelyn did not wave. They invited us into the building. I saw Henry eyeing us nervously. He was a tall, lean and intelligent-looking man in his late forties with dark hair, a dark beard and glasses. After we all crowded into their tiny office I quickly got to the matter at hand.

"Mr. and Mrs. Shane, we know that you are burning the bodies of aborted babies with animals in your crematory, and we would like to ask you to stop doing that."

Henry's eyes went wide, aflame with indignation.

"What do you mean by coming here and questioning what we do?" he said.

"Well, for one thing, what you're doing is illegal, isn't it?" I responded.

"Illegal? How would you know if it is?" asked Jacquelyn.

"Because you don't have a special license to do it."

"Why don't you check to see if we've got one before making an accusation? If you do something to bring scandal to my business— all I can say is you'd better have a damn good attorney!" Henry shouted.

"Look," said Jacquelyn, leaning forward on her chair, "We're running an honest business here. Abortion is legal. We're not doing anything wrong."

"I don't want to discuss legalities. I want to talk about morality," I told her.

"Hey, I'm not for abortion, and I'm not against it," Jacquelyn explained, "but I do think that under certain circumstances abortion is justified, like when the fetus is deformed."

"The issue here has to do with the way you are treating the unborn," I tried to explain. "These are babies, victims of injustice and you're actually helping the abortion clinics when you take them and burn them with animals. These unborn children are human beings just like you and me. You have to treat them with respect. You wouldn't burn a grown person just like you burn dogs and cats, hamsters, snakes and parrots, would you? These children were treated like garbage while they lived. We should give them the dignity in death that they didn't have in life."

"Look, what we're doing here," said Henry, "is the right and proper way to dispose of these fetuses. If abortion is legal then we have to dispose of them somewhere, don't we? Isn't it better that we burn them here than have them wind up in a trash dumpster? You shouldn't be criticizing us, you should be thanking us!"

"Mr. Shane, the difference between burning aborted babies with animals in a crematory and throwing them in the trash is purely academic. Both are degrading."

"Look," he said. "I'm in the cemetery business. I put bread on the table because I provide a service. But a dead body is a dead body. The difference is love. People care about these animals. They don't want to just throw them in a hole in the backyard. These animals have been loyal and obedient and loving and they deserve respect. People love their pets. So do I. I want to help keep the memory of that love alive."

He got up and went over to a large cage fixed to the wall behind him and took out a wild mourning dove. It was a common, attractive grey bird, the kind I often heard making its characteristically sad cooing in my own backyard. Henry brought the bird over for Sandy and me to admire. He stroked it lovingly.

"Look at this wonderful bird. Isn't it tragic that they are left out in the cold in the winter with hardly a thing to eat?" Henry said.

"Don't think I don't love animals," I said. "I've always loved them. Believe it or not, when I was nine years old I drew up a treaty saying that I would never harm one. But right now, I'm really just not particularly interested in this bird."

"What we're concerned about right now, Henry, is what's happening to the remains of the babies," said Sandy. "Pets buried here get more honor than the bodies of the babies. Please tell me that you don't just toss their ashes into the trash. Can I ask what you do with the ashes after you've burned the babies?"

"Don't worry," said Henry. "We bury the ashes separately from the pets."

"But in the same grave?" asked Sandy.

Henry did not answer. He walked back to the cage and set the dove carefully inside, then stared at it for a moment. "Some animals are better than people," he said. "A faithful dog is better than all those drug addicts, muggers, rapists and murderers."

For the Shanes, the value of a human being was determined by whether or not they were nice or productive people. Friendly, loyal dogs were more valuable than a criminal. It could not be wrong to burn the remains of the unloved aborted with those of cats and dogs who were good to their masters. After all, to the Shanes, the bodies of these fetuses had no more practical worth than these animals—if anything, they were worth less.

After an hour and a half of conversation, Sandy and I saw that the Shanes would not be convinced. As we stood up to leave, Jacquelyn opened the door of the office.

"Well, perhaps you'll hear from us again," I said.

"Oh, I'm sure we will," Jacquelyn replied.

Unable to persuade the Shanes to stop burning the fetal remains, Sandy and I decided to publically expose what they were doing in the hope of stirring community opposition. Ten days after our visit to Pet Haven, we were guests on the WVCY *In Focus* show, a popular local Christian television program. A few days before the program I asked the host, Vic Eliason, if I could show photos of aborted babies retrieved from the Chicago dumpster a year before, but it occurred to me that I didn't need photos. I had the actual remains of aborted babies retrieved from Vital Med. Vic agreed to let us show their bodies on the air.

When I walked into the spare bedroom of my apartment to gather the bodies, I caught a whiff of a nasty odor, but I could not find the source. The abortion clinics packed the fetal remains in a diluted formalin solution, a powerful preservative which gave off a distinct chemical smell. But this was definitely not a chemical odor. Only while unpacking the remains in the television studio itself did I find the cause. One specimen bag did not have any formalin in it, and the body inside had already begun to decompose. The smell of death overwhelmed me. The baby was about eleven weeks old, and I could see the lower half of the small, severed corpse. The legs were not stiff and intact like the other fetal babies, whose limbs were frozen by the formalin solution in the postures of their deaths.

I stared sadly at the limp body, taken in by the reality of death. I thought to myself, "Abortion took away this child's life. And now his remains are decaying, evaporating. Soon all traces of him will vanish as if he never existed."

Under the magnifying power of the TV lenses, the fragmented bodies became larger than life. The creases in a tiny hand, no larger than the nail on my little finger, were made plainly and beautifully visible. Two of the aborted babies were four months gestational age. One baby's rib cage was almost completely intact. It still held the fetal heart—strikingly similar in size and shape to the images of the Sacred Heart of Jesus I had seen on Catholic devotional badges.

The viewers of *In Focus* were shocked when they heard about Pet Haven. The humanity of the abortion victims was placed right before them. People were able to see that the bodies of human beings were burned with dead cats and dogs. The response was immediate. The following morning I had interviews with two radio stations, the *Milwaukee Journal*, and Channel 12 News, an ABC-TV affiliate. A reporter from the television station discovered that the Shanes' use of the crematory for the burning of human remains was indeed illegal. Henry and Jacquelyn had violated a zoning ordinance which allowed them to burn only animal carcasses but no other type of "waste material." For several days in a row, the black, sooty smokestack at Pet Haven was a familiar sight on the evening news.

The extensive news coverage helped spur pro-lifers into action. The week following the program, hundreds of phone calls poured into the WVCY studio. People wanted to know what they could do to stop the aborted babies being burned at Pet Haven or how they could become active in the pro-life movement itself. City Hall and the Department of Building Inspection received their share of phone calls from irate citizens as well. For three days in a row, my own phone rang every ten minutes. People asked me what they could do to stop abortion. Many people said that they had been active in the pro-life movement years ago but had dropped out, and were now inspired to return.

I was surprised by the volume and intensity of the response. Why should the news of aborted babies being burned with dead animals ignite such overwhelming outrage when abortion itself had not changed? What had changed was how the public was able to view abortion. The incineration of the bodies of fetal children with animals finally gave the public something tangible against which to measure the worth of the babies. Thousands of people were jarred into the realization that something indecent, something abominable, was taking place, beginning in the abortion procedure room and ending in the rising smoke of the Pet Haven crematory.

At first Henry and Jacquelyn refused to speak to the media, but after three days of constant news coverage, they decided to grant interviews to defend their practice. But the more the Shanes tried to justify themselves, the more their own words served to indict them. It was sad to watch. On March 23, a *Milwaukee Journal* article appeared with the headline: "Crematory owners defend fetal disposal." In it, Henry was quoted as saying, "The public is fine as long as they don't know what's going on." Jacquelyn explained that the public should not be so outraged, since "the firm accepted fetuses only from a few sources and it can't be two percent of our business." Henry went on to say that the pet cemetery charged for burning of the aborted babies "a flat rate for so many pounds." Henry tried to convey how little money he made from burning the fetal remains but only succeeded in emphasizing the unseemliness of his practice. The unborn were reduced to mere weight, valued by the pound.

In the week following the WVCY program, officials from the Department of Building Inspection paid a visit to Pet Haven. Henry cooperated with them in every way and explained in detail how the babies were burnt. This information was passed on to Milwaukee alderman Howard Tietz. Tietz and the Shanes appeared on a local late-night show, and Tietz, who vehemently opposed the Shanes' practice, described to the public how the fetal corpses were burnt. Because the bodies were wet with blood and formalin the usual heat level in the crematory needed to be raised to achieve incineration. To aid the burning process, dry and brittle animal carcasses were placed in the bottom of the crematory to serve as kindling. The boxes of aborted babies were placed on a shelf above the dead animals. Only in this sense were the babies burned separately. I later spoke with alderman Tietz in person, and he told me that when the temperature rose to a certain degree the specimen bags burnt and melted, causing the blood of the aborted to drip onto the animals below. In this process there was a certain reduction of one into the other. The crematory rendered all ashes the same.

* * *

On March 26, the *Milwaukee Journal* ran an editorial cartoon depicting a haunted-looking house in the distance, with bare trees hovering over it. Behind the house was a smokestack belching out thick black smoke. In the foreground was a large sign which read "Doggy Haven Pet Cemetery, 'We treat animals with dignity.'" Below that slogan was written "Fetuses also cremated."

The next day three hundred pro-lifers demonstrated in front of Pet Haven Cemetery and Crematory. Local media covered the event. Henry and Jacquelyn closed their business for the day. They had been issued a "cease and desist" order from the Department of Building inspection, and during this time they were forbidden to burn the aborted babies pending a public hearing. One lone old woman came out in the cold to counter-protest on behalf of the cemetery. She had two pets buried there. For two and a half hours this thin, elderly lady stood sternly in her gray coat, speechless and motionless, like a statue at the edge of the Pet Haven property. She held up a sign, a message meant for the pro-lifers: "Your presence here is degrading to all those resting here."

Some letters appeared in the local press defending the Shanes, some more peculiar than others. One such letter, printed April 7, ran in the *Milwaukee Sentinel*:

> Monica Migliorino (director of Citizens for Life) and alderman Howard Tietz have insulted every pet owner and every loveable and dedicated pet in the world. . . . Pets and pet owners have love and dedication in abundance, something Migliorino and Tietz apparently never heard of. . . . I would consider it an honor to be cremated with pets, rather than resting near some atrocious corpses such as Tietz and Migliorino.

On the day of the Pet Haven picket, the *Milwaukee Journal* printed an editorial which criticized the burning of fetuses with animals. The paper seemed concerned about the public relations fallout for the abortion clinics.

> If abortion clinics here had been looking for a way to generate even harsher criticism of their work, they could hardly have picked a more effective strategy than contracting with a pet cemetery for cremation of fetuses. Even proponents of the right to abortion must be troubled by the message that the practice of joint fetal/animal cremation sends.
>
> By expanding their business to include cremation of fetuses provided by abortion clinics, owners of [Pet Haven Cemetery] and Crematory apparently violated city zoning codes. Now [Pet Haven] says it will end the practice.

The abortion clinics, for their part, ought to negotiate contracts for fetus cremation with funeral homes or conventional cemeteries. The cost might rise, but the public's sense of outrage might diminish somewhat.

The editorial reads like satire, suggesting that the real problem is not abortion, but only that abortionists deny the fetuses a decent burial. The burning of aborted babies with animals is condemned only because it subjects the abortion business to public criticism. Indirectly, however, the editors admitted that the unborn are human—after all, what sense does it make to send "uterine tissue" or "blobs of cells" to a funeral home?—but they failed to confront the real issue at hand. The burning of the babies is an intrinsic part of the abortion ethic, compounded by the added insult of burning them with dogs and cats and parrots. The denigration of the aborted flows from abortion's attack on the sacredness of human life. One cannot be disentangled from the other.

On June 23, 1988, four months after we first learned about Pet Haven, the City of Milwaukee Zoning Board convened a hearing to determine whether to alter the Shanes' special-use permit. Over thirty pro-lifers were present to oppose any change. Henry and Jacquelyn undoubtedly felt overwhelmed and alone. Except their attorney, no one came to speak on their behalf. He argued that no special variance was needed since, as reported in the *Milwaukee Journal*, "human fetuses and animal carcasses were both tissue, and steps were taken to separate the burning processes for animals and human fetuses." In the end, the Shanes' request was denied.

While all of this was going on, Edmund and I continued our weekly pilgrimage to Vital Med with a few other pro-lifers from Milwaukee and Chicago. Just as Antigone was compelled to bury her brother despite the prohibition of law, so we performed the familial duties for small bodies left on the loading dock. God alone sees the hidden corpses cast out of our cities, lost in our sewer lines, buried in landfills, and vanished in the smoke of waste incinerators, denied even a burial of dust.

CHAPTER THIRTEEN

THE FIRST KINDNESS

"To forget murder victims is to kill them twice."
— Elie Wiesel

E DMUND informed me about an upper flat for rent directly
across from his small one-room apartment on 37th Street. He
lived only one block from Interstate 94 and only two short blocks
from a small neighborhood, in a valley, called Piggsville. And so
I moved from Milwaukee's east side to these relatively spacious
quarters. This arrangement meant that we saw a lot more of each
other. Indeed, we saw one another daily. Edmund was a handsome, thoughtful, quiet young man, and he took to pro-life activism quickly. He was not afraid to do the hard stuff, like block the
door to an abortion clinic or risk arrest. Following the Bread and
Roses sit-in we spent hours together sidewalk counseling. Edmund
had a deeply compassionate nature and was eager to reach out and
help the mothers scheduled for abortion.

Edmund came from a family sensitive to social justice issues;
indeed, he could claim a kind of pedigree in this regard. His father
William, a professor of history at Marquette University, was a
close friend of Dorothy Day, the founder of the Catholic Worker
Movement and wrote her definitive biography—nominated for a
Pulitzer in 1982. Inspired by Day's vision of a transformed, equi-
table community, William and his wife Rhea instilled in their

children a keen sense of justice and a will to break down the barriers of poverty and prejudice.

After weekly treks to the Vital Med loading dock, I stacked dozens of boxes filled with broken bodies in the spare bedroom that I used as a study. The house where Edmund lived had a nearly-empty basement, rarely visited by the two other tenants. It was here that we piled the largest share of the boxes: five feet high, twelve feet across, and six feet wide. Edmund covered the growing mountain of boxes with blankets and a tarp. I bought several air fresheners to mask the odor of formalin emitted from the boxes in my apartment. If I kept the door to my spare bedroom closed, the odor was barely noticeable, but perhaps over time I simply became used to the smell.

After several weeks of retrieving the bodies, the boxes were beginning to exceed our limited capacity to hold them. Sandy Schultz agreed to house some in her finished basement, as did Dan Zeidler, the former director of Wisconsin Citizens Concerned for Life. Edmund and I could have rented a storage room for the fetal remains or found a pro-lifer's empty garage to store them in, but we had a philosophical and spiritual aversion to doing so. As much as possible, we wished to treat the remains of these aborted human beings as we would the remains of any other person.

Those involved with the retrievals decided that the best course of action was to obtain as many of the bodies of the aborted babies as possible and, after a large number were in our possession, begin the arrangements for their burials. It would have been extremely time-consuming and expensive to bury bodies every two or three weeks as we found them, and we firmly believed that the babies deserved a well-planned and well-attended funeral. Whatever happened, we did not want a repeat of the clandestine burial of the five hundred babies from the Michigan Avenue Medical Center.

With a spare bedroom filled with the remains of aborted babies, I was indeed living with the dead. We had begun our retrievals in February of 1988. It was now July. As the months went by and the boxes accumulated, I began to feel not that I was burying the babies, but that the babies were burying me.

Just beyond a closed door in my apartment lay the dismembered bodies of unborn children. I began to know their isolation and understand that it is caused by the triumph of another individual in isolation—a lonely monadic self who must secure its own identity and power by suppressing or annihilating all who threaten to be in relation to it. Here lay these silent bodies, taken from a loading dock by the hands of a stranger, sitting quietly in a strange place. They were apart from their mothers, apart from their fathers, apart from the towns where they had been conceived. In them I knew the denial of mankind's most intrinsic bonds. *Roe v. Wade* was based on the premise—indeed, on the philosophy—that the woman stands alone. Abortion isolates the woman from all other human beings in the world. Under *Roe*, no one, not parents or boyfriend or husband, and much less a stranger, has any claim on the woman and her baby. In the philosophy of *Roe* there are no inherent human relationships. As Sr. Mary of Albany once told me—we are related to one another only if we choose to be.

* * *

Edmund and I told John Cavanaugh-O'Keefe about the discovery of the babies on the Vital Med dock. John was a very well-known pro-life activist leader; he pioneered the pro-life sit-in movement, or rescue movement, as it later came to be called. Between 1986 and 1987, John retrieved four hundred and fifty bodies from trash containers at Washington, D.C., abortion clinics.

John was also opposed to mass burials. He believed that each unborn child should be given an individual burial. Each unborn child is a unique member of the human race, and John wanted to recognize and ratify that uniqueness, instead of burying them together anonymously.

For this reason John organized Project Tobit, named after the Old Testament figure who, despite persecution, buried fellow Israelites slain by a despotic king. John, a former antiwar activist,

believed that what we did with the unborn, living and dead, fore-
shadowed what would happen to peace in the world. If we could
bury babies in mass graves, what kind of world violence were we
getting ready for? What kind of brutality were we prepared to
accept?

I wanted very much to do what John urged and give each child
an individual burial. If I had only a dozen bodies, or fifty, or a hundred, or even three hundred, perhaps it could have been done. We
could have found three hundred pro-lifers across the country who
could have organized three hundred funerals. But we had thousands of bodies. Edmund and I had retrieved over two thousand
of them ourselves. Tim Murphy and the other Chicago activists
had even more. By the time our retrieval efforts came to an end,
over five thousand unborn babies were in need of burial. Arranging
for that many funeral services would be a massive task. It probably meant that we would do no other pro-life work except arrange
burials for months to come. I did not want to be in the funeral
business forever.

Edmund and I decided on a sort of compromise between John's
vision and the volume of the unburied dead. We knew the particular cities where the babies had been aborted and we thought it only
right that the babies be buried in the cities where they may have
been brought into life and where they certainly had been killed. We
contacted pro-lifers in Raleigh, Fargo, Fort Wayne, Fairfield, and
Wilmington, DE, and tried to arrange the transportation of the
bodies by car to the various states. Sending them through the mail
or by the United Parcel Service was out of the question. That was,
after all, how they had ended up on the Vital Med loading dock in
the first place.

In July, 1988, Edmund drove his 1973 Super Beetle six hundred miles to Philadelphia to deliver a box of two hundred babies
killed at the New Jersey Women's Health Organization and the
Delaware Women's Health Organization to Joe Foreman, a well-
known activist and ordained minister. The bodies were then given
to pro-lifers in those states. Not wanting to spend Citizens for

Life's money, Edmund pawned his guitar to finance his Philadelphia excursion.

The unborn killed in Raleigh were buried at a cemetery in Chapel Hill, North Carolina. The funeral there was organized by Lucy O'Keefe, John Cavanaugh-O'Keefe's sister. I made arrangements with Charlene Crommit of the Diocese of Fargo's Respect Life Office to have the babies killed in Fargo transported back there. One hundred and forty bodies were placed in one small infant's coffin and sent by jet to North Dakota. The Fargo diocese paid for the jet, and Bishop John Sullivan sent his own representative to meet the small white coffin when it arrived at the airport. Sullivan himself presided over the burial service.

*   *   *

July 30, 1988, was a warm, sunny day as I drove with two friends from Milwaukee to Hillside, Illinois, a western suburb of Chicago. An hour and forty-five minutes later we passed through the ornate entranceway to Queen of Heaven cemetery, and walked to the small chapel in the mausoleum. A hearse was parked in the circular drive outside. I looked at the black funeral car and saw two large and exceptionally ornate beige adult caskets in the back. They contained the bodies of two thousand aborted babies from Vital Med to be buried that day.

We entered the chapel, and I took a seat in the pew near the front reserved for those who helped take the bodies out of the trash. Joe Scheidler was there, along with Tim Murphy, Jerry McCarthy, Brian Pabich and Peter Krump. Soon the chapel was overflowing with members of the funeral party. Then the processional hymn began and Cardinal Bernardin walked up the short aisle of the chapel and approached the altar.

Just one month before Joe Scheidler sat down with Joseph Cardinal Bernardin at the archdiocesan chancery office on Superior Street in the posh north end of the Chicago Loop. Joe, with other pro-life leaders in attendance, wanted to discuss their frustrations

with Bernardin's lack of serious support in the anti-abortion struggle. For years, Catholics active in the pro-life cause in his archdiocese felt they were very much on their own. Few priests provided
encouragement. Indeed, some were hostile to pro-life initiatives
and the archdiocese provided very little institutional backing for
pro-life work.

Joe and the other pro-life leaders hoped to change that. While
the cardinal listened intently, Joe suggested many ways Bernardin
himself could become more involved. Joe told him that there were
aborted babies that needed to be buried and asked the cardinal if he
would officiate at the burial himself. The cardinal agreed.

On this warm summer day everything was perfect. Bernardin,
was not only the primary celebrant for the babies' funeral Mass, but
he preached the homily as well. The funeral liturgy was marked with
the greatest dignity and solemnity. The caskets seemed suitable for
royalty, and most important, the burial was public, and there were
hundreds of people in attendance. After the Mass, the mourners
returned to their cars and followed the hearse through the winding
streets of the cemetery until it came to a plot at the far west end.
There the caskets were unloaded and placed on transport tables. All
those involved with the retrieval bore the caskets to the gravesite.

Cardinal Bernardin stood near the open ground, with Fr.
Coughlin at his side. Six hundred people gathered around to join
in the prayers at the side of the grave and also, unlike the burial for
the aborted babies from 30 South Michigan, several TV cameras,
photographers and journalists were on hand to report the event.
Bernardin blessed the ground, blessed the caskets and offered prayers
for the dead. In a matter of moments, the ceremony was over.*

---

* In many ways this July burial was the complete reverse of that nearly hidden burial of the aborted babies from 30 South Michigan and in some
ways prefigured a change that would come about in the attitude of church-
men 20 years later. In 2008 members of Citizens for a Pro-Life Society
helped retrieve the remains of thirty-three aborted babies altogether from
two Michigan abortion clinics, Alberto Hodari's WomanCare in Lathrup

Bernardin took some flak for officiating at the burial. Colleen Connell of the ACLU, the attorney who had fought to facilitate Peaches' abortion three years before, criticized the cardinal in a *Chicago Tribune* story:

> He allowed himself to be used in a shameless publicity stunt. It's one thing for a cardinal to say the Catholic Church is opposed to abortion. But it's quite another for him to participate in an action which demeans the personal privacy and integrity of women who may or may not be church members.

Connell failed to consider that some women—perhaps more than a few—would be comforted to know that their baby was given a humane burial. Connell also questioned whether laws had been broken by those of us who "provided the fetuses." Bernardin told the *Tribune* reporter: "I didn't ask where the babies had come from and I don't know what the legal consequences might be, but they would pale in significance when compared to the taking of innocent human life. I knew what I was doing, and what I was doing was a corporal work of mercy done in a very beautiful religious ceremony."

* * *

Two weeks before the Chicago burial Edmund built eight infant-sized coffins. He made them out of pine, painted them white, and

---

Village and Reginald Sharpe's Woman's Advisory in Livonia. When I approached the Archdiocese of Detroit to help facilitate their burials, chancery office officials, notably Msgr. Robert McClory and auxiliary Bishop John Quinn were eager to help and cooperated with me in the details of the burials. While the archdiocese was still very hesitant about media coverage, an issue that continued to frustrate me, nonetheless I detected that in 20 years an attitude shift had occurred in the Catholic Church toward pro-lifers and the abortion issue itself. The leery, distrustful mindset was gone, replaced with more respect for activists and a deeper sense of urgency about abortion itself.

affixed wooden crosses to the lids. We gently placed seven hundred and twenty-one aborted babies inside. Most of them had been killed by Dr. Ulrich Klopher at the Fort Wayne Women's Health Organization.

Edmund borrowed a trailer from his brother, hitched it to his car, and on the warm evening of August 3, we loaded up the trailer with the coffins and, along with our friend Greg Gesch, we began the thousand-mile trip to Edmund's family home in Lloyd, just outside of Tallahassee, Florida. Edmund's parents opened their home to us and the coffins were placed in Rhea's elegant parlor.

The burial for these aborted babies was scheduled to take place as part of a larger pro-life initiative. Don Treshman and Ed Martin of Rescue America had planned three days of nonstop pro-life activity in Tallahassee, which they called the Free Joan Andrews Campaign. On March 26, 1986, Joan and three other pro-lifers entered the Ladies Center, a Pensacola abortion clinic. Joan located one of the procedure rooms and tried to disable the suction machine by pulling on a plug that was permanently affixed to the wall. She was arrested and charged with burglary, criminal mischief and resisting arrest. In a bench trial, Judge William H. Anderson found Joan guilty of the charges. Anderson wanted verbal assurance from Joan that she would no longer engage in illegal activities to save the unborn. Joan, in conscience, could not give such a promise, whereupon Anderson, citing her lack of repentance, sentenced her to a five-year prison term. This punishment was far beyond Florida's sentencing guidelines, which recommended a year to thirty months for convicted burglars.

Joan believed she was called to practice non-cooperation with the judicial system, including her jailers. When the moment came for her to be taken from the court and escorted to jail, Joan sat down on the floor of Anderson's court and had to be carried out by the bailiffs. She continued her non-cooperation throughout her incarceration at the Broward Correctional Center, a maximum-security facility for Florida's worst female offenders. In addition to refusing to walk, Joan refused to be fingerprinted, ignored her work detail, and would not cooperate with other aspects of jail life. As a result, Joan lost time off for good behavior and was denied the right to attend religious services. She spent twenty-two months in solitary confinement.

By the time Joan was convicted, she was already a seasoned veteran of the pro-life rescue movement, having been arrested over one hundred times. In the early 1970s Joan attended St. Louis University and was very active in protests against the war in Vietnam. But in the end she left that movement, disillusioned with the anger, hostility and violence that too often attended anti-war demonstrations. In 1973, when *Roe v. Wade* struck down state laws protecting the unborn, Joan turned her activist energy to defending the unborn at abortion clinics. Joan's steadfast convictions were wedded to a very warm, gracious and compassionate personality. Many people in the pro-life movement were inspired by her spiritual and philosophical vision of the rescue of the unborn as an act of intense self-immolation.

Reporter Scott Eyman wrote of Joan while she was in prison. His article appeared in the April 19, 1987 edition of *Sunshine*, the Sunday magazine of the *Miami Herald*.

> She could be pretty, but she is beginning to look worn and old beyond her 38 years. She bears her afflictions with a joyful grace. . . . She lost her right eye to cancer six years ago and has a glass replacement, giving her face the unblinking, baleful stare of a stuffed animal. She dismisses the difficulty it causes her: "I have to be careful going down stairs."
>
> To look at her is to see someone rare, someone who has willfully chosen to mortify not merely her flesh, but her entire life. The unspoken logic is crushingly simple: If the babies with whom she identifies so strongly are unable to have a life, then neither will Joan Andrews. . . .
>
> The basis of Joan's non-cooperation is her feeling that, by sentencing her, the judicial system announced that the lives of unborn children are not worth defending—and that, were she to cooperate with her jailers, she would be implicitly agreeing

with that evaluation. To cooperate with her sentence would, in effect, be to admit her guilt.

Hundreds of pro-lifers converged on Florida's capitol to participate in rallies, marches and prayer vigils to bring attention to the injustice Joan was suffering and to petition Florida's governor Lawton Chiles to intervene in her case.

On Friday, August 5, the babies were buried at Roselawn Cemetery in Tallahassee following a service at Calvary Presbyterian Church. It was a humid, overcast day, and thunder rumbled in the distance as the graveside service began, but it did not rain. Adelle Nathanson, the wife of former abortionist Bernard Nathanson, was present, as was California congressman Robert Dornan. Tim Murphy and Andy Scholberg, who helped in the retrieval, were also there. The local television and newspaper media, already abuzz with the Joan Andrews story, covered the burial.

The white coffins Edmund had built were reverently carried to the edge of the deep hole dug out of the dark red earth. A voice rang out plaintively: "Sometimes I Feel Like a Motherless Child." When the song ended I addressed the mourners:

> We are gathered here today to perform the seventh corporal work of mercy, to bury the dead. Ironically, the last work of mercy . . . is the first kindness shown to these little ones killed in the abortion mills.
>
> Our Lord, hung on the cross, was held in scorn—reviled, hated, rejected by His own people. These unborn babies have been taken up into his suffering and when we took their bodies off of the loading dock, it was as if we had taken Christ off the cross.
>
> These are the very least of Christ's brethren, the poorest of the poor. Why are these aborted babies the very least? Because they're small, helpless, utterly and completely dependent? Yes. Because in terms of what the world values, they didn't contribute anything? Yes. But the real reason is because they received the least charity. Indeed, while they lived, they received no charity at all.

This is the key to ending the holocaust: charity. We must show real love toward those whom the world hates. We must become saints and be filled with the compassion of saints. . . .

A return to true Christian charity: this is what will end abortion. And it is not a very easy route, but it's the only one that will really work.

These are the bodies of God's children crushed up in a scream of "no" to Him. . . .

It is the faith of the Church that must sustain us, that enduring faith that teaches against all despair that the dead shall rise. These babies, baptized in their blood, shall rise. . . .

Jesus has promised it to us and to them. He shall wipe every tear from their eyes, and there shall be no more death, mourning, crying out, or pain, for the former world has passed away.

All those gathered around the grave sang hymns and offered prayers as we lowered the coffins into the ground. We did not want to leave the actual burial for the cemetery grounds crew. We wanted to bury the babies ourselves, as a personal act. A young man lowered himself into the massive grave, and Greg Gesch and another young man passed the coffins down to him. I took one long last look at the coffins below me. Then we took turns shoveling the red clay into the grave until it was filled.

Local media coverage of the Free Joan Andrews campaign was extensive. I was stunned when I picked up a copy of the next day's *Tallahassee Democrat*. A huge photo showing the young man who had gone down into the grave dominated the front page—but nothing was visible of him except his hands outstretched to receive a coffin. While the babies were rejected in life—it looked as if the earth had opened its arms to welcome them home.

CHAPTER FOURTEEN

THE BURIAL FOR NO ONE

"I'm not afraid of death. I am afraid of murder."
—Harry Caul, in the film *The Conversation*

METROPOLITAN was a non-descript two-story building near the corner of Wisconsin Avenue and 27th Street in a somewhat run-down neighborhood close to downtown Milwaukee, surrounded by lots of apartment buildings and old homes in need of paint and repair. It was one of the few abortion clinics that offered no other services except abortion. When it first opened, just after the *Roe v. Wade* decision, three doctors took turns doing the abortions: Neville Sender, George Woodward and Nathan Hildrich. Of the three, Sender was certainly the most committed to the abortion practice. He had boasted to the *Milwaukee Journal* that he had performed illegal abortions before *Roe v. Wade*, and he shocked pro-lifers when he told the *Journal*: "Of course we know it's killing, but the state permits killing in certain circumstances." Sender enjoyed harassing the protestors and sidewalk counselors outside of his clinic and made a regular practice of heaping insults and obscenities on the pro-lifers who faithfully assembled outside Metropolitan.

Carol Robbins was one of the most faithful sidewalk counselors at Metropolitan. She could be seen standing in front of the building nearly every day that the abortion clinic was open. Once in July, 1991, a good-looking young man strolled past her, stopping for a moment to look at a sign which displayed photos of aborted babies in the first trimester. Carol went over to him and gave him some pro-life literature which also showed aborted babies.

The young man looked at the pictures.

"What do you think about that?" Carol asked him.

"Hum," the man said. "It makes me hungry."

Three weeks later, the young man was arrested. When Carol saw the television news clips about his arrest, she gasped. The man was Jeffrey Dahmer who, over a period of thirteen years, had killed seventeen men. He cut up the bodies of his victims, dissolved the flesh, stored the skulls, kept body parts in his refrigerator and engaged in cannibalism. Dahmer lived in a dilapidated apartment building only two blocks away from Metropolitan.

On the day after Dahmer's arrest, the *Milwaukee Sentinal* front page headline blasted in larger than usual bold black letters: "Human Body Parts Found in Apartment." I was stunned by the headline. It could have been written about me. I thought how ironic it was that I too once had an apartment in which body parts from murdered human beings had been stored. The media was appalled by what Dahmer had done and presented his storage of body parts as a further denigration of his victims. If the media knew about the body parts in my apartment, what would they have said? Dahmer and I both had bodies in our homes. But where he had ruthlessly murdered and dismembered his, I was rescuing babies who had been ruthlessly killed and dismembered by abortion and tossed in the trash. My mission was to give them one shred of dignity in a short life marked by horror and sin. I was performing the last work of mercy: burying the dead.

*   *   *

Five weeks after we returned from Florida, Edmund and I awoke very early on Saturday, September 10. We assembled the bodies of six aborted babies in the last of the white children's coffins that Edmund had built and put it in the backseat of his car. I got into my Celica and followed him as we drove the short distance to Metropolitan.

When Edmund and I arrived, we parked on a side street around the corner. Edmund picked up the small coffin and we walked to the front of the building. We placed the coffin a few feet from the clinic's door and opened the lid. Metropolitan had dismissed the victims of abortion by shipping their remains to a place where they were treated like trash. Now, sitting on the doorstep in their white coffin, at least six of these severed bodies could not be so easily dismissed. Edmund stood next to the coffin while I stood on the sidewalk nearby. In my arms I held a tattered duct-taped box. It was one of the boxes from the Vital Med loading dock that Metropolitan had used to ship their fetal remains. The initials "MMS," and the return address of the clinic, were still plainly visible in the upper left corner of the box.

After about ten minutes, a squad car pulled into the parking lot. An officer came out and stood quietly on the sidewalk. A few minutes later, a dark-haired woman in her early forties wearing nurses' whites stepped out of the abortion clinic. It was Susan Corrone, the manager of Metropolitan. She took a few steps over to the little coffin, bent over it slightly, and peered for a second at the tiny broken bodies. Then she pursed her lips and shook her head.

"Nope, those aren't ours," she said.

"Yes they are, Susan," I said as I walked over to her carrying the Metropolitan box. I stopped several feet from her and pointed to the tattered cardboard container. "Maybe you don't recognize the babies, but you might recognize the box that they were shipped in."

She looked at me, puzzled and apprehensive. She took a few steps toward me, looked closely at the box, and read the return address.

"Well, I think I'll take that. That's our property." She grabbed for the box, and we tussled over it for a moment.

"Officer, this woman has clinic property! Tell her to return it!" Susan yelled, flushed and angry. She succeeded in wrenching the box from my grasp. The officer came over quickly. I expected he would immediately take charge and wield his authority. But he hesitated.

I spoke up. "Officer, she says I'm in possession of clinic property, but this was a box that the abortion clinic threw in the trash that contained aborted babies. I took the box and the babies out of the trash." Then I turned to Susan, who had taken a few steps toward the side door of the clinic, hoping to whisk the box inside.

"Susan!" I shouted. "It won't do you any good to take that box. I have more where that one came from."

To my utter surprise, the officer ordered Susan to give the box back to me. I wasn't used to police siding with pro-lifers. "I think this is her box now," he said. Susan came over and begrudgingly put the box back into my hands. The officer walked back to his squad, got in the driver's seat and sat there quietly keeping vigil over the scene.

While Edmund and I displayed the aborted babies at Metropolitan, hundreds of pro-lifers were beginning to fill Trinity Lutheran Church near downtown Milwaukee. The last of the Vital Med babies were about to be buried. The day before, Edmund and I went with two friends to Brett Funeral Home to place the bodies of the fetal babies in coffins. Thomas Wiseman, the owner of the funeral home, was a Catholic and sympathetic to our cause. He arranged to have six white child-size coffins donated by the Milwaukee Casket Company and provided three black hearses for transportation.

I felt ill at ease in the back room where we were escorted to carry out our task. It seemed as though I had intruded on a place that was meant to be forever hidden and secret. The bare, drab, utilitarian function of the room contrasted sharply with the elegant furniture, sweeping draperies and lush carpeting of the funeral parlors. As I was taken past those outer rooms and into the stark, grey place where the dead are readied for burial, I fully realized how immersed in death my life had become. I was jarred by the sight of the corpse of a full-grown man laying on a gurney. He was covered by a clean white sheet and a plastic curtain was drawn, but it only partially concealed him. We carefully took the tiny bodies of the aborted unborn out of their cardboard cradles, stained with blood and formalin, and laid them in the five white coffins.

After Susan Corrone returned the "babies' box" to me, I got back into my car and drove to The Brett Funeral Home just down the street from the abortion clinic. A reporter from the *Milwaukee Journal* and a photographer from United Press International were there to meet me at 9:30. When I arrived, Patrick Jasperse, the *Journal* reporter, was waiting for me in the parking lot. The backseat of my Celica was loaded to the brim with empty cardboard boxes from Vital Med; each one bore the return address of the abortion clinic from whence it had come. I wanted the media to see the boxes, if not the actual babies themselves, as proof that we were in possession of aborted babies and that indeed aborted babies were being buried that day. I wanted the victims of abortion to be as real as possible for the press. I showed Jasperse the boxes.

When we entered the funeral home, the five coffins were set out in one of the parlors. Jasperse observed the coffins briefly, made a few notes, shook my hand and said he would see me later at the burial. Soon a very young, short, dark-haired man came toting a camera. He was the photographer from United Press International and seemed far more interested in the bodies of the children than Jasperse. He took several photos of the coffins laid out in the parlor. I offered to open the lid of one of the coffins so that he could actually see the fetal remains. "Sure, I'd be interested to see them," he said. When I opened the lid of one coffin, hundreds of dark-red, blood-colored Whirl-Paks were revealed. The photographer nearly gasped.

I picked up one of the Whirl-Paks. Tiny feet of an aborted baby were plainly visible through the plastic. He took some photos of the open coffin and then left.

The wake for the children was to begin at eleven o'clock that morning. When I entered Trinity Lutheran Church near downtown Milwaukee, I was struck by the brilliance of the windows, their colors stunning against the church's dark carved wood. High above the sanctuary was another stained glass window that showed Jesus holding and blessing little children. By eleven the old-style German Gothic church was filled with over five hundred mourners. Edmund brought the coffin we displayed at Metropolitan into the church. In this coffin was placed, along with the other fetal children, the largest of the babies we had retrieved from Vital Med—a well-developed baby killed in the seventh month of gestation. The dismembered hands and feet, not yet covered with baby fat, looked like those of an adult, but in miniature. Edmund placed the open coffin on the bottom step of the sanctuary. Several mourners filed slowly past it.

From high in the choir loft, a soprano lifted her beautiful voice in a hymn written for the Lenten season:

> O come and mourn with me a while.
> See Mary calls us to her side.
> O come and let us mourn with her.
> Jesus, Our Love, is crucified!

The song continued as the five white children's coffins were carried slowly into the church and up the center aisle. The solemn procession was a step into a new sorrow; a sorrow that, until now, the world had not known. As the coffins were laid in front of the sanctuary I was struck by the realization that they contained almost three times as many people as sat in the pews.

A Lutheran minister preached on a passage from St. Luke's gospel: "Suffer the little children to come to me." Greg Gesch read Psalm 94:

> . . . Your people, O Lord, they trample down,
> your inheritance they afflict.
> Widow and stranger they slay,
> the fatherless they murder,
> And they say, "The Lord sees not;
> the God of Jacob perceives not."
> Understand you senseless ones among the people;
> and you fools, when will you be wise?

Shall he who shaped the ear not hear?
or he who formed the eye not see?

When the service was completed, the coffins were taken in procession out of the church. Edmund carried the small wooden one, and I followed behind. When we left the church we were bathed in sunlight. The coffins were placed in the three waiting hearses. One hundred cars lined up for a two-mile stretch behind them. With motorcycle police escorts, the procession wound its way through the streets of Milwaukee slowly making its way to Holy Cross Cemetery. Oncoming traffic had to be halted at several intersections to allow the procession to pass. How ironic, I thought, that a world that had not bothered about these unborn children while they lived now had to wait for them to pass in their deaths.

Spectators watched the scene, bewildered. One man standing on a street corner exclaimed, "Man! Whoever this guy was, he had to be rich!" Another onlooker asked one of the police escorts, "Who died?" The policeman shook his head and answered, "No one."

Hundreds of additional mourners gathered at the gravesite. The service began with hymns sung by a choir from Gospel Lighthouse Church. Father Gene Jakubek, a Jesuit priest known in Milwaukee for his ministry to the poor, read the gospel and delivered the graveside eulogy. Msgr. Fabian Bruskewitz, later the bishop of Lincoln, Nebraska, stepped forward and blessed the coffins and grave with holy water. During the ceremony, a woman who stood behind me leaned over and whispered in my ear: "I had an abortion twenty years ago. I'm offering this memorial service for my own baby."

When the ceremony was over, Edmund and a few other men lowered the coffins into the twelve foot-by-six foot grave. I looked into the dark earthen hole—the coffins set side by side. It finally seemed appropriate that these babies share the same final resting place. Many of them died on the same day, in the same place, at the hands of the same abortionist. Legalized abortion had woven their deaths together.

Local media coverage of the burial was extensive and for the most part favorable. The NBC affiliate's story was even poignant; the two-minute piece seemed more like a mini-movie than a news story. There were clips of the coffins being carried into the church, a portion of the sermon given by Pastor Ferdinand Bahr, and some shots of faces in the pews. Two of the women filmed were weeping. Viewers saw the coffins being placed in the hearses while the church bells tolled a low, solemn tone. A few of the mourners were interviewed, and the story concluded with video of the burial at Holy Cross. Strangely absent were the expected interviews with Planned Parenthood, the ACLU, or abortion clinic workers. In fact, it was completely devoid of derisive comments. In all my experience, this short piece was the most sympathetic news coverage of a pro-life event I had ever seen.

After the burial, CBS affiliate reporter Roseanne St. Aubin interviewed me at the cemetery. In keeping with secular media policy, St. Aubin insisted on using "neutral language" in her report, even referring to the fetal remains as "tissue" when she stated "the organizers [of the burial] would not give details on how the tissues were acquired." When the story aired, we found that St. Aubin had covered an angle most of the other reporters did not:

> Migliorino said the names of the women who had the abortions were on the bags containing the fetuses, but those names were buried along with the fetuses buried today, and the group kept no records. . . .
>
> It's not clear whether members of the group could be or would be prosecuted for the way the fetuses were acquired. Migliorino was not afraid of the possibility.

The camera cut to me. "We performed an act of charity for these children. The wrongness occurred when they threw them in the trash."

St. Aubin's remark about the possibility of prosecution was prescient. Six months after the burial, a summons was delivered to my apartment dated March 23, 1989. I opened the official-looking white envelope and discovered that I was now a defendant in the *National Organization for Women v. Scheidler* R.I.C.O. case. R.I.C.O., short for Racketeer Influenced and Corrupt Organization Act, was passed by Congress in 1970 as a means of stopping organized crime. The lawsuit was first filed in 1986 against Joe Scheidler, Joan Andrews, and John Ryan, a rescue leader from St. Louis. They were accused of being part of an illegal enterprise called the Pro-life Action Network or PLAN. The complaint was now amended to include not only the PLAN clinic blockades but also retrievals and burials of aborted babies. The NOW lawyers claimed that these actions amounted to extortion, since they were allegedly designed to close down abortion clinics. The fifty-page document described our retrieval of the bodies as "a ghoulish plot to steal laboratory specimens." The National Organization for Women accused us of threatening to reveal the names of the women whose aborted babies we had "stolen." Of course, we had never intended to make their names known, nor did we ever threaten to do so.

Now several new defendants were being added to the lawsuit, including Randall Terry, Tim Murphy, Andy Scholberg and Conrad Wojnar. NOW even named Vital Med as a defendant under the odd theory that the Illinois lab was somehow in league with us.

I spent several years litigating my defense. Since my involvement with the Pro-life Action Network was minimal, the Seventh Circuit Federal District Court in Chicago dismissed all charges against me in 1996. Joe and the other remaining defendants were finally exonerated by an eight-to-one decision of the United States Supreme Court on February 26, 2006, a full twenty years after the lawsuit had been initiated.

* * *

A month after the Milwaukee burial, Edmund, Dan Zeidler, and I went to the cemetery to take care of some final paperwork regarding the gravesite and the placement of the tombstone. On our way back to the cars we stopped by the babies' grave to say some prayers.

The infant section of Holy Cross is a very special place. The tombstone inscriptions express the great love parents have for their children. These tender, heartfelt expressions of love, affection and sorrow are not found on adult grave markers. The dates on the stones reveal that some babies died on the day they were born. Some of the inscriptions read: "Our angel, with us for a moment—with God for eternity," "Jesus adopted our son—Mommy and Daddy love baby," "Our treasure lies here," and "Tread softly—a dream lies buried here." The markers, like silent sentinels, stand with the sorrow of parental loss frozen into the stones.

Ironically, it was here among children who were loved, wanted and named that the aborted babies found a final home. Their grave, larger than the others and not yet covered with sod, was easy to find. Thirteen silk red roses, left by Edmund after the burial, covered the top of the grave. Many of the other children's graves had small toys and I was glad to see that someone left such a toy for the aborted babies. It was a stuffed toy rabbit wrapped in plastic to protect it from the rain. Through the plastic we saw a folded piece of paper fastened to the paw of the bunny with a rubber band. Overcome by curiosity, we carefully unwrapped the toy to investigate.

As Edmund stooped over the grave, Dan and I hovered over him. Edmund unwrapped the note and unfolded it. A message was written in a swirling, feminine hand:

> Please forgive me and maybe someday I can forgive myself. . . .
> I'll always wonder what you would have been, what you would
> have become. I can't stop hating myself right now, regretting
> the hardest decision I've ever made in my life, wishing I could
> do it differently now. But I can't. I will always remember this.
> It was a tough lesson to have to learn. . . . I pray to God and
> to you to forgive me so I can go on with my life and I swear to
> both you and the Lord that I will never ever do it again. Please
> forgive me so I can let go and go on!

Edmund refolded the note, bound it back onto the rabbit's paw, and placed the toy back inside its plastic shroud.

The woman's note seemed to indicate she believed her child was buried in this grave. Her note expressed an intense feeling that she had abandoned her baby, something she sensed deep within her being. By burying the baby we had returned the child to his mother. The burial gave the baby a human place in the world. The awful tearing of human bonds caused by abortion knew a more perfect healing. On a lonely day, one woman had come to this site, and her act of love banished her isolation. In her sorrow the order of the world, rooted in human bonds, was affirmed. From out of all the nameless, faceless children buried there, the mother claimed back to herself the one who was her own.

PART III

A DANGEROUS PERSON

CHAPTER FIFTEEN

SELECTIVE PROSECUTION

"What a number of the dead we carry in our hearts, each of us bears his cemetery within."

—Gustave Flaubert

EARLY in the morning of June 8, 1989, twenty-one pro-lifers carrying heavy chains and reinforced Kryptonite bicycle locks raced up the eleven flights of stairs of the Interstate Bank Building on Wisconsin Avenue near downtown Milwaukee. Huffing and puffing from exhaustion, we trudged down the long, narrow hallway and planted ourselves four rows deep in front of the door to Imperial Medical Services, owned by abortionist Dr. Milton Tarver. The activists sitting in the front row locked their ankles together in the U-shaped Kryptonite locks that we had reinforced by sheathing them in cast-iron pipes. Wendy Fulcher, who had been arrested several times at other Milwaukee sit-ins, wore a 5/8-inch-thick industrial chain around her waist, which was looped through the same kind of chain worn by the person next to her.

I had organized this sit-in, though many of those participating were new faces to me, people inspired by Randall Terry's Operation Rescue in which thousands of pro-lifers had been arrested in nonviolent clinic blockades. But there were old faces too, such as Robert Braun, who had been arrested with me when Citizens for Life's numbers were small and our mechanical methods less imaginative.

Soon the police arrived, and I saw another old face, Sergeant

Moe. He remembered me and greeted me by name. Several fire-men also arrived and hastily set to work drilling through the locks with pneumatic high-speed carbon-tipped drills. Wendy Fulcher's partner's chain was soon broken and he was immediately arrested. Still wearing her heavy chain belt, Wendy stepped over the remain-ing rows and stood next to me at the door, delaying her own arrest.

They used high-speed knives to cut the lock's metals shafts. Orange sparks flew and the ankles of the pro-lifers were burned by the heat. A physician who later examined two of them estimated their burns to be between second-and third-degree.

Those pro-lifers who were not secured by locks or chains were arrested first. The police pulled them from their stations, bending their wrists in the pain-compliance hold. The men cried out as they were forced away from the door, sending a wave of fear rippling through the rest of us. When Greg Gesch was arrested, the police officer held his wrist down so tightly that the bones in Greg's hand cracked under the strain.

While we were upstairs blocking the doors, picketers and side-walk counselors gathered in the parking lot eleven floors below. They were soon joined by the local news media. The police began loading the first of those arrested into the waiting vans. The ranks of pro-lifers blocking the doors began to thin. When it became apparent that those closest to the door would soon be arrested, Wendy Fulcher and I took hold of each other's arms and hung on to one another. Robert Braun, who was lying on the floor in front of me, wrapped his arms around my left leg. Sergeant Moe and his partner Officer Melewski, a tall, distinguished, white-haired vet-eran like Moe, waded over bodies toward the door. Moe placed his hands on Wendy's arm and began to pull.

"Monica, let go of her arm," Moe ordered.

"I can't let go, Sergeant. Babies are scheduled to die here."

"I am ordering you to let go," Moe commanded, his voice rising in frustration and anger.

"I'm sorry, I can't. I'm here to defend the unborn and I cannot let go."

"If you don't let go now, you're going to be charged with obstructing an officer."

This was not the Sergeant Moe I knew from our Bread and Roses sit-in. His kind and patient demeanor was gone. Today I was faced with an angry and determined officer of the law. Nonetheless, I remained silent and did not let go. It took Moe and Melewski only a few additional seconds of tugging to pry Wendy loose from my grasp. A moment later, two other officers came up and pulled me out of Robert Braun's grasp. I let my body go limp in passive resistance and was surprised that my wrist was not bent to make me walk. The officers dragged me several feet down the hallway and left me there. I got up and began to race back to the door but, before I could get far, I was tackled and handcuffed, and my ankles were bound with a plastic "flexi-cuff" strip. Soon, with a handful of other protesters, I was lying on the floor of the elevator making the eleven-story trip down to the police van.

When the van was filled, we were taken to the Milwaukee police station on State Street. I waited in the holding cell for about an hour before the door finally clanged open and a matron called out my name. I was led out and escorted down a long, narrow hallway to the booking room. When I entered, Sergeant Moe was seated on a chair near the door. He was calm and relaxed now, completely changed from the gruff and angry sergeant of police I had seen at the clinic. He had reverted back into his gentle and sympathetic manner.

I thought about his apparent double personality. At the clinic, Moe was acting in his professional capacity, as a man of authority who had other officers under him. Whether or not Moe was sympathetic to our cause, he had to do his duty. But the inner struggle between the public man and his private feelings was there. Even when he was ordering me away from the clinic door, I could sense that turmoil.

But now, as he sat across from me, he was calm. He smiled and looked at me fondly with his large blue eyes. The other officer in the booking room took my fingers, rolled them one by one on a glass covered with a film of black ink, and pressed each finger onto the white form. During the painless ritual I heard Moe remark to the other officer, "If I was ever in trouble, I'd want Monica to be around."

I was stunned. Was this the same man who one hour ago yelled at me and threatened to charge me with obstructing an officer?

Later that day I was called out of the holding cell again. Moe and Melewski stood in the hallway outside and led me to another small room. Moe informed me that he was referring my case to the Milwaukee County District Attorney's Office, recommending that I be charged with criminal obstruction of an officer. I was disappointed and a bit shaken. When Moe had made his threat, I was not entirely certain what he meant by it. I knew there was a city charge of resisting an officer and thought perhaps I would be in for an additional city ticket besides the expected citation for disorderly conduct issued to the other twenty pro-lifers.

"I've got to do what I've got to do," Moe said in an apologetic tone. The criminal charge of obstructing an officer carried a maximum nine-month jail sentence and a ten-thousand-dollar fine. Moe's large eyes and friendly face reflected a sense of regret, even a feeling of guilt that his role as an officer compelled him to treat me more harshly than others.

As he had done in the past, the pro-life Milwaukee district attorney E. Michael McCann recused himself from my case. And once again my nemesis, Jeffrey Kremers, was assigned as special prosecutor. A week after the sit-in, a pretrial hearing took place in a small room at the district attorney's office. Sergeant Moe and Officer Melewski were present. I arrived with Wendy Fulcher and three others who had participated in the rescue. Kremers sat behind a desk, arms across his chest, his red, bushy eyebrows knit in a frown. Moe and Melewski stood next to the desk and the five of us squeezed into chairs in front of it.

Moe described the sit-in to Kremers: "I responded to a call regarding a disturbance on the eleventh floor of the Interstate Bank Building at Wisconsin and Eighth Avenue. We arrived on the eleventh floor and encountered a group of demonstrators blocking the doorway to a doctor's office where abortions are performed. We informed everyone that they were trespassing and ordered everyone to leave. The protesters refused to do so."

Moe glanced through his bifocals at a small record book and continued:

"When I placed a Miss Wendy Fulcher under arrest, Monica grabbed on to her and would not let go of her. I told her to let go several times and she refused to obey my order."

"Monica was not only holding on to me," Wendy explained to Kremers, "I was holding on to her! We were holding on to each other!"

I then explained that many of those participating in the rescue held onto each other—that Robert Braun, for example, had held onto my leg. We also explained that several of the pro-lifers were locked together and that it took far longer to remove them than to pull Wendy and me apart.

"It's unfair that Monica be singled out," Wendy said. "If she's going to be charged with a state charge, then so should everybody." The rest of our group agreed.

Kremers smirked.

"But Monica's different," he said. "She was told to obey an order. She didn't. Besides, no one else in this protest has a criminal record."

"Robert Braun does," I reminded Kremers.

Marshall Cheitlan, a young pro-lifer, yelled at Kremers angrily: "You've already decided that you're going to charge Monica. Coming here to try to convince you of anything was a waste of time!"

"No," said Kremers as he shook his head, "I have *not* come here with my mind made up."

"But you act like it is!" said another voice.

"No. I'm here to assess the facts upon which to make a decision. I'm in the process of making up my mind."

"Then charge everyone the same," Wendy urged again.

"Monica acted differently and she already has a criminal record."

Again I reminded Kremers about Robert Braun.

"I do not have any authority to charge Robert Braun. I've only been given authority to decide Monica's case."

"You can get the authority to charge everyone, can't you?" asked Wendy.

"Today we are deciding Monica's case." Kremers argued.

Marshall stirred in his seat with frustration as Kremer's continued: "And I find that the criminal charge of obstruction of an officer is warranted."

Marshall exploded. "You are an unjust man! You're just out to get her!"

Kremers yelled back in anger, "Well, not only am I going to charge her with obstructing an officer, but I'm going to charge her with criminal disorderly conduct and criminal unlawful assembly as well!"

My friends and I sat stunned. I looked over at Sergeant Moe, but his face was expressionless. I don't think he expected this outcome. I had entered the pretrial conference facing a possible nine months and a ten-thousand-dollar fine and left it facing twenty-one months and a twenty-one-thousand-dollar fine. Kremers was painfully aware that blockades of abortion clinics had significantly increased despite his prosecution of pro-lifers. If Kremers wanted to stop my leadership activity, he now had his chance. I   hired   a young attorney, Bill Kerner, a devout Lutheran committed to the pro-life cause, to defend me. His commitment was reflected in his legal fees; for this trial, he charged me only a thousand dollars. Bill had very ably defended me in a sit-in case from 1987, and I was confident in his skill as an attorney.

He filed a complaint against Kremers for selective prosecution. A prosecutor is guilty of selective prosecution when, with malicious intent, he singles out for a more serious charge a defendant from other defendants "who are similarly situated." Even if Kremers believed the obstruction charge was warranted, I had two extra criminal charges piled on top of me, when everyone else received only city tickets.

My case was assigned to Judge Louise Tesmer, a former state representative with a relatively good pro-life voting record. She opened the hearings on selective prosecution, but suddenly recused herself from my case, citing her pro-life views. My case was then assigned to Judge Dominic Amato, who also had pro-life sentiments. But he too quickly recused himself. I eventually wound up in Judge Charles Schudson's court. He announced to us that his wife was "solidly pro-choice" and had even once or twice participated in the efforts of the Milwaukee Clinic Protection Coalition, a group of dedicated proponents of legal abortion that regularly showed up at Milwaukee clinics to escort women arriving for their scheduled abortions. These "clinic defenders" aggressively interfered with pro-lifers' attempts to talk to women and persuade them away from their decision to abort. Bill Kerner could have filed a request for substitution of judge. But Schudson appeared conscientious, thoughtful and honest in his disclosure. We thought he would give me a fair trial.

Still, I was extremely frustrated with the attitude of the judges who were against legal abortion. It was very common for pro-life judges to take themselves off cases involving pro-life defendants, as if somehow their position disqualified them. However, judges who supported legal abortion, like Judge Patricia McMahon, in my experience never recused themselves. The problem with pro-life judges who removed themselves from pro-life cases is that they left pro-lifers at the mercy of judges totally unsympathetic with, and at times even hostile to, our cause. A pro-life judge may not, by law, be permitted to allow pro-lifers a necessity defense, but judges have a great deal of discretion on penalties. Pro-life judges who did hear cases tended to be lenient in sentencing, while pro-abortion judges tended to be harsh.

Schudson set the hearings on selective prosecution for May, 1990—nearly a year after the sit-in. Meanwhile, Edmund and I planned a dedication service for a monument which was erected near the grave of the twelve hundred aborted babies at Holy Cross Cemetery. Donated by the Milwaukee Monument Company, the polished red granite stone stood five and a half feet tall. A picture of Jesus holding children was carved on the front of the stone. Auxiliary Bishop Austin Vaughan of the New York Archdiocese was our special guest speaker for the service. Bishop Vaughan, a white-haired, kindly intellectual, had by then participated in several sit-ins in New York and elsewhere on the East Coast. He had also served a three-day jail term for blocking the door to an abortion clinic. On August 28, 1989, about six hundred people gathered for the graveside service.

Just one month after the dedication service, on September 30, 1989—a beautiful, warm sunny day—Edmund and I exchanged marriage vows at St. Bernard's Parish near Milwaukee. As Edmund and I prepared to walk down the aisle, dozens of pro-lifers led by evangelical pastor Matt Trewhella, founder of Rescue: Operation Milwaukee, piled themselves in front of the doors to Affiliated Medical Services. Meanwhile, pro-abortion demonstrators stood across the street from the downtown clinic. They held a large sign which read "Congratulations, Monica and Edmund: May Your Choice Increase and Multiply." It was a very unexpected—if somewhat odd—sentiment from the opposition.

After the wedding, Edmund and I set up our household in my two-bedroom upper flat. Edmund was only twenty-nine years old at the time of our marriage, and I was an old maid of thirty-six. We had a three-day honeymoon, cut short by a trial scheduled for October 4, 1989, in front of Milwaukee Circuit Court Judge Thomas Doherty. We were on trial for a clinic blockade we had done on October 10, 1987, at Metropolitan Medical Services. Not only was our honeymoon cut short, but so was our time together as newlyweds.

Just three months after our wedding, Edmund and I were separated by jail sentences handed out by Judge McMahon. On January 11, he entered the Community Correctional Center, a run-down, crowded jail that once was St. Anthony's Hospital. We kissed each other goodbye at the door, and he began a twenty-day jail term for the rescue he had done at the Milwaukee Women's Health

Organization, the clinic operated by Reverend Elinor Yeo. A week later, I entered the same jail to begin the forty-five-day term for the first rescue in Milwaukee at Bread and Roses. For two years our sentences had been deferred pending appeals that had gone all the way to the Wisconsin Supreme Court as a challenge to the constitutionality of the Criminal Trespass to a Medical Facility law. When the Wisconsin Supreme Court upheld the law in a five-to-two vote, our attorneys asked a federal court to hear our case, but our petition was refused.

"Honeymoon Over" was the headline above society columnist Meg Kissinger's article for the *Milwaukee Journal* that appeared the day before our sentences began. She described how Edmund and I, newly joined in marriage, were now separated by the start of his jail term. Edmund and I had work-release privileges and occasionally met in the early morning in the student cafeteria of Marquette University where I taught theology courses.

Robert Braun also began his one-month jail term for the Bread and Roses rescue on the same evening that I entered jail. When I arrived at the Community Correctional Center, I saw Robert in the parking lot. His wife Violet had just dropped him off, and I greeted him warmly. In my hand I clutched the same small crucifix I had laid before me on the defendants' table during our trial. I passed the crucifix to Robert. "Here," I said, "please take this. I want you to have it." Robert, although a Protestant, accepted it, his eyes full of gratitude. He thanked me and nodded his head. Then he walked alone through the doors of the jail.

Having been arrested several times for blocking the door to abortion clinics, I had been inside jails before, but only in temporary lockups. This was my first real jail term. On a forty-five day sentence, with time off for good behavior, I would be out in thirty-four days. The female dormitory was on the top floor of the prison, five floors up. After my belongings were searched, I was led up the elevator by two grim female guards, escorted to a room with lockers, and strip searched. I was then given a dark green prison uniform to wear, at least two sizes too big for me, and led to a bunk in a large room at the end of a narrow hall. I was given the upper bunk. The room was occupied by fifteen other prisoners.

After I settled myself in the dormitory room I decided to check out the jail's day room. This was a large common space with chairs, tables, a couch and a TV set. Standing near a window I saw a familiar face, the serene and gentle Carol Robbins, who had handcuffed herself to the Bread and Roses suction machine. She had entered the CCC nine days before me to serve the ten-day sentence handed down by Judge McMahon. The sight of my good friend on the first night of my own incarceration comforted me greatly. However, I would soon be without her company; Carol was released from jail the next day.

That night I prayed as I lay down on my bunk—a stiff pallet that served as a mattress and a folded-up towel that served as a pillow. I decided that the only real way I would make it through the jail sentence was to accept absolutely everything about the injustice of it. I would not be bitter. I would not be angry. I would not wish that things were different. I would not act as if I had rights and they were being trampled upon. I tried to put on the attitude of Christ who, as God, had all the rights in the universe but gave them up to suffer for others. I found the key to enduring jail with peace: a total surrender of my will to the fact of being in prison.

Jails like the Community Correctional Center are extremely noisy places. For virtually every waking moment, there's nonstop racket—the constant chatter of fellow inmates, the blaring television, metal lockers clanging open and closed. One of the most difficult aspects of prison life for me was the inmates' incessant use of profane language. I always tried to avoid taking the Lord's name in vain and shied away from using obscene speech. I was suddenly taken from my genteel Christian surroundings and plunged into the world of the "f" word." It seemed to precede and follow every other word spoken in the jail. Crude speech about sexual intercourse was common. My manners, demeanor and lack of profane speech singled me out among my inmates. They sensed I was different.

On the first night, several inmates asked, "What're you in for?"

I told them I was in jail for trying to save babies from abortion, that I had sat down in front of the door to an abortion clinic. Nearly all the inmates were astonished and appalled that I was sent to jail for what they considered comparatively harmless actions. To those who committed crimes of violence or fraud, what I had done didn't seem like a crime. "Man, you don't belong here at all," said one. "Those folks killing them babies belong here—not you! I hate abortion. I hate it!" exclaimed an inmate called Black. Her real name was Karen, but everyone called her Black, and she seemd to prefer it. She had small, raised, crisscrossed scars on her arms and her front teeth were missing.

Black was a cocaine addict, in jail for selling drugs. She had been jailed three or four times before. For her, being released from jail and being incarcerated again was a way of life. Like several of the inmates, she was openly lesbian. She spent most of her time in the dayroom smoking cigarettes and playing cards. One day while dealing out a deck of cards, Black turned to everyone and announced loudly: "Hey! Monica's white. I'm black. Monica likes men. I don't like men. Monica don't like abortion. I don't like abortion. Hey, least we got somethin' in common!" She laughed heartily, and I laughed too. One thing I was totally unprepared for was the pervasive lesbianism I found in the jail. Several inmates were quite open about their sexual preferences and had lesbian lovers.

My bunkmate was an emotionally volatile woman, twenty-three years old, and, like most of the other inmates, was jailed for possession of drugs. In my first days there I threatened to report her while she attempted to have a lesbian encounter with another inmate beneath my bunk. I tried very hard to get along with her, but in the days following my threat to report her to the guards she went out of her way to annoy me, rocking the bunk while I was trying to read or playing her radio loudly. Once during a bunk-rocking episode, I leaned over the side of my bunk and said, "Tanisha, knock it off." She proceeded to rock even harder. "You just be careful. Sometime when you're not lookin', I'm gonna get you. Oh yeah—we're gonna have ourselves a real blanket party." A blanket party, I later learned, was when inmates who wanted to frighten or get even with another inmate would catch their victim off-guard, often in the dead of night, throw a blanket over her head and beat her mercilessly. With her head covered, the victim would have no way of knowing who did the actual beating. Perhaps I should have taken my bunkmate's threat seriously, but I didn't think she had it in her to resort to such a thing. In any event, nothing ever happened to me.

I had a lot of respect among the guards as well as the inmates. Many of them treated me with an unusual deference, telling me they were against abortion and respected me for "bein' in jail for doing somethin' good" and for "standin' up for what you believe in." One of my dormitory mates was a tall blond woman, a topless dancer who was serving a sentence for drunk driving. I was amused that her judge had given her work release privileges so she could go to her topless dancing job. One day she told me, "This place is called the Community Correctional Center, but Monica, you don't need any correction." Another inmate, jailed for prostitution, came up to me in the hallway. With a perplexed look on her face, she shook her head and asked, "What are you in here for?" She peered at me intensely. "You look awfully innocent."

When I opened my locker one morning, I found that a letter had been dropped inside. I opened the envelope and unfolded a piece of yellow-lined paper. With misspelled words and bad punctuation it stated:

> Dear Monica,
>
>   Well I don't know if I'll see you befor I leave or not. So I thought a short note would have to do. I hope your time in here passes quickly, and all your other cases in court are droped and you have no more time to do in here. . . . I know I've only known you a short time but you have given me a new insight into my life. Thank you so very much. . . . Maybe someday you can take me to mass?

Keep in touch . . . if you want. You'll be in my thoughts.

Yours,

Mary

P.S. I wouldn't mind to help you in your rescue efforts.

Mary was the topless dancer. She had been released the night before. When I read her words, joy spread through me. Before I left the jail, I received another letter from a woman in her late forties, Sandy. A cocaine addict, she was in the CCC on a three-month sentence for drug possession. She was an intelligent woman with a great sense of humor. She and I had several discussions about God, the Bible and the Church. She was a Catholic who had not practiced her faith for many years. I encouraged her to go to confession and Mass. She was nervous about going to confession, since she had not gone for many years. I suggested she see Father Bill Kurz, a Jesuit at Marquette University, who was a kind, understanding, and devout priest.

Sandy was released several weeks before me. After she got out, she visited another inmate who was on work-release at a restaurant Written on the restaurant's napkin she sent me a note through her.

Hi Monica,

I hear you're down in the dumps. Smile cuz I saw Fr. Bill tonight and I feel great and I want you to feel good also. Cuz you had a lot to do with it. I know you're used to saving babies but you saved a big one! Me. Smile! I write soon. Hang in there.

A friend always,

Sandra

P.S. I'm doing good.

* * *

On a cold, dreary January day I was rudely awakened by one of the guards. "Come on Miller, you've got a court hearing today." As I walked sleepily through the day room, I saw the clock on the wall.

It was four-thirty in the morning. I knew I had a hearing in front of Judge Schudson, but it was not scheduled until eleven o'clock that morning. I quickly tried to get ready. Two other inmates also had court appearances. I asked one of them why we had to get up so early. She said, "I dunno. That's when they takes you and when you gets over there you sits and you waits."

The policy did not make any sense to me, especially since the place we were being taken was the Safety Building directly across from the jail. I was trusted with work-release privileges and could come and go to Marquette University on my own, yet I was not permitted to leave the jail and walk across the street to attend a trivial court-business hearing.

After we ate a quick breakfast, my two companions and I were handcuffed and herded into a sheriffs' transport van. Several other male inmates, already seated inside, hooted and whistled as we climbed aboard. Amused, I laughed quietly to myself. A county trooper started up the loud rumbling engine and we made the one-minute journey to the Safety Building, which housed courtrooms, the county clerk's office and the district attorney's office. The top floor was a jail.

We were taken to the jail by an old, creaking elevator. A female guard escorted us to a small room and removed our handcuffs. Then she left, locking the heavy metal door behind her. The room had a long wooden bench against one wall, as well as two large, heavy office desks, one wooden and one metal, stacked on top of each other. We waited there for hours.

I prayed for a while and tried to sleep on the hard bench. Failing that, I chatted with my two African American companions about their families, their children, their boyfriends and their drug addictions. Finally the door opened, and the same female guard who had locked us in the room now ushered us out. We were taken down a long hallway to a foyer area that preceded two large double doors. Male prisoners were also brought in to join us.

To our right was an open door to another room. I peered inside. A male prisoner wearing the usual orange jumpsuit was sitting on a stool. His bare foot was shackled with a handcuff to a metal ring on the floor. I was completely unprepared to see a human being bound this way. I had never seen such a thing except in movies or television. The whole room was lined with tiny cubicles and stools, and each space had a ring on the floor to bind the prisoner. More than anything I had experienced in jail, this sight overwhelmed me with the reality that I was indeed in prison. I was in a totally different world, a world set apart, a world underneath the world I had known: a world for criminals, cold and sometimes cruel and full of humiliation. My eyes caught the eyes of the young man shackled there, and he seemed to sense my shock and my pity.

I heard the sound of chains clanking together and turned around. Male guards were approaching our group holding ropes of chains in their hands. We were told to stand in a straight line front to back with female prisoners first. I stood third in line behind my two companions and in front of a black male prisoner. Our hands were bound together with cuffs and a chain was looped around our waists. Another long length of chain was threaded through the chain belts we wore, binding all of us together.

The metal double doors of the jail hallway opened and we were led to an elevator. We descended in silence. The only noise was the hum of the elevator's motor. It stopped with a small jolt, and its doors opened suddenly into the bright hallway of the sixth floor of the Milwaukee County Courthouse. Years before, when I was on trial for the rescue at Bread and Roses, I saw for the first time uniformed prisoners bound in chains paraded through the courthouse hallways. I was shocked and disturbed by the spectacle. Now I was a prisoner like them, acutely aware of the rattling chains.

*   *   *

I was released from jail in the middle of February, 1990. Edmund and I were happy to resume a more normal married life. A few months later, in early May, the hearings for the Imperial Medical Services case began. It was made known that of the twenty-one people arrested, I was the only one who received criminal charges, even though several other rescuers held on to each other and had to be pulled apart. Milwaukee County District Attorney, E. Michael McCann, took the stand and testified it was the policy of his office that demonstrators would not be charged criminally unless there was a possibility of violence. He also testified that no one in Milwaukee County had been charged with unlawful assembly for twenty years—not since the Vietnam War, and only then if an antiwar protest turned violent or there was damage to property. This was significant, since according to standards set by the American Bar Association and accepted as Wisconsin's legal policy, a prosecutor was supposed to consider the prolonged non-enforcement of a statute to be "non-enforcement with community acquiescence." McCann also testified that it was the policy of his office that the charge of obstruction of an officer not be made "except for those cases in which the defendant directs force at the officer which results in injury to the officer or tearing of the officer's clothing." According to this standard, I should not have been charged with that either.

In an unusual move, my attorney called Jeff Kremers to the stand. Kremers testified that he "did not see any need to consider the policies or guidelines used by the district attorney's office in the charging of the crimes." Kremers believed he had the authority to act independently, as he alone saw fit, without reference to the usual policy of the district attorney's office, even though he was acting as an assistant prosecutor within that office.

Bill Kerner tried to show that Kremers was not simply interested in prosecuting crimes, but that he was ideologically motivated to bring these charges against me—in other words, his commitment to legalized abortion clouded his sense of fair and just application of the law. Kremers never hid his anger and contempt for me and other pro-lifers. If he was not ideologically motivated, then why take all these cases as a special prosecutor and slam me with three criminal charges, all so contrary to the usual policies of the district attorney's office? Why did it matter so much to him that

I should receive, at his hands, three criminal charges while those who blocked the doors with me, and delayed their arrests even longer than I did, received only city tickets? If I had any doubt that Kremers was indeed a supporter of legalized abortion, those doubts were laid to rest when Kremers took the stand in the selective prosecution hearings. My attorney asked him: "Do you have any strong feelings on the issue of abortion and whether or not they should be available?"

Kremers responded: "I believe it is the private right of a woman to decide for herself whether or not she should have to carry a pregnancy to term and that the state has no business legislating or impacting on that woman's right up to some period of time—I'm not prepared to say when in the pregnancy—that the rights of the unborn person supersede the rights of the mother."

On May 6, 1990, Judge Schudson ruled against our motion on selective prosecution. He said Kremers was not guilty of acting without due discretion in charging me, that there was no real evidence to show he intended to suppress the free-speech rights of pro-lifers or that he acted out of personal vindictiveness. My trial on the three criminal charges was summarily set for the following November.

I was frustrated once again by the legal system. I could not shake the feeling that something was horrifically out of balance—indeed unjust—with Kremer's charges, and Schudson had done nothing to correct the imbalance.

But something else was out of balance. I was not just upset, I was *exceptionally* upset. There was a reason for my exaggerated emotion: I was pregnant. For the first time in my life, and just shy of my thirty-seventh birthday, I was having a baby. On the day Schudson made his ruling I was about a month into my pregnancy. Although I didn't know it at the time, my hormones were having their way with me.

Edmund and I were extremely happy about the baby. The day I learned I was pregnant, I entered the room that we used as a study. It was late at night and the room was totally dark. I sat in a chair, closed my eyes, and reflected upon the presence of this new, hidden someone growing so quietly and mysteriously within me. A new life was in the world—our child. I thought how ironic it was for me to sit there now, with my own hidden baby in the very room where I once housed the bodies of the rejected unborn.

Over the next few weeks, however, I was dogged every day with a grim premonition. I felt somehow that our baby would not live. I was pursued by this unshakeable feeling, almost as though I could not believe or imagine that I would have a living unborn child. After so many months of living with, touching, and burying the dead unborn, I could not fathom that this child would actually live and be born. I was so used to the dead that I expected our child would die as well.

On May 12, 1990, Mother's Day, I began to feel a slight cramping. I tried to deny that this minor physical pain meant anything and hoped that everything was alright. Five days later, on May 17, I experienced severe cramping. It was my thirty-seventh birthday and Edmund had prepared a special birthday dinner. I sat down to eat the meal. I had not yet told him of the severe cramps that were becoming more painful by the minute.

I put one bite of food in my mouth and swallowed it. I stared at the plate but couldn't eat more. I was overcome with grief and burst into tears.

"Edmund, we're losing this baby."

He looked at me, his eyes full of pity. I walked into the bedroom and collapsed in sorrow and physical pain. Tears streamed down my face. Soon I began to pass blood in heavy clots and reddish, spongy-looking placental tissue.

My miscarriage was in full swing. I went into the bathroom. I tried to save everything, not knowing if a small, perhaps even invisible part of our child might be there. Because of my experience with the aborted unborn, I was ultra-sensitive that no part of our baby, no matter how small, would be disposed of in the toilet and find his burial in a sewer.

I passed several clots and bled profusely. I began to feel weak.

Since I had never been pregnant before, much less miscarried, I didn't know what to expect. We went to see my physician, Dr. James Linn, a pro-life obstetrician, at St. Mary's Hospital on the east side of Milwaukee. At the emergency room I changed into a gown and lay down on a narrow bed that was little more than an examination table.

Dr. Linn came into the small cubicle and explained to me that there was a small chance of infection if the body parts and placenta did not pass through. He suggested a D&C. I consented.

A few moments later a suction machine was wheeled to the end of the cubicle. The sight of it startled me. In my mind a suction machine was synonymous with abortion, and now this same instrument was going to be used on me. I had to make a deliberate mental effort to separate the suction machine from killing. I was given a local anesthetic. Nevertheless the D&C was extremely painful. If this was what a suction abortion felt like, it was anything but a "gentle suction" like I had read about in abortion clinic literature. Dr. Linn turned off the machine and told me that he had extracted some tissue.

When the suctioning finally ended, when the noise of the machine cut off—the room was filled with silence, a silence that marked the end of my pregnancy. I was now utterly empty of all traces of that dearly wanted baby. My deep sorrow burst forth in a profound sob of anguish. Edmund laid his head on my chest and wept also. I had a child. Now I did not. I had life within me. Now I did not. The hidden person had died and was gone from my body. I thought I had known the depths of sorrow when I took the broken bodies of the aborted unborn out of the trash. I was wrong. The loss of this child was a deeper grief for me. Perhaps, though, the loss of our own baby would not have caused me such a sense of being bereft had it not been preceded by all those other losses—the children of other women.

When the physical ordeal was over and I was ready to leave the emergency room, I had to sign a medical form. It listed the reason I had been admitted to the hospital. I was jarred by the words:

"incomplete abortion." I had to pause while my rational mind beat back the furious sense of insult. Even though I knew it meant I had a spontaneous miscarriage that required a D&C, the word "abortion" had become in our culture simply too loaded a term.

A few days later, Edmund and I went to the pathology lab of the hospital to pick up the remains of the miscarriage. Although no discernible body parts could be found, Edmund and I were perhaps overly scrupulous to bury whatever remains we had. We received a paper bag that contained a small plastic jar. On the jar was written "POC"—products of conception—the same letters we had so often seen written on the bags that contained the well-formed miniature children killed by abortion.

On a warm day in May, Edmund and I walked past the grave makers of the infants buried at Holy Cross Cemetery until we came to a newly dug grave. The freshly opened earth lay but a few feet from the large grave of the twelve hundred aborted babies. Edmund placed a small cedar box into the grave. Father Kurz officiated at the short ceremony attended by another Jesuit priest, Fr. Earl Muller. Our pastor Msgr. Bruskewitz, Marquette philosophy professor Mary Rousseau, Matt Trewhella, Sandy Schultz, Christine Le Blanc and a few other friends gathered at the gravesite.

I knew that it was entirely possible that we were not burying any actual fetal body parts at all, but Edmund and I had another reason for the grave. This little plot of earth was a mark in the world that our little unseen child did live once and will forever remain a part of us. We named the child Gesu-Marie. The stone that was soon set on the grave bore the name of the child, the date of the miscarriage, and an inscription: "Our Unborn Child—We will see you in Paradise."

Our wanted baby shared the earth with those unwanted. The earth bound them together. The memorial stone that had been dedicated on that hot August day nine months ago towered behind the graves. After the earth covered over the place for Gesu-Marie, I once again read the memorial stone's inscription: "This monument stands as a testimony to the sanctity of human life. Among these

graves of children are included preborn babies, victims of abortion."
Beneath this was a quote from 1 John 3: "The reason why the world
does not know us is that it did not know Him. . . . We are God's
children now."

The words on the stone were now carved into me as Edmund
and I laid what remained of our first child into the earth. This
unseen child, now a neighbor to the unwanted unborn, bound us
to them forever in a way not expected, in a sorrow never dreamt.

CHAPTER SIXTEEN

A DANGEROUS PERSON

There's never been a true war that wasn't fought between two sets of people who were certain they were in the right. The really dangerous people believe they are doing whatever they are doing solely and only because it is without question the right thing to do. And that is what makes them dangerous.

—Neil Gaiman, *American Gods*

"WE, THE jury, find the defendant, Monica Miller, guilty of disorderly conduct. . . ."

"We, the jury, find the defendant, Monica Miller, guilty of unlawful assembly. . . ."

"We, the jury, find the defendant, Monica Miller, guilty of obstructing an officer this fourteenth day of November, 1990."

The jury foreman read these words at the conclusion of my three-day trial for the sit-in at Imperial Medical Services. Even though I had held little hope that I would be acquitted, the words stung my ears. My very able attorney had done all he could, and Judge Schudson had made attempts to keep the trial a fair one. He permitted me to tell the jury what education I had concerning the medical facts of prenatal development and, although I was not permitted to discuss the facts themselves, he did not censor my language as Judge McMahon had done. But I knew that without a defense of necessity on behalf of the unborn, there was little to prevent the technicalities of the law from prevailing.

219

But I had a few technicalities of my own, upon which I could launch an appeal. A prospective juror who openly stated that she belonged to the National Organization for Women and contributed to Planned Parenthood was not struck for cause—that is, removed by the judge on the suspicion that she would not render impartial judgment. She described her pro-choice activism as extensive, including pro-choice marches, legislative lobbying and letter-writing campaigns. Schudson refused to remove her since he thought her position on the ethics committee of a Catholic hospital demonstrated that she could be reasonable and unbiased in her thinking. Bill Kerner and I naturally felt rather differently, especially considering that NOW was currently suing me and others in the federal class-action RICO lawsuit. Kerner ended up having to use up one of his preemptive strikes to remove her.

My sentencing hearing was set for early the following year. On January 12, 1991, Edmund and I entered a courtroom already filled with reporters and television cameras. Kremers had recommended to Judge Schudson that I be sentenced from sixty to ninety days in jail and fined five thousand dollars. Bill Kerner brought in a number of pro-life activists to testify on my behalf. Christine Steeno, a pro-life activist who had had an abortion several years prior, stated how she came to regret what she had done. She also told the court that she and her husband were presently the foster parents of a one-year-old boy named David, whose mother was talked out of an abortion by Jim Fanson, a local pro-lifer. Technically Fanson committed trespass to talk to the mother, but today this little boy and his mother were in the court. The boy's mother told the court how grateful she was that someone had come into the building to speak with her just before she was about to have the abortion.

Bill Kerner informed Judge Schudson that I wished to exercise my right of elocution. The trial transcripts record what I said to the court:

> Perhaps it is even redundant to say so, but these people have
> come to court to show the value of trying to protect human life,

and the enormous great good that can come from intervening in abortion and the business of abortion. This is [David], a human life that was saved by a man who actually went in [the building] and got the girl out. . . .

I want you, Judge Schudson, to understand why I didn't let go. I could have. I wanted to, but I didn't because I knew that if I let go of Wendy Fulcher, I would have betrayed those children. I would have said my comfort, my liberty, is more important. I couldn't do that. If it had been a born baby who was going to be torn limb from limb behind the door that I was standing in front of, everyone would understand perfectly well why I could not let go of a fellow rescuer so that we could buy more time for that child.

I was buying time for that child. If it had been your child or Jeff Kremers' child, you would have wanted me to do that, at least that, to hold on to somebody so that the baby would live. So that's why I'm here, because I refused to let go for the sake of human life.

The second thing is, I really do not ask for leniency for my own sake. There is only one reason why I would want you, Judge Schudson, to be lenient. The only reason I ask for leniency is for the sake of human life. You know in your own heart that we were there to protect human beings from being killed by abortion. That really to me is the only reason. If you don't have it in your heart to be lenient for their sake . . . there's nothing more to it, then, as far as I'm concerned. . . . Leniency must be for the children, your Honor, and not for myself.

At this point I gave Schudson a pamphlet on fetal development with Lennart-Nilsson photos of the growing child in the womb. Bill Kerner then addressed the court and asked Schudson to be lenient because I had acted to save human beings from being put to death. And while I was not permitted, by law, a defense of others, Kerner asked Schudson to consider that I acted in defense of others as a mitigating factor in my sentencing:

I think that someone who exercises a decision to save a human life—that the law does not recognize—is one of the highest forms of heroism. It's the kind of thing that was done by the Underground Railroad in the last century. It's the kind of thing that people were imprisoned for and executed for in the last century.

And . . . I think you should recognize that people who act with these motivations are entitled to not be treated as though they were out there causing trouble for no purpose. They did have a purpose and their purpose was to save lives.

Kerner asked Schudson to give me the same sentence the others arrested that day had received, which meant that he simply give me credit for the time I was incarcerated on the day of the arrest. I told Schudson I would neither pay a fine nor accept probation because of the restrictions it placed on what I deemed to be an act of charity. Kerner then gave Schudson another brochure. It was from Imperial, and it advertised the abortion center's "super saver days"—days on which special discount prices were given on abortions. We had hoped to introduce the pamphlet into evidence during the trial to show that the abortion center was a crass business whose goal was to churn out a high volume of abortions, but Schudson prohibited us from presenting it to the jury. After Kerner handed the pamphlet to Schudson, the judge turned to Kremers, whose turn it was to speak.

My principle reaction, your Honor, is I think that Ms. Miller in her statement has, in fact, criticized everyone else who's sitting at counsel table with her, everyone else who was at the demonstration that day, and probably ninety-nine percent of the rest of the people in the country that exercise their First Amendment rights to free speech along the same lines that take the same position that she does, and she has done that by saying: Judge, what I did, the reason I could not let go is because I would have betrayed the cause, I would have betrayed those unborn children, I would have betrayed why we were there.

Everybody else then . . . betrayed that cause by letting
go or by leaving or by not interfering in the lawful arrests
that were being carried out by the police officers. She has
set herself above everyone else. She's the only one that is so
righteously committed to her cause that she can do whatever
she wants to do and she shouldn't have to suffer any penalties
for it, regardless of what the law in this country is.

I don't think she should be treated like everyone else,
because she didn't act like everyone else. She went beyond
what everyone else did.

Why does Ms. Miller have to go to the lengths she did
and cause this community's already overburdened criminal
justice system to deal with her attitude and her belief that she
can do whatever she wants regardless if it includes obstructing
an officer or causing the kind of expenses that she did to the
police department, the fire department, the legal system, and
everyone else involved in this? I think she should be treated
much more harshly than the other people, and she has asked
for that, and I think that's what she deserves.

Schudson seemed perplexed as to why Kremers did not recom-
mend the stiffest sentence possible. It was interesting that Kremers' answer included a recognition that "she was the only one
charged with State charges in this case. I think there are adequate
reasons for that, but it's a fact nonetheless." Perhaps this was a
slight admission that he was, after all, not entirely comfortable with
having charged me with three criminal counts. He also noted that
the manner in which I obstructed Officer Moe was "towards the
lower end of the continuum."

After the closing statements were over, Schudson focused
his attention on me:*

THE COURT: Ms. Miller, a question for you. Assume for
a moment that the Court accepts everything that you have

---

* Again, these are taken directly from original court transcripts with some
minor editing for flow and clarity.

presented and applauds your conscience and commitment. Why don't you do more? What is it that leads you to draw the line where you draw it? Why, for example, didn't you tackle the officer? Why didn't you take more actions if this is truly your personal commitment to save lives? How can you justify limiting your actions as you do?

DEFENDANT: Because I want to present these actions nonviolently.

THE COURT: Why?

THE DEFENDANT: Because we have to deal with not simply saving the baby, but we have to—we have to be a witness for the mother who's going to kill her child, because ultimately . . . even if we had closed the clinic for the day, and frequently we do that in rescues, we still have the outreach to the woman. That is ultimately the thing that must be accomplished if she is not going to come back and kill her unborn child.

Now, that would be the same reasoning why I wouldn't advocate bombing an abortion clinic, for example, because you are not there for the woman. The bomber bombs the place but he is removed from the situation. And ultimately, it's because I want to do what I do—and I know we don't share the same religious faith—but I'm sure you can appreciate my position on this—I do what I do because I want to enter into the suffering of Christ. I don't want to be a person of violence. I want to lay down my life for my neighbor, and to do that I have to be one who becomes vulnerable in the situation involving a rescue.

What's going to overcome abortion is not bombing clinics. It's not marches in the street. It's not even political action. Ultimately, we're dealing with a profound spiritual crisis of the human heart in this country. The only way to overcome something like that is love, through true sacrifice of the inner self in which you, myself, whomever, lay down their life. I must refrain from actions that would cause harm to others, while yet providing an action that is defending others. So that is my philosophical position that I hope at least adequately answers your question.

THE COURT: Well, I'm not sure whether it's really a relevant issue or not, but as long as you frame it in terms of attempting to assist life in a way that does not harm others, then perhaps the question of criminal justice resources would become important. If, after all, you select a strategy that necessarily brings about the intervention of dozens of police officers and fire fighters who are therefore not available to assist others in emergencies, is that something you would consider as something that might, while assisting life on one hand, have a negative impact on other lives elsewhere?

THE DEFENDANT: I'm not responsible for whether the police, the fire department are going to come and open up an abortion mill.

THE COURT: Why do you say that?

THE DEFENDANT: Because that is their decision. I'm there to protect life. They're actually in league with the legal system.

THE COURT: Sure, so you know they're going to come—

THE DEFENDANT: If they come, it's their fault, it's not mine. I'm doing what is positively correct, a positively correct action. They're doing a negatively incorrect action. The problem with your question is that you don't recognize the scheduled killing of innocent unborn children as an emergency situation.

I'm engaged in doing good, as a moral dictate of natural law, do good and avoid evil. I am doing good. I cannot be responsible ultimately for the way the fire department is going to respond to my defense of human life. I still have a moral obligation to defend that life. They don't have to be there. They can say no. They have to take perhaps the ramifications for it down at the fire department headquarters.

Schudson now suggested we "role-play," and assumed the part of a friend who was trying to persuade me that his legal means of saving lives were just as effective as my methods. He wanted me to engage in a simple give-and-take conversation with him.

THE DEFENDANT: The rescue is the appropriate response to a human being who's about to be put to death.

THE COURT: So as your colleague, I'm just wrong in not taking that extra step with you?

THE DEFENDANT: Maybe you're not called to it. It's not your vocation. It's not what God is asking you to do. That's something you have to assess in your own conscience.

It's important to be consistent here. We have to treat unborn children like human beings, and if a human being was on the street being pulverized and torn limb from limb, I wouldn't just write my congressman, I wouldn't just get a picket sign and say please stop doing that, I wouldn't just try and persuade an assailant from beating and tearing limb from limb this helpless child. I'd put—at least I'd put my own body between the assailant and the victim. That's the act of protection. That's the act of love.

THE COURT: Let us assume that there is a mother who has been reached. Let us assume perhaps even on that day a woman came to Imperial and gave you full, convincing evidence that she had received very careful, comprehensive counseling. You know exactly the counseling received, you know who provided it, you're satisfied that this person has provided the best, most comprehensive counseling in this area.

Consider further that in addition to that counseling, this woman was willing to pause and talk with you for the time you thought necessary, an hour, three hours, whatever, and consider at that point, after all of that, after you had taught her everything and were satisfied that she understood and had learned everything, she said with all due respect, I have decided to abort. What would you do?

THE DEFENDANT: I would lay down my life in front of that woman and I wouldn't let her go kill her baby, for the same reason if it was a born child—which I think makes our situation much clearer—if she had all the counseling in the world . . . just because she thinks this is best and has had all the proper counseling doesn't make it correct, doesn't make it right, doesn't make it just. Besides, I don't do this alone.

There are others there so that our presence there is going to be effective in terms of being that wall of defense between the assailant and the victim.

THE COURT: Well, as you can see, what we're coming to is perhaps some better definition here. I'm very impressed by what you and your lawyer have said about the virtue of providing every woman with the opportunity for full counseling. . . . And yet now what I'm hearing perhaps would suggest that counseling and the fully informed decision is not the issue.

THE DEFENDANT: It's not the only issue. The other issue is truly offering protection to the baby even should the mother refuse the aid, the information that we offer. That baby still deserves to be treated like a human being, to be loved, to be defended, to be given an act of love in this world before they die. That's what the rescuer is going to do. The rescuer is perhaps the only person who will truly love the baby before he dies so he doesn't leave this world unloved, unwanted, unaccepted.

THE COURT: One of the, I think, most vexing areas here with which most everyone would have to have great sympathy for you relates, interestingly enough, to law. We will go to this dry area of law for a moment and find, I think, a focus where others would share your frustration. After all, they might say: Look, here we have a subject on which lawmakers have differed and changed over time. Here we have actions [the abortion practice] that are lawful that just a few years ago were unlawful, that perhaps a few years from now may be unlawful again.

So I think one might argue on your behalf, how fair is it that the weight of criminal law of society come down upon you when your philosophy has been consistent . . ? Why, then, can one day a person be a heroine for such actions, consistent with law, and the next day be a criminal, jailed for the same actions . . . ?

Now, I ask you to offer advice. How does a judge, sworn to uphold the law as it stands—how does a judge, even one

who may be in full agreement with you, ignore his or her oath,
ignore the legislative mandate, in order to say by virtue of my
agreement with your philosophy, I choose not to provide the
criminal law consequences as the Legislature has mandated?
How could a judge do that consistent with the judicial oath?
THE DEFENDANT: Your Honor, you have asked me one
of the most important questions that the pro-life movement
has pondered for these last 18 years. I have an answer. I don't
know if you're going to like it.

We're living in a situation in which the law is unjust. It
allows millions of innocent human beings to be killed. You
have to ask yourself, I think, your Honor, what does it mean to
do justice, truly . . . ? I do have some experience with the legal
justice system—the problem as I see it with the justice system
in this country is that it has become virtually positivistic, and
I think you're probably aware of what positive law is about.

If I say that the black man is only three quarters human
and the law says that, it is therefore the fact. If the *Roe v.
Wade* decision says the unborn are not persons, and therefore
when I go to an abortion clinic and protect them, I'm not
protecting anyone who is being harmed as the law sees it,
this is madness. And I believe that in order for this wholesale
injustice that's gripped our entire nation—4,400 babies die
every day by abortion—you have to say, no, I will not be a part
of this injustice.

. . . To a pro-lifer—now, I hope you can appreciate this
without being offended—but to a pro-lifer, abortion is a
Holocaust. I don't say it's entirely analogous with the Third
Reich and what went on there. There are differences. But you
have to ask yourself—I want to ask every Judge: could they
have upheld that system that under law allowed Jews to be
put to death?

Schudson suggested that perhaps an important difference
between abortion and the Nazi extermination of the Jews was
that under Hitler there was no debate over "whether persons
should be exterminated" as opposed to *Roe v. Wade* and legislative

decisions that respect the differences that people have on abortion. I responded:

> Let us please realize that the *Roe v. Wade* decision of January 22, 1973 was done by judicial fiat. Nobody voted for it. The most you could say is that arguments from the Texas State's Attorney were presented, but the Court wanted abortion, it was going to get abortion, and it gave us abortion. The so-called legal mandate represents disrespect for human life with the protection of law. The unborn don't get a chance to oppose their deaths.

Schudson ended the sentencing hearing by stating that he was going to take at least a month to make his decision. He warned all parties that they could "expect to be very dissatisfied," but added, "I assure you I will do my very best to provide a decision, that includes not only law but love." The sentencing was scheduled for February 22, 1991.

A few days after the hearing I composed a letter to Schudson. In it, I told him that I thought he was "a man of conscience—that he desired to be such a man." I was impressed with what I perceived to be his honest probing for the truth. Yet something still troubled me about him. A system of government that allows for freedom of debate was very important to this judge, and I wrote that I had the definite impression that he believed in this principle so strongly that so long as it was upheld, it didn't matter what injustice might take place. In my letter, I suggested that the "freedom to debate" should not take place in a moral void, in which "truth is beyond us—all we can do is debate."

I wrote Schudson about the bodies of the unborn we had retrieved from the trash at the Northbrook, Illinois pathology lab. I included three photos of the victims; one from 30 South Michigan in Chicago. One showed the arm and hand of a fourteen-week-old fetal child. I explained:

> To see these bodies there was to see a complete and horrifying abandonment, as if the edge of the dock was the edge of the

world where the unborn had been cast adrift apart from all human care.

To me the photo of the hand . . . still connected to the arm torn at the shoulder speaks of the utter loneliness of the aborted child. The hand is unconnected to a body and looms out of nothing, yet in this void the child's hand speaks his humanity and speaks the horror of his alienation.

I know that Schudson had said that all parties would be dissatisfied with whatever decision he would make and, although I expected him to be fair, I still hoped that on February 22, the advocates of legal abortion might be the more dissatisfied party. Two weeks prior to the sentencing, Schudson did something that gave my attorney and me a tremendous sense of hope. Schudson called Bill and asked him for a copy of the pamphlet printed by Dr. James Dobson and Focus on the Family. The pamphlet was very well designed, featuring the Lennart-Nilsson fetal-development photos. Kerner had tried to introduce this pamphlet into evidence, since it was used by a sidewalk counselor to talk a couple out of an abortion during the sit-in. Then, about a week prior to the sentencing, Schudson told Kerner that he had decided not to use the pamphlet. Instead, he was going to incorporate into his sentencing statement the photos of the aborted babies that I had sent to him. I was elated at the news.

There was one important piece of information about me that Schudson did not know and that I deliberately withheld from him. At the time of the sentencing hearing, I was seven weeks pregnant. When Bill Kerner filed the pre-sentencing report, which is supposed to inform the court of any personal circumstances which might influence a judge's sentence, he knew about my pregnancy; but I insisted that he not mention it. He agreed. I felt that if the judge was going to be lenient, I wanted his leniency for the sake of the unborn on whose behalf I had acted. I did not want him to make his sentencing decision based on sympathy or concern for my unborn baby but not for the others.

Edmund and I walked back into Schudson's court on February 22. I was just over three months pregnant and still not showing. We took our seats in the rear of the courtroom and waited for my case to be called. The media already had assembled in the rear of the court and several pro-lifers had come to give me their support. I leaned over to Edmund and said, "I'm preparing myself for the worst."

"What's the worst?" he asked.

"A three-month sentence—the most Kremers asked for." I replied. I did not believe Schudson would give me anything harsher than that, but I fully expected to spend some time in jail.

When the judge finished the other court business, my case was called. Jeff Kremers strode haughtily over to the prosecutor's table. Bill Kerner and I went over to the defendant's table. I felt a rush of nervousness as I took my now-familiar seat. I clutched a small crucifix in my left hand and prayed silently.

Judge Schudson, cloaked in his robes, sat at the elevated judge's bench. It struck me as odd that the slightly-built Schudson always appeared larger and taller when he sat behind his bench. He announced that he had prepared a twenty-one page sentencing statement that he intended to read. Everyone assembled in the courtroom knew how unusual it was for a judge to prepare such a lengthy statement, and even more unusual for a judge to read it all word for word. Before he began, Schudson told the court that he hoped his statement would give guidance to other judges who had pro-life cases before them. He directed the bailiff to pass out copies of the document to each party in the case and to the members of the press.

Schudson began reading. I listened intently. About two minutes into his statement, a bolt of joy shot through me. Schudson was quoting a story from Herman Melville's *Moby Dick* about the black slave cabin boy Pip, who, taken on one of the whaling ventures, jumped from the small whaling boat into the sea to become a castaway in the immensity of the ocean where:

Melville writes: "The awesome lonesomeness is intolerable. The intense concentration of self in the middle of such a heartless immensity, my God! who can tell it? . . . The sea had jeeringly kept his body up, but drowned the infinite of his soul." Hauntingly, Monica Miller wrote to the court in terms that would have enveloped Melville's seaman. She enclosed this photo of an unborn, fourteen week fetus, tossed in the garbage dumpster along with other aborted children behind a Chicago abortion center.

Where Melville wrote that Pip's "awful loneliness is intolerable," Miller described the "utter loneliness of the aborted child." Where Melville wrote that "the sea had jeeringly kept his finite body up but drowned the infinite of his soul," Miller described "the hand connected to the arm torn at the shoulder, unconnected to a body and looms out of nothing." And where Melville wrote that Pip, the traumatized castaway, walked "the greater quarter deck on high . . . with angels, and beat his tambourine in glory," Miller described this child's hand that "in this void speaks his humanity and speaks the horror of his alienation."

Thus Miller understands that abortion not only terminates the lives of unborn children, but devalues the humanity of all who live. She understands that at different times laws have devalued slaves and unborn children, but that laws do change. She rejects the notion that while waiting for laws to change, abolitionists should have closed the underground railroad, sanctuaries should have turned away Jews, and anti-abortionists should only sing hymns at the clinic doors. The "horror of alienation" she describes has become her own, as well as that of unborn children and any society that would devalue life.

His words elated me. The judge understood, and perhaps, for the sake of the babies, I would have no sentence or at least an extremely light one that would reflect the fact that the unborn deserved to be protected. More importantly, Schudson was doing something bold, perhaps even unprecedented, exonerating a pro-lifer in recognition that the unborn are human beings that deserve to be acknowledged and defended.

Schudson continued:

> [H]owever, one could very well accept her beliefs about abortion without necessarily concluding that her strategy is acceptable. Even while approving her view, one might seek to consider certain understandings of law, life, and American society that expose her crimes as less just than she maintains.

My joy evaporated. I tried to maintain my composure as I sat in my seat at the defendant's table. As Schudson's voice continued to unravel his text, I gripped the edge of my seat with one hand. With the other I held the crucifix so tightly that it dug into my palm. I tried not to tremble. I realized that I had been cruelly teased. Each word he spoke carried me closer to dejection, anger, frustration and sorrow.

First Schudson mischaracterized *Roe v. Wade* as a Supreme Court decision that allowed states to place significant restrictions on a "woman's right to choose." Then he entered into a lengthy philosophical discussion on the American experience of the struggle between the "American individual and the American aggregate." He relied on the views of Yeshoua Arieli, a professor of American History at the Hebrew University in Israel and the author of *Individualism and Nationalism in American Ideology*. Schudson quoted Arieli, saying that the "strength of American nationalism rested upon the tension between these two poles." Schudson explained that what is important for America as a nation are not answers to issues like abortion, "but our continuing determination to seek them":

> With that recognition, many responsible, sensitive Americans are coming to be both pro-life and pro-choice. They believe that life begins at conception and writhe at the thought of each unborn child crushed or consumed. However, they, along with Jefferson, are prepared to "maintain the common right of freedom of conscience"—to accept that their view

is not the only view and that other, equally responsible and sensitive Americans have reached other conclusions. They are prepared to regret and protest abortion, but accept that other individuals are guaranteed the equal opportunity to reflect and choose.

I believe Schudson was telling his courtroom audience more about himself than about Jefferson. Undoubtedly he thought of himself as one of the "responsible, sensitive Americans . . . coming to be both pro-life and pro-choice." Next, he told the courtroom that my comparison of abortion to the Nazi holocaust was flawed, particularly so in that I failed to recognize that abortion was, in his view, the result of "a painful yet deliberative process" in which the Supreme Court and the legislatures "have tried to respond with moral and legal consideration for the unborn children and for the women who would seek to make their own painful choices." He believed this democratic process qualitatively differed "from that which produced a single, undebated, demonic decree demanding the destruction of all Jews." It would seem that as long as the killing of the innocent is first debated, the final decision that facilitates killing is not "demonic."

Since I failed to acknowledge the importance of that difference I failed to acknowledge the "significance of democracy"—and therein lay my crime. I failed to acknowledge the "fundamentally differing views" of others as equally as legitimate as my own and thus had to "accept the consequences should she assume for herself the absolute, unqualified authority to obliterate the differing views of others." I wondered if Schudson thought blacks who illegally protested segregation in the South were as bad Americans as I was. In my copy of Schudson's statement, I saw that the following was italicized for emphasis:

> *Monica Miller is not being sentenced for her beliefs or for her efforts to rescue unborn children . . . but for dangerous criminal conduct that obstructed police, threatened safety, and violated constitutional rights.*

Schudson continued:

> The defendant has concluded that her principles are superior
> to those of the United States Supreme Court; that her strategy
> is justified even if others sharing her view do not embrace her
> techniques . . . this court concludes that the defendant, for
> all her admirable qualities, is a dangerous person who cannot
> be expected to respect the rights of others with whom she
> disagrees.

Schudson then launched into a lengthy litany of my crimes,
which he stated "victimize the community at many levels."

> First, ironically, the crimes victimize the unborn children
> the defendant is determined to save. To the extent that her
> strategy is perceived as fanatical and dangerous, it undermines
> support for the passionately reasoned arguments that others
> offer in opposition to abortion. Second, her crimes victimize
> others who share her philosophy. To the extent that she is
> perceived as one who maintains the absolute correctness of
> her own strategy, she will be viewed as one who implicitly
> rejects the lawful strategies of others.
>   . . . At other levels the communities' victimization is
> even more apparent. First, women . . . are denied their
> Constitutionally-protected right to choose. Next, women
> needing medical services are denied the opportunity to obtain
> them. . . . The community is further victimized because the
> defendant's crimes require a substantial law enforcement
> response that inevitably reduces essential services to other
> citizens . . . .
>   Finally, the defendant's crimes victimize democracy. Her
> crimes convey a clear message: if you are certain you are right,
> you may break the law; if the Supreme Court says you are
> wrong, you may ignore it.

Before Schudson completed the reading of his statement
he characterized my crimes as "serious and dangerous" and thus
declared that he was going to give me the maximum prison

sentence possible. He also cited the fact that I had already been in jail for "similar crimes" before and "she has not been deterred . . . women wanting to choose [abortion] deserve to be protected from her." Schudson gave me a sentence of three months for disorderly conduct, nine months for unlawful assembly, and nine months for obstruction of an officer. But Schudson ordered that the sentences be served concurrently since, as he stated, "punishment at its best is tempered by mercy." Ironically enough, my sentence, stemming from one rescue, totaled nine months. At that time it was one of the longest jail sentences given to a pro-lifer for an abortion clinic sit-in. Schudson stayed the sentence pending the outcome of the appeal I planned to pursue. My appeal was taken up by Richard Martin, a very pro-life and extremely able public defender in the Milwaukee County appellate division.

The hearing concluded and everyone in the courtroom spilled excitedly out into the hallway. Jeff Kremers passed me on his way to the nearby elevators. He and I looked at each other. He smiled, face aglow. He had prevailed well beyond even his own expectations. I was soon surrounded by reporters and gave several interviews. A *Milwaukee Journal* reporter, pad and pen in hand, asked me: "So, Ms. Miller, the judge described you as a 'dangerous person.' What is your response to that?"

"Anyone who has gone against the grain of society for what's right has been considered a dangerous person," I answered.

Chris Gorski, the manager of Bread and Roses, was interviewed at her clinic. She told the *Milwaukee Journal* that when she heard about my sentence she "jumped for joy." Her jubilant response undoubtedly reflected the sentiments of all the pro-abortion activists in Milwaukee and across the United States.

Of the twenty-one pro-lifers who had blocked the door to the Imperial Health Services, I was the only one who had received a sentence of any kind. By the time my friends went to trial on their city tickets, Sergeant Moe and Officer Melewski had retired from the police force. They did not show up for the trials and thus the other pro-lifers' charges were dismissed.

The reporters eventually dispersed. Edmund and I left the courthouse. As we descended its steps on that cold February day I felt the joy of the child growing within me and the weight of the nine-month sentence that lay in my future. I tried to recall something Schudson had said in his sentencing statement. He made certain remarks, perhaps to soften his otherwise harsh words, perhaps out of genuine respect, or perhaps because, like his commentary on *Moby Dick*, these statements gave him a chance to wax eloquent. In light of my "civil disobedience," he referred to Thoreau and Martin Luther King, Jr.

He quoted Thoreau's statement that "the true place for a just man is also a prison," and King's remark that "Words cannot express the exultation felt by the individual as he finds himself . . . behind prison bars for a cause he knows is just." The words offered a thin mantle against the bitter February air.

CHAPTER SEVENTEEN

OUR DAYS OF BOLDNESS

"We have reached a point in this particular technology where there is no possibility of denial of an act of destruction by the operator. It is before one's eyes. The sensations of dismemberment flow through the forceps like an electric current."

—Warren Hern, Colorado abortionist,
author of *Abortion Practice*

BY THE end of April, 1991, I was five and a half months along in my pregnancy, proudly "showing" and feeling quite well. On April 25 I awoke early, dressed quickly, ate breakfast and grabbed three bananas to get me through what I expected to be an eventful, stress-filled morning. I drove fifty minutes east on Interstate 94 with heavy chains, three pairs of handcuffs and three kryptonite bicycle locks in the trunk of my car.

Finally I came to a familiar sight—the Wendy's overpass, or what was officially called, the Forest Park Oasis, a complex of fast food shops, restrooms and a Mobil gas station built over the Illinois toll road. Wendy's was the most visible restaurant from the expressway. As I parked my car, just east of the entrance to the overpass, I saw a cluster of familiar faces gathered in the parking lot—pro-lifers from Milwaukee, including Matt Trewhella, leader of Missionaries to the Preborn. There were about forty present, fifteen of them from other states. I walked over to Matt.

"He's here, inside," Matt said to me as he tilted his head toward the Wendy's, "Just as I predicted."

There was a small group of pro-lifers standing at the front end of a large, black and gray late-model Mercedes Benz. Two of them were in the process of sliding themselves underneath the car's front end. As quickly as a woman five and a half months pregnant could manage, I dashed back to my car, opened the trunk and grabbed a kryptonite lock and a pair of handcuffs. I raced back to the Mercedes and gave the kryptonite lock to one of the men, who by now had nearly the full length of his body under the vehicle. Someone else slid partially under the car to help the man attach himself to the axle. I gave the handcuffs to another who expressed an interest in having them.

Suddenly Matt rushed over to the car. "He's coming!" he said in a low voice, but loud enough for all to hear. "Everyone gather around the car," he instructed with a tone of near desperate urgency. It was 9:43 a.m. The group surrounded the car just as a tall, rather balding, gray-haired man with white at his temples exited the oasis. He wore a blue sport coat and black pants and carried a white paper bag and a Styrofoam cup. Even though a horde of people was surrounding his vehicle, he strolled to his car with the calm of someone about to take a Sunday drive. I recognized Aleksander Jakubowski, the abortionist at the Bread and Roses clinic, but I had not seen him since the day he testified against us in Judge McMahon's court. In those four years his appearance had changed very little.

On this April morning, with his car completely encircled by pro-lifers in the parking lot of an Interstate 94 overpass, I was impressed with Jakubowski's stoic demeanor. He did not appear to be the least bit angry or upset by an obvious attempt to keep him from traveling to Bread and Roses, where he was headed to do abortions. Jakubowski did not live in Wisconsin, but in Presbury, an exclusive subdivision in Aurora, Illinois, a western suburb of Chicago. He traveled to Bread and Roses three times a week where he now did abortions through the twenty-first week of gestation. Perhaps Jakubowski was not ultimately surprised to find himself the target of a protest. By now he was used to being confronted by pro-lifers. Members of Missionaries to the Preborn had been blocking the door to Bread and Roses every day the clinic was open for the previous eight months. A few of the Missionaries had been arrested over a hundred times.

For about a month, members of the group had followed Jakubowski and noted that he always, without fail, stopped at the overpass on his way to Bread and Roses. The April 26 *Chicago Sun-Times* quoted Clara Trewhella, Matt's wife, as saying: "[Jakubowski]'s a creature of habit . . . almost every Tuesday, Thursday and Friday he stops at the oasis long enough to buy a newspaper, go to the bathroom and call the clinic to see if there are any picketers there." It appeared the primary reason for his stops at the oasis was to place his "Is the coast clear?" phone call to the abortion clinic.

When Jakubowski walked over to the car, he assessed the situation for a second, but said nothing. The pro-lifers also said nothing. He quickly turned on his heel and walked back into the Wendy's. "I went in to call [the police], and they came and took over from there," Jakubowski told the *Sun-Times*. Within five minutes a dozen Illinois state troopers arrived to confront what certainly was one of the most unique and unusual "disturbances" ever to occur on the Interstate.

Three state troopers walked over to the Mercedes, bent down and looked at the two pro-lifers stretched out beneath the car. Other state troopers huddled together with Jakubowski. It was apparent that he and the troopers were devising a plan for his "escape." In a few moments they all walked into the Wendy's. In another minute an unmarked police car, a Chevy Caprice Classic, suddenly sped to a stop in front of the oasis doors. The car's passenger door was flung open and troopers quickly ushered Jakubowski out of the Wendy's. Everyone was caught off guard by the "get away" tactic, except for a very earnest young man named Tom Burke, who had come all the way from Kansas City to attend the rescue. He grabbed the top of the open passenger door with both hands and held on to it with all his strength. Troopers instantly descended on him and tried to pull him off the door, but Tom would not let go, and the door was bent at the hinges. His attempt prevented the driver from taking off with Jakubowski, and other pro-lifers had time to run to the car and surround it. A few of them placed themselves directly in front of the Caprice and prevented it from moving. Two others slid underneath the car, and Steve Wagi, a sixteen-year-old who had blocked the door at Bread and Roses dozens of times with his mother Elizabeth and sister Beth, handcuffed his wrist to the front end of the car. I was amazed by the scene. In fifteen years of pro-life activism I had never seen such a serious, genuine and intense effort by pro-lifers to prevent an abortionist from killing the unborn.

Troopers pulled Burke off the door and to the ground, and cuffed his hands behind his back. He resisted passively and was carried off to the squad car. Another rescuer who had told Matt he came "only to offer up prayers" was arrested when, in the heat of necessity, he also tried to grab the door. Rather amazingly, however, the troopers arrested no one else, not even Steven Wagi who removed himself from the car when it was obvious the troopers had abandoned this failed plan.

Troopers again huddled with Jakubowski. Pro-lifers stood nearby, tense and anxious. The troopers then surrounded the abortionist and escorted him through the doors of the oasis. Remaining troopers immediately stationed themselves in front of the doors and blocked us from following. Jakubowski was being hustled through the oasis where a squad car was waiting for him on the other side. A few pro-lifers, however, were already in the oasis and, anticipating the new strategy, they raced to the other end. Bursting through the doors on the other side, they sat down in front of the squad car parked fifteen feet from the building. Jakubowski got into the car's front passenger seat. Staring straight ahead, he nonchalantly continued to sip his coffee. But with the car blocked, it did not go anywhere.

Since the path through the oasis was fenced off by troopers, the remaining pro-lifers did something extraordinary: they walked along the narrow cat walks on either side of the overpass. Five and a half months pregnant and carrying a large camcorder, I clumsily and carefully climbed over the catwalk gates.

When I arrived at the west side of the oasis, more pro-lifers had surrounded the car. Additional state troopers arrived, as well as a S.W.A.T. team with a very intimidating German Shepherd police dog who, thankfully, was never turned loose on us. Troopers pulled pro-lifers away from the car and let go of them as if they were sacks of potatoes, and many simply got up and dashed back to block the car again. One stretched himself under the front of the car and handcuffed himself to the undercarriage. A trooper knelt down on his upper leg in a kind of genuflection while another trooper equipped with a bolt cutter slid his body half way under the car and cut the pro-lifer loose. He was then cuffed and taken into custody. Officers tried to yank Ralph Ovadal, a Missionary to the Preborn, off the front bumper. For several minutes troopers tried to pry him loose, but he held on tenaciously. When a trooper slammed his palm down on Ralph's arm, his hand slipped off the bumper. But Ralph was able to crawl back and hold onto the car again before being dragged away. This happened twice until a trooper was specially assigned to block Ralph after he was dragged away from the car for the third time. The troopers pulled Missionary to the Preborn Jim Ketchum away from the driver's side of the car and used a submission hold on his hand to get him to cooperate. Ketchum's hideous shrieks of pain pierced the air as he was dragged away from the car.

By noon Jakubowski still had not been escorted away. All this time he sat in the squad car, seemingly impervious to the drama taking place all around him. Finally, the troopers came up with "escape plan" number three. Jakubowski got out of the squad car and stood near the doors of the oasis with several troopers. He was escorted suddenly into the building and the remaining troopers blocked the doors. Pro-lifers rushed the doors in an effort to block Jakubowski's getaway. Troopers grabbed several of them and pulled them back.

In their third attempt to help Jakubowski "get to work," the troopers came up with a clever plan. We quickly surmised that he was being taken down to the interstate, and indeed he was. He was taken through a door led to a staircase that led to another door that opened directly onto the busy road. There sat a squad car waiting for its passenger. Jakubowski got into the car and it quickly sped away. Jakubowski had escaped. Realizing what had happened, some pro-lifers raced to the catwalk on the north side of the oasis. The troopers rounded up as many as they could, but some slipped through and managed to lower themselves to the steep embankment. They ran down it and onto the expressway in hopes of blocking the waiting trooper's car, but it was too late.

We scrambled to our cars, parked on the east end of the oasis, and raced up the tollway hoping to arrive at Bread and Roses before Jakubowski. The two men chained to the abortionist's car were unlocked and walked away from the Mercedes without being arrested. A state trooper got into the car and turned the ignition, but it would not start. A raw potato had been inserted inside the car's exhaust pipe. The Mercedes was towed to a service garage in Gurnee, Illinois. There the state troopers reunited the abortionist with his vehicle, and Jakubowski drove himself the rest of the way to Bread and Roses.

Several protestors, who had had been at the Wendy's overpass, arrived at Bread and Roses and waited for Jakubowski. The black Mercedes was seen approaching the parking lot, Jakubowski at the wheel. Over two dozen pro-lifers swiftly walked to the door of Bread and Roses and sat down. It was three in the afternoon, and Jakubowski was four hours late. Eleven women scheduled for abortions had left. While Jakubowski was held up at the overpass, sidewalk counselors successfully persuaded two of the eleven to keep their babies and took them to a Milwaukee crisis pregnancy center. Only one woman, intent on getting her abortion that day, opted to wait.

The police arrived, and within half an hour twenty-seven pro-lifers were arrested. Finally, Jakubowski, his stoic demeanor never shaken, walked through the door of Bread and Roses and killed the unborn baby of the one remaining woman.

Throughout the Wendy's overpass rescue I was disturbed by how utterly determined the state troopers were to assist Jakubowski to get out of the oasis. They all knew that he was on his way to perform abortions, but it made no difference to them. We pleaded with the troopers and tried to show them that, by helping this man, they were facilitating the deaths of innocent human beings. Yet they acted with exceptional tenacity—almost as if they needed to prove that they could thwart our clever scheme.

Of course, I expected the troopers to make an effort to "rescue" Jakubowski, but it was the fervor with which they applied themselves to the task that, from a pro-life point of view, was frustrating, disappointing and even perplexing. During the demonstration I confronted a sheriff's department captain. "Hey, I'm Catholic," he said. "And my wife just had a baby five months ago. I don't believe in abortion, but ma'am the law's the law."

The overpass rescue generated a great deal of media attention. In several articles printed in the *Chicago Sun-Times* and *Chicago Tribune*, Jakubowksi was portrayed as a victim who needed to be "freed" and "rescued" by state police. Jessica Seigel of the *Tribune* even characterized the overpass rescue as a "strategy" that was "part of the escalating harassment against doctors and clinic bombings." In another article Seigel wrote about how the "tough and sometimes violent tactics" of pro-lifers were causing doctors to quit doing abortions and contributed to an "11 percent decline in abortion services nationwide." She again linked the overpass rescue to a concern on the part of abortion providers "about a rash of fire-bombings and arsons in recent months." This kind of reporting led readers to believe that the overpass rescue was simply another act of harassment and violence. Siegel did mention that "about 60 to 75 abortions are performed each week" at Bread and Roses. But, unlike the tactics of pro-lifers, abortion was never characterized as violence.

Carol Ashkinaze, in an April 30 *Sun-Times* column, described the overpass rescue as an "ambush" performed by the "lunatic fringe."

[I]t is bewildering not only to hear the thugs and scofflaws who trapped a doctor at an Illinois rest stop for two hours Thursday defend their tactics, which included knocking a policeman to the ground and causing hundreds of dollars worth of damage to a squad car—but also to hear those tactics described by Chicago's own Joseph Scheidler, who looked on admiringly, as "the wave of the future."

If there is anything reasonable people on both sides ought to be able to agree on, it is that a Milwaukee-based group really did cross over into the lunatic fringe when its members deprived Jakubowski of his freedom by pursuing him across state lines, chaining themselves to his car, and interfering with the police who tried to escort him to freedom.

That little exercise in what one described piously as an attempt to stop the "killing of children," by which I presume she meant partially formed fetuses incapable of life outside the womb, not only waylaid him; it also took 30 Illinois state troopers and sheriff's officers away from their traffic posts and patrols for hours on end, without regard for the real live adults and children whose lives might be endangered as a result.

The reporter's dismissal of the unborn as "partially formed fetuses" who, unlike born human beings, were not "alive" seemed to me very far from reality. This was especially so now that I was pregnant with my own baby, a baby who I felt move, a life so precious and dear. Three and a half months after the Wendy's overpass rescue, I gave birth to our first living child—a daughter. Born August 15, 1991, Edmund and I named her Bernadette.

*   *   *

The Wendy's overpass rescue was a kind of rehearsal for what would happen in Milwaukee in the Summer of 1992. The Missionaries planned what Matt Trewhella called the "Short Term Mission." Beginning on June 15, 1992, and lasting for six weeks, the Short Term Mission brought activists together from all over the country to participate in a series of rescues at abortion clinics. For weeks prior to the start of the mission, local media hyped the event as "abortion foes" preparing for massive clinic blockades. The publicity actually helped turn the event into a major anti-abortion activity and made the mission something much bigger than it would have been otherwise. Pro-lifers who would not have been attracted to the mission, or perhaps would not even have known about it, now wanted to participate. A lengthy article appeared in the June 7, *Milwaukee Journal*, taking up the whole front page of the News Plus section. Entitled "Target: Milwaukee," it reported:

> In just two weeks . . . a confrontation between those who seek to eliminate abortion and those who want to keep it as an option is expected to take place closer to home: on the streets of Milwaukee, in front of the city's six abortion clinics.
>
> Organizers claim the demonstrations scheduled for six weeks beginning June 15th, will take place on a scale not seen before in Wisconsin.

Milwaukee abortion providers were thrown into a state of panic. Milwaukee city officials including Mayor John Norquist, Police Chief Philip Arreola, and City Attorney Grant Langley teamed up with Wisconsin Attorney General James Doyle and sought a temporary injunction to prevent the blockades. Norquist and Doyle were known to support legal abortion. Doyle's sister, Katie Doyle, became active that spring in the newly formed Milwaukee Clinic Protection Coalition. The group, formed in response to the impending rescues, trained volunteers to surround women entering abortion clinics so that sidewalk counselors would have little, if any, opportunity to speak with them.

The injunction stipulated that members of Missionaries to the Preborn, Youth for America, a group co-sponsoring the event, and thirty-five named defendants (including Edmund and me) had to stay twenty-five feet away from the property of Milwaukee abortion clinics, as well as ten feet away from anyone seeking ingress or egress from the abortion clinics. Most of the named defendants were not served with the injunction before the start of the mission, and it had little effect on the clinic blockades.

On the first day of the Mission, June 17, 1992, pro-lifers gathered at the Wisconsin Women's Health Care Center at 86th and Brown Deer Road, located on the extreme north side of Milwaukee. While a large group of pro-abortion demonstrators shouted "Pray, you'll need it, you're going to be defeated," thirty pro-lifers ran for the door of the abortion center and were arrested. Some of those arrested included teenagers and even a few children between the ages of nine and twelve. In 1991, many children had participated in Operation Rescue's Summer of Mercy, a series of blockades at the Wichita, Kansas, clinic of George Tiller who specialized in third trimester abortions. A few teenagers had blocked the doors to Bread and Roses within the past year. Indeed, teenager Beth Rella, often accompanied by her mother Elizabeth Wagi, was arrested more than any other person in Milwaukee, no less than 176 times, mostly at the weekly rescues at Bread and Roses. In the Short Term Mission, Brian Longworth, a good-looking and very earnest twenty-one-year-old leader of Youth for Life, was chiefly responsible for the very visible presence of young people in front of Milwaukee abortion center doors.

When I arrived at the Wisconsin Women's Health Care Center at 7:30 a.m., hundreds of pro-lifers were already there, lined up along the sidewalk facing the large parking lot in front of the office building that housed the clinic. A nearly equal number of abortion supporters, their arms locked together, had planted themselves along the lot's perimeter to act as a human barricade. The two opposing sides of the abortion war were literally facing off. The police were everywhere.

I walked up to the clinic and noticed Joe Foreman standing near the entrance to the parking lot. Joe had worked closely with Randall Terry, but earlier that year, at the invitation of Matt Trewhella, he moved his family to Milwaukee and took a leadership position with the Missionaries. Joe and I exchanged glances. If a rescue was going to occur, we would all have to make a dash for the door and try to get as many pro-lifers as possible past the police. I looked at Joe and pointed toward the clinic and Joe nodded in acknowledgment. I turned toward the building and broke into a run. As dozens of other pro-lifers followed suit, the police chased after us. When I was half way across the lot, an officer grabbed me and pulled me to the ground. About fifteen others were also apprehended. As I was prone on the parking lot being handcuffed, I could see the feet of other pro-lifers running past me. Many of them successfully eluded the police and sat down at the entrance of the building.

At the end of two hours, a total of ninety-nine pro-lifers had been arrested. About one third were juveniles, the majority of whom were fourteen and over. Everyone received a city ticket for disorderly conduct. Rescues such as this continued for weeks at the various Milwaukee abortion clinics. The injunction did not have the effect the abortion providers had hoped it would. The Short Term Mission continually attracted newcomers, and the rescues went on unabated. Many participants came from out of town, and if they were served with the injunction, they simply ignored it.

* * *

Citizens for Life made its own contribution to that summer's anti-abortion activities. Two years ago, when the Continental Bank Building refused to renew his lease, Milton Tarver was forced to relocate his abortion clinic. He moved Imperial Health Services to 64th and Capitol and now occupied the bottom floor of a small two story building. On Monday, August 3, 1992, two large barrels, filled with hardened cement, were placed in front of the clinic's south door. PCV pipes ran through the center of the barrels, just wide enough for an adult male to slip his arm through. Two holes had been cut in the center of each pipe opposite each other. A metal rod was slipped through the holes and held in place by the cement surrounding the pipes. Four pro-lifers, with metal clips duct taped to their palms, inserted their arms through the pipes, slipped the clip around the rod, and became part of the heavy immoveable objects.

A junk car was parked at the clinic's north entrance. A front-page article in the August 4 *Milwaukee Sentinel* described the fire fighters' efforts to remove it:

> Firefighters spent about five hours cutting apart the car that blocked the clinic's front door and held two protesters. The car's doors were welded shut and its windshields were fortified with wire grilles. Two men had their arms encased in a pipe, attached to the car by about 100 pounds of concrete. . . . The two protesters' bodies were partially inside the car. Holes cut in the floorboards allowed them to sit on the pavement.
>
> Firefighters took the car apart piece by piece, then cut through the concrete that held the men in the car. Once the men were lifted out, the pipe on their arms still had to be carefully cut.

For weeks I had carefully planned this blockade, hoping that members of the Milwaukee Clinic Protection Coalition would be caught off guard, and they were. When a dozen of them arrived, all they could do was watch the scene. WVCY reported that a rescue was in progress, and over a hundred pro-life picketers arrived. Two fire engines, as well as several police squad cars, were parked on the street. Police and firemen were everywhere; so were reporters and TV camera crews. *The Sentinel* reported that Milton Tarver had to cancel his appointments for the day and "was furious about the blocking tactic." Matt Trewhella and his friend Mike Skott, came to observe the rescue. Mike saw me standing nearby as I nervously watched firemen force open the car with the "jaws of life." He walked over and whispered: "This is just as it should be, Monica, an abortion mill totally under siege!"

On August 7, 1992, four days later, the Short Term Mission climaxed with a rally at Mecca, a sports arena downtown. Ten thousand people—an unprecedented number—attended the event, which had the flavor of a huge tent revival meeting. Indeed, the theme of the rally was personal conversion. The preachers on stage called participants to repent for their apathy, for having done nothing while millions of unborn children perished in abortion.

It was a major pro-life event, but I was not there. Earlier that day the Wisconsin attorney general, James Doyle, held a press conference, announcing on television that he had issued a warrant for my arrest. I knew police were looking for me at the rally, intending to take me into custody. Doyle charged me with two criminal counts of violating the injunction. I was accused of blocking a woman who sought to enter the Summit Women's Health Organization during a June 27 rescue and for refusing to produce a key to a kryptonite bicycle lock worn by one of the pro-lifers who blocked the door to Imperial.

Edmund and I knew that when the police didn't find me at the rally, they would show up on our doorstep and whisk me away. We wanted to avoid my being taken on the whim of the officers. While thousands of pro-lifers filled Mecca with prayers, hymns, and speeches, Edmund and I placed eleven month-old Bernadette into her car seat and drove to the home of Joe and Kay Crnkovich. Happy to help out pro-life "fugitives from justice," they agreed to let us spend the night. The next morning we drove to a friend's lakeside cottage four hours north of Milwaukee. As we drove up highway 45, thousands of pro-lifers gathered in front of the abortion clinic at 86th and Brown Deer Road, hundreds of whom sat down in front of the clinic's entrance.

The front page of the August 9 edition of the *Milwaukee Journal* blared: "546 arrested at abortion clinic rally." Below the headline was a large aerial photo of Brown Deer Road and the clinic's parking lot. Four thousand pro-lifers had showed up at the clinic. Pro-lifers closed down the westbound lanes of traffic to prevent the travel of police vans that were carrying other pro-lifers to jail. This tactic was intended to slow down the arrest process so the rescue itself would be prolonged. This clinic blockade turned out to be the largest in the history of the pro-life movement.

After fourteen years of activist pro-life leadership, I could only gaze at the photo with a sense of amazement, and also regret that I could not participate in this historic pro-life demonstration. But I knew that, with our growing family, I could not take the risk. I had every intention of turning myself over to the sheriff's department, but I wanted to delay the arrest and get my affairs in order. I had just discovered that I was pregnant again, three weeks along. When I was arrested on June 17, running toward the abortion clinic door, I was one day into the pregnancy—unaware of the new life within me. Having already suffered a miscarriage with our first baby, I did not want to risk losing this one. To eliminate stress, in what was an inherently stressful situation, I felt I needed to be in some control over what was about to happen.

After three days at the cottage, Edmund and I returned to Milwaukee and I handed myself over to the authorities. Standing before a court commissioner, I pled not guilty to the charges. A hearing, which was twice postponed, was set before Milwaukee Circuit Court judge Daniel Konkol. Seven months after the warrant had been issued, and when I was a very hefty and obviously eight-months pregnant, I finally walked back into Konkol's court. My committed pro-life attorney, Craig Parshall, had filed a motion to dismiss. After a twenty minute hearing I walked out again a free woman. Konkol dismissed the charges against me based on lack of evidence in the state's written complaint. He was not convinced that my alleged knowledge of the whereabouts of a key constituted aiding and abetting the blockade of Imperial Health Services. As to the second charge, the complaint stated that I had "attempted" to grab a woman who was entering the abortion clinic, meaning I had never really done anything to prevent her ingress or egress. In reality, I had simply extended my hand to offer her a piece of pro-life literature. The two young assistant states attorneys present at the hearing seemed embarrassed at the outcome of the whole proceeding as I happily and, enlarged with the life of my unborn son, somewhat laboriously, departed the courtroom.

*　*　*

Ten months after we blocked the entrances to Imperial, I drove up a narrow strip of road called North Lake Drive. On this warm

June morning in 1993 I eyed the large homes and secluded estates and enjoyed the beauty of the wealthy northeast Milwaukee suburb. I thought to myself, "Fox Point is definitely posh." But I hadn't come to take a casual drive, and I forced myself to pay closer attention to the street signs. I was in search of a specific home. I eventually spied the street I wanted and turned right onto a blacktopped, wooded residential road. It was early Saturday morning, and a few residents were out jogging or walking dogs. Then the road took a turn to the left, and there was the house—a contemporary, sprawling ranch. It was set back from the street, with plenty of trees and shrubs obscuring my view. I could tell from the property's location that the back of the house was right on Lake Michigan.

From the looks of his abode it appeared that Dr. Neville Sender had done well for himself. With Metropolitan, his old abortion clinic closed, and his abortion partnership with Woodward dissolved, Sender, in his late sixties, now performed abortions at Summit. Because of pro-life activism, abortion providers admitted that fewer and fewer doctors were getting into the abortion business. Considering the shortage Summit's owners were undoubtedly happy to have this skilled veteran abortion practitioner working for them. For years Summit, like many clinics across the country, had been forced to import out-of-state abortionists such as George Miks and Susan Wickland from North Dakota, where there was only one abortion clinic. Several abortionists became known as "circuit riders" because they traveled from state to state on a circuit of abortion clinics desperate for their services.

On Wednesday June 21, 1993, I returned to Neville Sender's driveway. It was 7:45 in the morning. Several other pro-lifers had assembled, picketing along the road across the street from his home. A van carrying twelve other pro-lifers drove through the nearby streets. It occasionally passed by Sender's house on its continuous circular route. A Fox Point police officer arrived. He drove into Sender's long driveway, up to the garage and turned the squad car around. He then came back down the driveway and stationed his squad car toward the driveway's end, leaving enough room for another car to pass. The officer, a young man, leaned against the front fender of the car. This may well have been the first time the small, elite suburb of Fox Point had ever seen a picket for any reason.

Several minutes passed. The picketers, who walked in a narrow circle, were completely silent. All that could be heard on this warm, bright, first day of summer was the singing of the birds in the many trees and shrubs that lined the road. The sound was idyllic and beautiful, like in a fantasy—far removed from the real world.

As I picketed, my eyes were fixed on the driveway. Another half hour passed. Then, at 8:22 a.m., Neville Sender came down the driveway in his black Saab. I shouted loudly, "Get to the driveway!" In a flash the picketers, many with signs still in their hands, ran toward the car. Sender brought the car to a halt as thirty to forty people now effectively blocked his path. He could continue only at the risk of running over the pro-lifers, many of whom actually sat immediately in front of the vehicle, so he remained in his car and waited.

Our new rescue strategy was a consequence of the injunction that finally did force us to alter our blockade methods. The injunction specifically prohibited blocking clinic doors and the terms "ingress and egress" were interpreted to mean entering or exiting in close proximity to the protected abortion facilities. To get around the injunction, we devised strategies that achieved the same effect as an actual clinic blockade. Thus the "driveway rescue" tactic was born.

Ten minutes into the rescue, the Fox Point police captain arrived, dressed in a casual beige sport jacket—his official uniform. He was a kindly, dark-haired, somewhat overweight, middle-aged man and a law enforcement officer unused to dealing with protestors. With a camera in his hand, Sender got out of his car and began to take pictures of the crowd that sat in his driveway.

The Fox Point police captain addressed us: "You're on private property. You're being asked to leave."

No one responded.

He tried again: "You've all been informed. This is an illegal assembly—you're on private property."

We began to quietly recite the Lord's Prayer. When the prayer was over, one pro-lifer shouted at Sender, "Neville, you know it's wrong. You said it was wrong." She was probably referring to Sender's statement printed in the local paper some years ago: "Of course it's killing but the state permits killing in certain circumstances."

Upon hearing her yell I cautioned everyone, "No talking. No talking. Be prayerful, be peaceful." I did not want the rescue to turn into a shouting match between the pro-lifers and Sender, and I believed it was important to keep a quiet demeanor.

Sender, mocking my command, turned to the group and said, "No talking." He then approached us as if to make a speech to the group sitting on his property.

"Be understood about one thing. You do not intimidate me. Not one little bit. I will do whatever is right and proper under the law. I obey. I obey," he lectured the rescuers in his distinctly British accent.

He meant that abortion was legal and that doing them violated no law and that, indeed, by doing legal abortions he was in fact an obedient person, a good citizen—a person of law and order. It was ironic for Sender to speak this way since he had told the media some years earlier, rather proudly, that he had performed illegal abortions before *Roe v. Wade*.

Most of the rescuers began to sing "Amazing Grace." A few others softly intoned the prayers of the rosary. The birds continued to make their morning songs in the trees.

Sender stood before us and made another speech:

> You guys are not going to stop me from doing what I want to do. You know I've been picketed. I've been in the process for years and years and years, ever since the 1973 *Roe versus Wade* decision. You haven't stopped me one little bit, and it won't stop me. The only way I'll stop doing abortions is when abortions are not required, when abortions are illegal and I won't do them. Until that day, no way Jose. What you guys must know is that, in about 18 months from now, you know the abortion issue is going to be almost null and void. RU–486

is going to be issued, and most of those kinds of abortions will be a very private matter, and you won't know a god-damn thing about it!

He then turned and walked away and stood near his car. It seemed strange that Sender kept emphasizing how he would do what the law required. Perhaps he needed to reassure the community that now he was a law-abider, though he did give himself a loophole by saying that he would stop doing abortions when they were "not required." Sender was also not a good prophet. The French abortion pill RU-486 was not available in eighteen months. Under the threat of boycotts from pro-lifers, U.S. drug manufacturers would not market the pill. It did not become widely available until the year 2000 and it never did replace surgical abortions performed in free-standing clinics.

A minute later, Sender approached the group again. His hands thrust into the pockets of his pants, he silently stood before the sitting crowd for several seconds and stared at the faces before him. Perhaps he was mentally composing his next discourse. He took his right hand out of his pocket and raised it up as if he were about to give a lecture to a class of college students: "In spite of all the protests, there are still about the same number of abortions performed in this country this year, last year, and it'll continue to be. You haven't made one little dent."

The lecture completed, Sender then turned and walked back to his Saab; but when he got there, he turned around, walked a few paces and addressed the sitting pro-lifers again.

"You know what chutzpah is? It's gall, it's cheek. That's what you have, because you don't respect anyone else's opinion."

He turned around and took two steps toward the Saab. Then he turned back again. "I wouldn't expect you to know what chutzpah is. I think a lot of you are very ignorant."

Sender went back to his car and stayed there, his speeches apparently completed. The Fox Point police captain walked over to the driveway, and now he addressed the group.

"We gave you twenty-five minutes to make your point. You are now being asked to move across the street to allow the doctor to leave. If you do not, you will be subject to arrest."

He waited a moment for a response, but his words were met with silence. He spoke again: "I'm telling you for the second time this is an illegal assembly. You are being asked to leave to allow the doctor to exit his property. You've made your point—or you will subject yourself to arrest."

The police captain's efforts had all the force of Andy of Mayberry. It seemed that he really did not want to arrest anyone. Like so many other police officers, he didn't understand that we were not there to "make a point" but there to prevent Sender from getting to the abortion clinic. Those sitting in the driveway were prepared to be arrested if necessary.

When his second warning was also met with silence, the Fox Point police captain bent down and started to drag one of the pro-lifers away from the driveway, taking him a few feet and depositing him on the street, whereupon the pro-lifer simply crawled back to his original position. Other officers dragged pro-lifers from the driveway, and the pro-lifers all crawled back. The Fox Point police were under the impression that once a person was taken away, the person would stay put. Such was not the case. Their efforts at first seemed a little comical, and they soon realized that their method of clearing the driveway was ineffective.

A half an hour went by. Sender sat in his car, police officers stood nearby, the pro-lifers continued to block the driveway, waiting for something to happen. At last ten more officers showed up, imported from Bayside, a small town north of Fox Point. A few minutes after they arrived, a bus pulled up at the driveway of Sender's home. Every pro-lifer knew what this meant. Slowly, methodically, and without violence, the arrests began. We were handcuffed with plasticuffs and carried to the door of the bus. There an officer wrote a number on the prisoner's forehead and he or she was photographed and carried onto the bus.

Forty minutes later the driveway was finally cleared. Sender started his car and drove into the street. He turned right and slowly crept northward. Suddenly three pro-lifers threw themselves in front of the car, forcing Sender to stop. One was a college student named Joshua, who grabbed hold of the front bumper. Another rescuer was Steve Gaenslen, a Milwaukee firefighter. Just as he lay down in front of the car, two officers grabbed him and carried him to the other side of the street. Steve sat on the pavement while one officer remained standing over him. The third man, Jim Valentine, a tall, heavy-set man, remained sitting near the front of the car while officers tried to pull Joshua from the car's bumper. Two more police officers ran to assist them. I yelled at them, "As soon as that so-called doctor leaves here, unborn children will be put to death. Stop helping him!"

The policemen continued to struggle with Joshua. They finally pried his hands off the front of the car. He struggled to free himself from their grasp to regain hold of the bumper, but the officers wrestled him to the ground as he screamed hideously. I could not see what they were doing to cause him such pain. Linda Schmidt who stood nearby, ready to place her body in front of Sender's car, cried out, "Take it easy with him!"

Sender's path was now clear, but when Steve Gaenslen saw that Sender was about to drive away, he dashed toward the car. Two policemen instantly pulled him back and held onto him as he lay face up in the street. Another officer motioned to Sender and shouted: "Go, go, go!" Sender stepped on the gas and sped off.

I walked up to the officer and said to him, "You're arresting the wrong people." I pointed in Sender's direction. "There's the murderer. He just left here in a black Saab."

Joshua was half-dragged, half-carried to the bus, but remarkably, Jim Valentine and Steve Gaenslen were not arrested. Sender's arrival at the abortion clinic had been delayed two hours. A sidewalk counselor stationed at Summit later told me that, while we were blocking Sender's driveway, a woman had been talked out of an abortion.

The bus in front of Sender's driveway began to pull away and the police dispersed. Only a handful of pro-lifers stayed behind, quietly praying the rosary across the street from Sender's home. The rescue in Fox Point had come to an end. Soon, even those who lingered to pray went home, returning the street to the only sound left, the sound that had initially greeted us—the carefree lyric of the birds.

No one who observed the Sender driveway rescue, its orderliness, the number of people involved, their enthusiasm, their willingness to make sacrifices and risk arrest, would ever have predicted that soon a radical and devastating change was about to take place within the activist pro-life movement. Sender falsely prophesied that in eighteen months a new abortion method would render such demonstrations obsolete. Instead, within eighteen months, one of the most significant social protest movements in American history—a movement in which thousands of people had blocked the doors to abortion clinics—would nearly cease to exist.

CHAPTER EIGHTEEN

P.O.C.

I was put into a jail . . . for one night, and as I stood considering the walls of solid stone, two or three feet thick, the door of wood and iron, a foot thick, and the iron grating which strained the light, I could not help being struck with the foolishness of that institution which treated me as mere flesh and blood and bones, to be locked up. . . . I did not for a moment feel confined, and the walls seemed a great waste of stone and mortar. . . . In every threat and in every compliment there was a blunder, for they thought my chief desire was to stand on the other side of that stone wall. I could not but smile to see how industriously they locked the door on my meditations, which followed them out again without let or hindrance, and they were really all that was dangerous. As they could not reach me they had resolved to punish my body; just as a boy, if they cannot come at some person against whom they have a spite, will abuse his dog.
—Henry David Thoreau, *On the Duty of Civil Disobedience*

LESS than a month after Sender's driveway rescue, I sat on the couch holding Joseph, only four months old and still nursing. Bernadette, just six weeks shy of her second birthday, sat on the floor nearby, contently coloring a picture of a farm. Soon I would be leaving them and they would have no idea where I was going. Richard Martin called to tell me now, a tone of disappointment in his voice, that the Milwaukee Supreme Court upheld the appellate court's decision, which had ruled against my appeal of Schudson's decision.

And so on a hot July evening in 1993, at seven o'clock I turned myself over to the Milwaukee County Sheriff's Department to serve my nine-month prison sentence. Edmund went with me to the familiar door of the Community Correctional Center. We waited in silence. Soon it was my turn to check in. We kissed each other goodbye.

A matron led me down a long hallway past the elevator I had taken to the fifth floor when I was in this jail the first time back in 1990. Since then the women's lockup had been moved to the first floor on the far south end of the building, and since this was a full work-release women's dorm, uniforms were not required. The matron was Miss Holloway, a middle-aged African American woman, and she led me to a room near the end of the hall. There, behind the closed door, I was strip searched, the first of many I would endure during my prison stay. Then, the humiliation over, I gathered my things and followed Miss Holloway to a set of heavy metal doors. As soon as they swung open I was hit with the din of loud voices, not unlike the boisterous noise of guests at a New Year's Eve party.

I walked into the large, drab women's dormitory. Miss Holloway escorted me to a locker where I could keep my few approved possessions. Two inmates stood nearby, watching me fill my locker. One of them spoke up: "Oh brother, one of them pro-lifers." I shot her a half-smile. "You could do worse." I had deliberately chosen to wear my "Citizens for Life" t-shirt, with its emblem of an unborn baby surrounded by the words "Life is worth giving." It would have been easier to allow myself to simply blend into the jail population, but I felt that I could not in good conscience hide my identity. I wanted my jail time to be a witness to the unborn. Pro-lifers who went to jail in the 1990s referred to themselves as P.O.C.s— "prisoners of conscience"—but the acronym had a double meaning. It was a conscious way for us to identify with the unwanted unborn—called "products of conception," or P.O.C.s, by abortion providers.

The first thing inmates want to know upon entering jail is when they will be released, and I was no exception. I entered the jail on July 12, 1993. Miss Holloway informed me that I would be released February 2, 1994. With time off for good behavior, I would do seven months of the nine-month sentence. It was only seven months, but February seemed like an absolute eternity. Whenever I thought about how far in the future it was, I was seized by a dreadful sinking feeling, as though an impassable chasm of time lay between me and the day I would be free. But I made a deliberate effort not to dwell upon the date of my release. I knew that if I were going to serve this sentence in peace, I had to concern myself with only one day at a time. I was grateful for doing what I considered soft time; I had child care and work release, which meant I would be out of the jail on house arrest for ten hours of each day Monday through Friday. I was also permitted to teach my theology classes twice a week at Marquette University. Since I was still nursing Joseph I had hoped to be on house arrest at least fourteen hours each day including weekends, but the extended time was denied.

As I took a look at my new surroundings, I was unsettled by feelings of resentment and apprehension. I wanted very much to do this prison sentence with a sense of serenity, but now that I was in the jail I felt an anger I did not expect. I was angry at the strip search, angry at the noise, especially angry that the matron showed me to an upper bunk right across from the guards' room and directly beneath a fluorescent ceiling light. It bathed my bunk in an intense brightness, and to make matters worse, it was never extinguished, even at night.

I lay awake late into the evening, staring into the blaring light above my face. I knew from my previous jail experiences that complete and utter surrender to the circumstances of incarceration and all its deprivations was the key to peace. I tried to enter into the heart of Christ. He had every right to protest the injustices done to Him, but instead He acted as if He had no rights and gave Himself over completely to the suffering laid upon Him. I knew I had to act as if I had no rights—no more liberty, no more expecting to sleep where I wanted, to wear what I wanted, to do what I wanted, to associate with whom I wanted, to hear what I wanted, or to see what I wanted.

This is not to say that I never took steps to ease the prison time. The next morning a prison matron whom I recognized from my previous stay was on duty. Her name was Miss Monroe and I knew her to be reasonable and fair. I noticed there were a few open bunks in less illuminated parts of the dormitory. I asked Miss Monroe if I could move, and she gave me permission. I asked friends to send me books and a Walkman with tapes of classical and spiritual music. Within a matter of weeks I had a tape of The Three Tenors and of Catholic singer and composer John Michael Talbot. John Broderick, a pro-life attorney from New York, sent me *War and Peace* and *Anna Karenina*. Fr. Paul Quay from Loyola University in Chicago sent me St. Augustine's *City of God*, and my friend Chris Le Blanc sent me a book on St. Augustine's use of metaphor, along with a commentary on modern art by E. Michael Jones entitled *Degenerate Moderns*. The jail did not permit inmates to bring in books themselves, so I had a local bookstore send me *City of Joy*, a story about a doctor's experiences in India, G. K. Chesterton's biography of St. Thomas Aquinas, and a biography of St. Francis of Assisi. The jail did permit inmates to bring in Bibles, prayer books and rosaries.

When I entered the Community Correctional Center I had been nursing Joseph around the clock, but now that I was gone he began to prefer the bottle to nursing. After ten days of being away from him, Joseph, despite my many efforts to encourage him, would no longer nurse at the breast. I mourned the loss of my closeness with him. The sentence had taken this precious mother-child intimacy from me. I was prepared to lose my liberty and the comforts of home, and endure certain humiliations and indignities, but I was not prepared for this. Like everything else, I had to surrender this as well. Joseph, on the other hand, appeared quite happy and well adjusted, and he apparently did not miss the nursing.

As was the case with my first incarceration, I was treated with a certain amount of respect by the other inmates. Many of them told me they were shocked that I was in jail for blocking the doors to an abortion clinic, and with a lengthier jail term than many of their own. On one particular day, a young woman named Olivia came up to me as I sat at a table and said, "I want you to know how much I respect you for what you did. I'm in here for messin' up, but you're in here for doin' somethin' good." It was always humbling to hear them say such things. Many of the guards were also sympathetic to me and openly told me they thought it was wrong for me to have been sent to jail.

Before I had ever served time in jail, I had always been perplexed by a certain episode in the Bible. When Christ was crucified, one of the thieves who hung on a cross near to Him recognized Jesus as an innocent man. I had always wondered how this "good thief" recognized Jesus' innocence. Did he know who Jesus was before he hung on a cross beside Him? Did someone tell him who Jesus was? I believe the thief did not need to be told. My personal experience showed me that criminals are simply able to detect when someone among them is not a criminal.

On the second day of my jail term, one of the inmates pointed me toward a young and very quiet prisoner. She said, "That's Randie. She used to work at an abortion clinic." She told me that Randie had worked at the Imperial Health Center for two years before Milton Tarver, the abortionist, fired her for credit card fraud. Convicted of that crime, she was now serving time. Many women who came to Imperial paid for their abortions with credit cards. Randie had access to their names and their card numbers and made purchases for herself. I was in jail for blocking the doors to an abortion clinic, and right across the room from me sat a woman who had worked at that very same clinic.

By the evening of that second day, I had gotten up enough courage to talk to Randie. I approached her bunk apprehensively. She was putting on a clean set of sheets the guards had passed out earlier that day.

"Hi, I'm Monica Miller." I tried to be as friendly as possible.

Randie looked up at me as she continued to make up her bunk. Her face was set like stone.

"Yeah, I know who you are. I recognized you."

Later that week, I wrote a letter from jail about the conversation I had with Randie:

> I spoke to her for about 10 minutes, but her whole attitude was cold, hard, and angry. She also seemed depressed, unhappy, sullen. But she did converse with me in her cold, angry way. She told me she worked there [at Tarver's clinic] two years and quit at the beginning of summer.
>
> I asked her how she felt about working there and she said "It was the woman's decision." I said "Your job involved you in taking innocent life." But she kept saying "I didn't do anything, it was the woman's decision." She admitted that she did assist Tarver in the abortions. I tried over and over again to help her realize her involvement with the process of killing. I asked her "Do you think the unborn are human?" and she agreed! She said, "Yes, they are. They have a heart, a brain and everything."
>
> I asked her "What if a woman was stabbing her born child—would you help her do that?" She said: "No" I asked her "Would it be okay for me to stab you just because it was 'my decision'?" She said: "That would be your decision and it would be my decision to live or die. People got to die anyway."
>
> I talked about how human life belonged to God, how human life is sacred. She has a Bible on her bed. I tried to impress on her that she participated in doing evil, that she participated in the killing of the innocent. She listened but continued to justify it all by saying, "It was their decision—we didn't force them to choose abortion."
>
> We ended the talk with her saying, "What about women who have miscarriages—is that their fault?" Of course, I pointed out the obvious. A miscarriage is not an abortion. Women who have miscarriages don't deliberately kill their babies—the babies die from natural causes and that many women mourn their deaths.
>
> I am not sure that anything I said will make any difference. Randie will be in here until Sept. 6 but she goes out for work

at 12:00 P.M. and doesn't come back until 1:00 A.M. and I am out for most of the day and we can't talk until after 11:00 P.M., so I won't really have too many opportunities to speak with her. . . . Please pray for her. . . .

Because I wasn't sure I would be able to talk to Randie again, I felt I had to get to the heart of the matter right away in my first conversation with her. I did have another opportunity to speak with her again the following evening, but she was just as icy and cold as before. "God wants you to be with Him, but, Randie, abortion involves the taking of human lives, the spilling of innocent blood."

"There ain't no blood on *my* hands," she retorted. "I used gloves."

Late that night, as I sat quietly on my upper bunk, I looked over at hers. Randie sat on it cross-legged, her Bible open in her lap. She seemed entirely recollected and absorbed. The noise of the inmates, the crude language and obscene words—the constant chaotic world of the jail—was not her world now. The ex-abortion worker was reading the Bible, alone in her bunk. I doubted that this had anything to do with what I had said to her, but it seemed clear that something spiritual was going on within her. As I watched her, I prayed for her.

One week later, a second ex-employee from Imperial Health Services arrived at the CCC. I was already surprised that one of Milton Tarver's workers was in jail with me—now I was amazed to learn that here was another! Her name was Patrice, serving time for retail theft. Unlike Randie, Patrice was at ease, open and friendly. She had only worked at Imperial for two months before quitting. She told me that she did not get along with Tarver, but she said that she sometimes assisted Tarver with the abortions. When Tarver told her that he was ready, Patrice said, "I flipped the switch on the suction machine."

She did not seem to be particularly concerned or regretful over her role in the abortions, but she agreed nonetheless to write a notarized affidavit that documented the abuses she had witnessed at the Imperial Health Center. In the affidavit she described Tarver's assembly-line approach to abortion. He shouted at the staff when they failed to fill the appointment times. With a woman lying on a table in each of his four procedure rooms, he would dash from one to the next. "Always in a hurry," Patrice described him. He did the abortions so fast that often there was not enough time for the anesthetic to take effect. In addition, Tarver did not give women their full dose of twilight sleep when they requested it, even though they were charged for the full dose. Because of his speedy surgical methods, fetal parts were often left in the woman, necessitating a re-suctioning later.

I made several copies of the affidavit and mailed it to the sidewalk counselors at Imperial, who in turn gave it to the women entering the clinic. While I was home on child-care release, the sidewalk counselors told me over the phone that at least two women did not go through with their abortions after reading it. I also sent a copy of the affidavit to the Wisconsin Medical Examining Board and requested an investigation of the clinic. Several weeks later I received a letter from the Board stating that it had declined an investigation since the complaint did not come from an actual patient.

Because this was a work-release jail, inmates were allowed to see doctors and schedule treatment on their own. One night an inmate named Rosilyn came up to me and said in a low voice, "Mary Harris—over there on that bunk—told me she is getting an abortion." Sitting upright, a blanket wrapped around her, sat a rather unkempt black woman with a blotchy complexion. I wasn't sure what to do with Rosilyn's information. To approach this woman would, of course, be extremely awkward. I climbed up to my bunk to think things over. Here was a woman, jailed with me, whose unborn child was also in the same room. I could not simply ignore Mary and her baby.

I gathered my courage and walked over to her. She was still sitting on her bunk, wrapped in her blanket. Her face was a blank mask, dull and foggy, like someone half-asleep. She had the look of someone who had seen a lot of abuse in her life. I stood by the bunk.

"Hi, Mary, I'm Monica."

She glanced up. "Hi."

I took the liberty of sitting on the edge of her bunk.

"I'm in jail because I blocked the door to an abortion clinic."

"Oh yeah?" she said, still staring blankly, emotionless.

"Yeah. What do you think about it? Abortion, I mean."

"I don't know. Guess I don't like it."

"How come?"

"Um, I guess if you make a baby you should take care of it."

"Yeah, me too. I feel the same way. So, you'd never have an abortion yourself?"

"Naw-uh, no."

"Good," I said. "You take care now."

"You too."

I got off the bunk, utterly confused. What was going on? Mary's anti-abortion attitude seemed spontaneous and genuine. I went back to Rosilyn.

"I talked to Mary. She said she was against abortion. Are you sure she told you she's getting one?

"Yes, yes. She told me she was getting one. She's going to get one."

I didn't know what to do. Either Mary was lying to Rosilyn, or Rosilyn was lying to me, or Mary was lying to me. But I knew that Rosilyn herself was very much against abortion; she had told me her feelings about abortion when she first learned why I was in jail. I trusted that she was telling me the truth, so, as awkward as it was, I decided to talk to Mary once more.

Again I crossed the carpeted floor to Mary's bunk. "Mary, um, you know if you ever need help with a problem pregnancy, I would help you."

"Okay."

"You're not considering an abortion, are you?"

"No," she responded confidently, without hesitation. "I ain't even pregnant."

There was nothing more for me to say or do. I thought perhaps Rosilyn must somehow have been mistaken. But two days later Rosilyn came up to me and said, "Mary had an abortion today."

"How do you know?" I asked, frustrated.

"She told me. Other inmates know about it."

I didn't know what to believe. I hoped Rosilyn was wrong. Whenever I saw Mary's sleepy face, I wondered what the truth was.

One week later Mary Harris, her sentence completed, was released from the Community Correctional Center. The day after she left, I returned from child-care release and stood in line by the guard's room, waiting to sign myself back into the jail. An inmate came up to me and handed me a tiny newspaper clipping. The little article stated:

> Woman Identified: The body of a 28-year-old woman found in a garbage bin was identified by police Wednesday. Mary Harris of Milwaukee was found dead Tuesday in the 2400 block of North 10th Street, Detective Lt. Raymond Sucik said. The woman was found by city sanitation workers. Police had no suspects and were continuing to investigate the incident.

On the day of her release, Mary was murdered and her body thrown into the trash. Like Mary's abortion, her death was a mystery. I never learned the circumstances of her killing, but the violence done to her filled me with sorrow. I had tried to save an unborn child that I wasn't even sure existed, not realizing it was Mary who needed to be saved from a similar fate.

* * *

The lower bunk directly to my right was occupied by a slender, blond and very pretty inmate named Jessica. Two years ago she and her boyfriend Jay, desperate for drug money, held up a convenience store with a toy pistol. They had a child out of wedlock named Anthony. Jessica, recovering from her addiction, left Jay and married another man who adopted Anthony as his own. By the time she entered the Community Correctional Center, Jessica was making a real attempt to get her life back together. She was also pregnant with her second child.

Jessica told me that when she was fourteen years old she had had an abortion at Milton Tarver's abortion center and that she regretted it deeply. Jessica told me that she received absolutely no counseling at Tarver's clinic. She also said that she told Tarver she was unsure about getting the abortion, but felt pressured into it by her boyfriend, who was with her. "The people at that place treated me like I was nothing. It was obvious I was really upset about this—the abortion, I mean—but that didn't seem to matter to them." I had hoped Jessica would file a complaint with the Wisconsin Medical Examining Board to support Patrice's affidavit, but she said that doing so would bring back too many painful memories.

"You have no idea how much I hate that man," she said of Tarver, "but I can't take the stress, Monica, I just can't. I'm sorry."

Jessica was seeing Dr. Allen Babbitz for the child she now carried. Babbitz was a former abortionist; during the 1980s he worked at the Milwaukee Women's Health Organization and at the Summit Women's Health Organization with his partners Paul Burstein and David Nash. Babbitz, dressed in surgical greens, would often walk across the street from Mt. Sinai Hospital, where he was on staff, over to Elinor Yeo's abortion clinic. Babbitz and his partners agreed to stop doing abortions when St. Mary's, a Catholic hospital, wooed them over to their facility in the hope of benefiting from their extensive obstetrical practice. The fact that a Catholic hospital had hired three abortionists, offering them full benefits and privileges, caused a great scandal. The hospital justified their offer because, as part of the deal, the doctors had to quit doing abortions.

One night I returned from child-care release to find Jessica seated on the floor at the farthest end of the dormitory. Several other inmates were crowded around her. The conversation was loud and lively, and Jessica seemed particularly tense and agitated. I walked over to see what was going on. As soon as Jessica saw me

she blurted out, "Oh Monica, Dr. Babbitz told me my baby might
have Down's syndrome. I can't believe this is happening!"

Dr. Babbitz had informed Jessica of the results of an alpha feto-
protein test, which is used to determine fetal abnormalities. Because
of her own experience with Tarver, Jessica was opposed to abortion,
but she was confused now about what to do. Babbitz suggested that
labor be induced in the fifth month of gestation. The baby would be
born too prematurely for any effective life-saving procedures. The
baby, in short, would simply be left to die. Pro-lifers referred to
this as the "induce-and-let-die" abortion, although it more closely
resembles post-natal infanticide. Several years later, Jill Stanek, a
labor and delivery nurse at Christ Hospital in Illinois, would lead a
movement to have such procedures banned. She was compelled to
speak out when a Down's syndrome baby at five-months gestational
age was forcibly expelled from the womb and placed in a closet to
die amongst the soiled linens. She held the tiny life until he gasped
his last breath. In 2002, President George W. Bush signed into law
the Born-Alive Infants Protection Act outlawing the practice.

Later that evening, as Jessica lay awake on her bunk, I told
her, "Jessica, what Babbitz is proposing is just abortion without the
name." I pleaded with her to reject the procedure. Jessica flew into a
rage. "You don't get it, do you, Monica? I know you're pro-life and
all, but this induced labor will spare my child a life of suffering!"

Jessica's attitude toward me turned cold. Two horrible days
went by, and though her bunk was right next to mine, Jessica did
not speak to me. On the evening of the third day, when I returned
to jail from my child-care release, the captain of the prison, a burly
red-haired man, immediately called me into the guard room.

"I have received a complaint from Jessica that you are harassing
her about her private decisions," he said. "I'm giving you a warning that if she complains again you'll be sent to Franklin and your
child-care privileges will be revoked."

Franklin was the main Milwaukee County prison just south of
the city. The last place someone in the Community Correctional
Center wanted to go was Franklin. I was devastated that Jessica

had made a complaint about me. I had befriended Jessica. I had listened to her talk in detail for hours about the tests she was going through and all her fears about her baby. I felt trapped. If I never said anything to Jessica again about her decision, a baby's life might be lost, and if I did, I risked losing the ability to care for my own children. I was angry with the captain's lack of concern for the life of Jessica's child.

"You know," I said to him, "Jessica is going to kill her baby. Is that what you want her to do?"

"That's her business, and you've had your warning," he snapped impatiently.

"I have to follow my conscience," I said. "I'll talk to her if I feel the need to."

"Then you're going to Franklin."

"A baby's life is at stake. Don't you care?"

"It's not up to me to care."

"You should care."

"It's not my business."

And with those words the captain opened the door to the guards' room and motioned for me to leave.

I did have an option. Jessica had been in the Franklin jail two years earlier when she was pregnant with her son Anthony. While there she had been befriended by two pro-life women, Susan Day and Maura Heiss, members of Matt Trewhella's Missionaries to the Preborn, who had been jailed for a sit-in at a local clinic. Susan and Maura still kept in touch with Jessica, and while Jessica was home for child care they could easily call or even visit her. I called Susan from the jail phone. In desperate tones I explained my predicament and that I needed her and Maura to intervene. Susan assured me that they would visit Jessica and speak with her.

A week went by and Jessica still did not speak to me. I knew, however, that she was in contact with Susan and Maura, and I prayed daily for her and her baby. One night, while I was sitting on my bunk, Jessica lay on hers with her hands cupped behind her head. Suddenly, breaking her silence, she said to me, "I'm having a baby girl, Monica. I've had a lot of ultrasounds and she might have Down's syndrome. But I know I can love this baby, Monica. I love this baby now. I know God's in the middle of all this and that this baby might have Down's syndrome for a reason. I know I have to trust God."

All the tension and worry instantly fell away like a heavy pack that suddenly falls when the straps are cut. I listened silently while she spoke, but my spirit erupted in prayer, in a litany of gratitude to God that Jessica accepted her baby. In the weeks that followed, I gave Jessica all the support I could and always made myself available to listen to her. She decided to name the baby Madelyn.

When Jessica's due date was upon her, a judge permitted her to complete her sentence on house arrest. When the baby was born, there was more than the usual cause for rejoicing. Little Madelyn was a beautiful, healthy baby. She did not have Down's syndrome after all.

Jessica's temptation to abort her baby and my deep concern for her made my jail experience even more stressful than it otherwise would have been. The jail environment itself was, of course, very stressful and oppressive.

Because this was a work-release jail, we were strip-searched every time we returned from work or child care. It was a most humiliating procedure, and I dreaded it. But six weeks into my sentence, I found I had something else to dread. I was informed by Miss Holloway that I would have to "drop." This meant going into the bathroom with the matron and urinating into a cup while she watched. These "drops," as they were called, were necessary for the purpose of running a drug check. The matron watched to ensure that the inmate did not tamper with the sample. Any inmate in the work-release jail who had drugs or alcohol in her system would have her work-release or child-care privileges revoked and she would be sent to Franklin.

How I wished I could have simply rebelled against it all. How I wished I could refuse to cooperate with the rules and demands of the prison. I knew I was not guilty of any crime, and I felt that this whole experience was unjust. I held on to a fellow protestor in defense of the unborn. I wished, for the sake of continuing my witness to the humanity of the unborn, that I could stand up to the jail system that claimed me to be guilty for doing what was right. I sat in the prison day-room and held the small plastic urine cup that Miss Holloway had just handed me. As I waited, dreading her summons to the bathroom, I thought about Joan Andrews.

When Joan Andrews was in Broward federal prison in Florida, she did not cooperate with the demands of the prison system. At Broward, Joan never consented to strip searches, urine drops, or even being fingerprinted. Once, when Joan was being transferred from one prison to another, guards tried to subject her to a strip search. She refused to comply. In a letter Joan wrote to her sister, she described her experience:

> What occurred was a very bad forced strip search with a male officer and about five female officers. The female officers could have handled it, as the two did when they handcuffed me to the bars. As soon as I showed passive resistance here, to the extent of merely clutching my clothing about myself, the male officer said I was asking for it. With that he and the others managed to pull or tear off my clothes (the male officer cut off some with scissors) . . . [S]ince it is well known I am a non-violent pacifist, they knew I did not carry any concealed weapons on me. They knew I was clean in every way.
> Susan, I wasn't hurt except for a few bruises and lacerations . . . [but] emotionally I feel as though I went through an attempted rape with all the brutality and degradation . . . [E]xperiencing it, despite the clarity of dread beforehand, had a powerful, radical influence on me . . . it brought home to me even more clearly the dehumanizing attacks on the dignity of the prenatal children, the newborn handicapped, and the elderly or infirm "unwanted." And because of this I realized that my non-cooperation must entail accepting nothing from the prison, no care beyond the bare necessity to maintain life. I will eat . . . enough to stay alive, but I'll accept no other things beyond one set of clothing for my body . . . I will not

accept the comfort of mail via the prison. I will not accept paper and envelopes, except to write the family and when I have a need to write to Father Cusack, my spiritual advisor.

As I sat there with the cup in hand, I yearned to give the kind of witness Joan had given. I thought: "If more pro-lifers refused to cooperate the way Joan did, perhaps legalized abortion would come to an end." Yet I cooperated. I now had two small children. I was no longer the young, carefree college student I had been when I first participated in clinic blockades. I cooperated so I could care for those who now depended on me. I found some spiritual solace in the cooperation. I tried to give myself over to the deprivations and indignities in the spirit of Christ who allowed himself to be put to death. I hated the injustice, but I tried to endure it for His sake.

One evening as I lay on my bunk listening to a tape of *The Three Tenors*, an inmate tapped me on the leg to get my attention. Her name was Amelia—in jail for prostitution. "Hey, Monica—you got any of them pictures of the dead babies—somebody wants to see them."

I had brought with me some of the photographs that Edmund and I had taken of the aborted babies we found in the trash. If I were in a conversation with an inmate about abortion, I sometimes took them out of my locker to show her the reality of abortion. It became known among the prison population that I had the photos.

After I got them out of my locker, Amelia escorted me to the woman's bunk. I sat down on the floor, opened the envelope and started sharing the photos. Soon a small crowd of curious inmates gathered around.

One of the women was Carmen, a handsome, Hispanic, twenty-one-year-old cocaine addict. She sat on the floor across from me. Carmen had had nine pregnancies since the age of fourteen. She was pregnant with her ninth child now. Of those nine pregnancies, six of them ended in abortion. Carmen had more abortions than any woman I had known. The photos passed from the hands of one inmate to another and finally into her hands. She was utterly dumbfounded when she saw the pictures. Captivated by the obvious humanity of the children she shook her head back and forth.

"I'm a killer," she said, "I'm nothing but a killer. These are real babies!"

I did not expect Carmen's immediate and honest reaction to the photos. Undoubtedly, she really didn't know the truth about the humanity of the unborn child until this very moment.

The images then passed to Camille. She was a large, tough, quick-witted black woman who was also a cocaine addict. Although she was a lesbian, Camille conceived a child while drunk at a party. Her daughter, whom she cherished, was now two years old. Camille stared at the photos, stunned by what she saw. The graphic images of the broken bodies shocked her into new depths of reality and emotion. Her feelings were frozen by the tragedy the broken, twisted bodies had caused her to penetrate.

I knew this feeling. Many years ago, when I first saw the photos of aborted babies in the "Life or Death" brochure, I went into a kind of shock. My emotions were frozen as I was utterly unprepared for the horror and sorrow that the crushed bodies revealed to me. It is the reaction of that last pure part of the soul confronted by the desecration of the holy—a desecration beyond what one can imagine.

Yet these unspeakable, unimaginable crimes took place and continue to take place. They are part of a terrible truth, as if a veil has been torn away to expose a glimpse of Hell. The sight makes us tremble and weep, and the shock solidifies within us a great, absolute "No," as we refuse to be part of this terrible darkness. Our being is filled with a resolve to stand against it. Nothing in this glimpse of Hell can be right, and the evil of it all is incarnated in broken bodies that cry to you for justice. Once you see the bodies with the right mind, you can never go back. They have taken you into their world.

In 1987, after I had helped retrieve the bodies of the aborted babies from the alley behind the Michigan Avenue Medical Center, I would occasionally shudder spontaneously if I saw a trash bag standing upright and tied at the top or if I happened to walk down the street and pass by a trash dumpster. On a few occasions I would shudder if I passed a building—usually low, modern and non-descript—that reminded me of an abortion clinic.

I think I was experiencing, in a very mild form, what a soldier back from war might experience when reminded of the atrocities he saw on the field of battle. Certain sights, certain sounds, even certain smells transport me back to the dark nights when we came face-to-face with the unwanted, aborted unborn. If I see a baby's foot cocked in a certain position, I recall the foot of one of the aborted babies we had photographed. If I see a baby's hand held up in just a certain way, the hand of one of the aborted babies comes to mind. When Edmund and I brought our tiny newborn daughter Bernadette home from St. Mary's hospital for the first time and laid her on our bed, I looked at her small clear eyes. But then I thought to myself, "I have seen other eyes"—eyes out of their sockets floating free.

The inmates gathered around me to see the pictures. Truth was unleashed without a single obstacle in the way of its bursting forth. Very rarely have I ever seen such quick, sure, and honest human response to the reality of abortion as these women about me expressed.

After several minutes I put the photos back in my locker and returned to my bunk. I lay down and closed my eyes knowing God moved in the room. I felt for my Walkman and put the headphones over my ears. The strains of *Nessun Dorma* entered my head and carried me away.

CHAPTER NINETEEN

TO MARVEL AT THE FIREFLIES

"The nonviolent resister not only refuses to shoot his opponent but he also refuses to hate him."
—Martin Luther King, Jr., *Stride Toward Freedom*

MY ALARM clock rang on Friday, August 20, 1993, at its usual time and I began to stir slowly from my bunk. I put on my shoes and hoped that a bathroom would be free. I had been in the jail just over a month and was becoming used to the environment and the routine of jail life. Mylissa, an inmate with a reputation for being cocky and outspoken, came to my bunk. She was serving an eighteen-month sentence for a third drunk driving conviction.

"Hey Monica, did ya hear? An abortionist got shot last night."

"What?" I asked, startled. "Who? Which abortionist?"

"I dunno," she replied, turning to walk away. "I think in Kansas someplace."

When I arrived home for child care I called the Missionaries to the Preborn to find out what happened. At 3:00 p.m. on August 19, three pro-lifers stood outside the Wichita, Kansas clinic operated by Dr. George Tiller, an abortionist who specialized in third-trimester abortions. Two of them were sidewalk counselors, and the third was a picketer. A woman approached who said her name was Ann. She said that she was not pro-life. One of the sidewalk counselors said she had an intense expression in her eyes, and thought that perhaps she had had an abortion at Tiller's clinic and was going to vent her anger, as sometimes happened, against the pro-lifers outside.

At 7:00 p.m., Tiller, having completed his abortions for the day, drove slowly out of the clinic parking lot. As one of the sidewalk counselors tried to hand him a pro-life pamphlet, Ann approached suddenly with a pistol and shot at Tiller four times, blowing out the glass of the driver's side window. The bullets struck Tiller's arms, but he was not seriously wounded. It was not clear if Ann, whose real name was Shelly Shannon, had attempted to kill him or to wound him so that he would not be able to perform abortions.*

When I first heard the news, I became frustrated and angry. This was not the first time an opponent of abortion had attacked an abortionist. Earlier that year, on March 10, Michael Griffin, a newcomer to the pro-life movement, shot and killed circuit-rider abortionist David Gunn at Pensacola Medical Services clinic. Gunn performed abortions at two Alabama clinics, a clinic in Georgia, and two in Florida. A small group of protesters, led by local pro-life leader John Burt, were picketing in front of the clinic as usual. As Gunn walked toward the building from the rear parking lot, Griffin approached Gunn and told him not to kill unborn children that day. Gunn brushed Griffin aside and continued toward the clinic. Griffin shot him three times in the back.

When news of Gunn's murder erupted in the media, I was torn and confused over the morality of such actions. The killing of abortionists by pro-lifers was unprecedented, but killing in defense of life was not. I tried to evaluate the taking of human life in defense of oneself or others according to the moral tradition of the Catholic

---

* Shelly Shannon's shooting of Tiller would only be the first act in a two part drama that, seventeen years later, would eventually claim the abortionist's life. On a Sunday morning, May 31, 2009, Scott Roeder stood in the rear of Reformation Lutheran Church—the church attended by Tiller. Described as having an "eye-for-eye hatred of abortionists," Roeder shot Tiller dead in the middle of the Sunday service.

Church. At least, academically speaking, I began to conclude that the use of force against anyone who attacked innocent human life could not be condemned on the basis that it was *intrinsically* immoral. As a budding theologian, I insisted that critical thinking be applied to this issue as any other moral issue.

I believe that the tragedy of abortion can only ultimately be resolved through non-violence. Nonetheless, my first musings on the subject were hasty and imprudent. During my sentencing hearing I told Schudson that I believed the use of force in defense of the unborn was not necessarily immoral, yet I was also very clear that such violence should not be used, violent acts would not bring an end to abortion, would not persuade women to turn away from abortion, and that only acts of self-sacrifice in the pattern of Christ were the real answer to the slaughter of the unborn. Many activist leaders, however, believed that the use of force against an abortionist was justified, assuming that the killer acted in the defense of life—and in the wake of the Griffin shooting, they were swift to express that view to the media. The ambivalence some pro-life leaders expressed about the shootings was rooted in anger and frustration, and in some cases an inability to think critically through the moral issues involved. Many pro-lifers were angry that the media swiftly condemned the killing of Gunn, while the millions of lives lost to abortion were deemed worthless and insignificant.

One of those who defended Michael Griffin's actions was Paul Hill, a Presbyterian minister in Pensacola. In the wake of the Gunn murder, Hill, who frequently picketed the Ladies' Center abortion clinic, founded a letterhead group called Defensive Action. He drafted a statement and gathered signatures in support of it. It read:

> We, the undersigned, declare the justice of taking all Godly action necessary to defend innocent human life including the use of force.
>
> We proclaim that whatever force is legitimate to defend the life of a born child is legitimate to defend the life of an unborn child.

> We assert that if Michael Griffin did in fact kill David Gunn, his use of lethal force was justifiable provided it was carried out for the purpose of defending the lives of unborn children. Therefore, he ought to be acquitted of the charges against him.

The statement was signed by twenty-four people including Matt Trewhella, Andrew Burnett, Paul deParrie and Cathy Ramey of *Life Advocate* magazine. Roy C. McMillan, an activist in Jackson, Mississippi, and husband of ex-abortionist, Beverly McMillan, was also a signer. At the top of the list was Michael Bray who had been convicted in 1985 for his part in the bombings of Washington, D.C., abortion clinics. One Catholic priest signed the statement: Fr. Thomas Carleton, who was serving several months in a Massachusetts jail for blocking the door to an abortion clinic.

Joe Foreman helped Paul Hill compose the statement. In the end, however, Joe decided he could not put his name on the final version. He informed me about the statement when it was being initially drafted and I asked him for Paul Hill's phone number. I wanted to talk Paul out of issuing the document. I was particularly troubled by Hill's statement that "all Godly action necessary" could be used to defend the unborn. What did such a statement mean? The greatest weapon pro-lifers' possess to prevent abortion and to convert hearts and minds, I believe, is living a life of nonviolent self-sacrifice according to the teachings of Christ's Beatitudes, and this statement neglected that.

While home on child care release, I called Paul Hill. He was extremely polite and very open to discussing his views. In his pleasant, Southern accent, he said, "'All Godly action' means whatever can be justified biblically and the Bible reveals to us that God does not forbid the taking of lives of people who commit murder. Indeed, God made a covenant with Noah and tells him that 'Whosoever sheds man's blood, by man shall his blood be shed for in God's image was man made.'"

"But Paul," I argued, "Christ also gave us the Beatitudes.

Putting the Beatitudes into action to save the unborn—those are our weapons."

"Do you have any children, Monica?" he asked.

"Yes, two so far."

"Well, wouldn't you use force against an aggressor to defend them if they were attacked?"

"Yes, I would, but the systematic killing of the unborn is different. How do we even know that the unborn will be saved by shooting the abortionist? We can save babies other ways, like the rescues and sidewalk counseling. Even picketing can save lives!"

"I think the Bible is clear that deadly force can be used to defend our lives or the lives of our neighbors. When I say 'all Godly action can be used,' that's part of the Godly action. It's a question of our responsibility toward our neighbor. I think it's wrong to say that we would defend our own children against being attacked by shooting the attacker, but that somehow this same defense is not allowed for the unborn. They are people as precious as our own children."

"Okay Paul, you say that killing an abortionist is justified, but don't you have any doubts about your position?"

"Well, Monica, just because something is justified does not mean it's necessarily the wise thing to do. I don't do it, for instance, because it wouldn't be wise."

"Okay—good, tell me how it's not wise?" I asked.

"Well, there's lots of things to consider. You know that if you do use force against an abortionist, for instance, you'll suffer in prison and there might be others who are dependant on you and also you'd be taken away from doing pro-life work—things like that."

"Well, Paul, maybe we should consider the harm to the movement. And besides, Christian ethics requires that if we can defend life short of killing the unjust aggressor, even in defending our own children, we have to use those methods. There are lots of practical and effective ways to defend the unborn without resorting to violence. We disagree, morally and politically, and I hope you'll not circulate your statement. I think it can be shown that just as many babies are saved from abortion by someone who sidewalk counsels outside a clinic as by what Michael Griffin did." Before the conversation ended, Paul emphasized that he picketed outside the Florida clinic every week and would continue to do so, but felt strongly that Michael Griffin's action needed to be defended.

Sixteen months later Paul Hill must have overcome his belief that using force was unwise. On July 29, 1994, he shot abortionist John Britton and Britton's bodyguard James Barrett to death with a shotgun as they arrived at the Ladies' Center. He also wounded Barrett's wife. Hill acted as his own attorney during his murder trial, and asked the judge for a defense of necessity but it was denied. Hill, therefore, chose not to try to defend himself on mere legal technicalities. He was convicted and sentenced to death, and on September 3, 2003, the State of Florida executed him by lethal injection. At his sentencing hearing he told the jury which was to decide his fate: "You may mix my blood with that of the innocent unborn."

In February, 1993, one month before Michael Griffin's killing of Gunn, a bill was introduced in the House of Representatives by Congressmen Charles Schumer of New York and Constance Morella of Maryland. Originally it was called the Access to Clinic Entrances Act but was finally named the Freedom of Access to Clinic Entrances Act, or the FACE act. Senator Edward Kennedy introduced a similar bill in the Senate one month later.

The new federal legislation did not appear overnight and was not designed as a response to the lethal attacks against abortionists. For months abortion advocates had been looking for a way to halt what had come to be called the rescue movement. An April 1993 news release from the National Abortion Federation, issued just before the hearings on the bill, stated: "The members of NAF called upon Congress to provide federal protection for abortion providers and women who seek their services." Attached to the press release was a NAF survey, "Incidence of violence and disruption against abortion providers." The survey included peaceful blockades of clinic doors and even constitutionally-protected picketing. Picketing was listed under the section entitled "Disruption," which also included "hate mail, phone calls, and bomb threats."

FACE was introduced to suppress the rescue movement. But the killing of David Gunn provided already eager pro-abortion politicians with a powerful excuse to quash what they perceived to be harassment of abortion doctors.

In April, 1993, the Judiciary's Subcommittee on Crime and Criminal Justice held hearings on the FACE bill. Among the pro-lifers who testified against it were Randall Terry, Joe Foreman, Jeff White of Operation Rescue: California, and Joan Appleton. Prior to her conversion to the pro-life position, Joan had been the director of Commonwealth Women's Clinic in Falls Church, Virginia. She testified that when rescues occurred at her clinic, the National Organization for Women sent women there who, for the benefit of the media, passed themselves off as customers and pretended to be emotionally upset at the pro-lifers' presence.

Several clinic workers testified before the Subcommittee. One was Jeri Rasmussen, the director of the Midwest Health Center in Minneapolis. She told members of Congress: "I hope to make real for you what it is like to go to work in the morning and not know if you will make it home at night. And, when you are home, to know that the latter-day Ku Klux Klan has plans for you."

Rasmussen described in detail how pro-lifers picketed her home and circulated a flyer in her neighborhood which she said contained "misinformation" on how she "regulary 'killed/murdered babies'" and which invited anyone to "visit, call, write, or pray for me at my home or clinic." She told the Subcommittee how this activity invaded her "very precious privacy" and how even though she sought and obtained ordinances against the picketing of her home, she was still exceptionally frustrated that the pro-lifers managed to get around the law. She insinuated that federal legislation was needed to protect her and other abortion providers from harassment. Rasmussen told of the phone call she received at 1:10 a.m. from someone who warned her "not to kill babies." Then at 7:00 a.m. that same morning, a hunk from a cement block came flying through her dining room window with a note again telling her "not to kill babies." She lamented how she was forced to change her life; afraid to walk alone anymore for fear that she was being followed, for fear that if she was in trouble no one would be able to hear her call out. Near the end of her speech, Rasmussen said: "We need the Congress of the United States to say no to these domestic terrorists. I am no longer free to enjoy a nightly walk in the summer, to hear the frogs and the crickets and marvel at the fireflies that twinkle on my path."

On May 26, 1994, President Bill Clinton signed the FACE bill into law. The language of the bill was sweeping and unprecedented:

> Whoever by force or threat of force or by physical obstruction, intentionally injures, intimidates or interferes with or attempts to injure, intimidate or interfere with any person because that person is or has been, or in order to intimidate such person or any other person or any class of persons, from obtaining or providing reproductive health services . . . shall be subject to penalties provided in subsection (b).

The penalty for the first conviction was to be an unspecified fine, imprisonment for not more than one year, or both. Upon a second conviction, the penalty would be increased to no more than three years, an unspecified fine, or both. In its very next section, the FACE bill specifically addresses the penalties for "an offense involving a non-violent physical obstruction." It called for imprisonment up to six months, a fine of not more than ten thousand dollars, or both. The penalty for a second conviction is a jail term of up to eighteen months, a fine of not more than twenty-five thousand dollars, or both. A federal conviction that carries a possible eighteen-month jail sentence is a felony. Now, any pro-lifer convicted of violating FACE more than once would be considered a felon. In addition to the criminal penalties under FACE, abortion clinics could bring civil action against activists with statutory damages of five thousand dollars, triple punitive damages, and injunctive relief.

The law even empowered the Attorney General of the United States to sue pro-lifers who violated the FACE law. In this way, a law that so many legislators said was necessary to prevent violence at clinics, also targeted nonviolent pro-life activists.

FACE, buttressed by the growing imposition of local injunctions, had a swift and devastating effect on pro-life activism. Indeed, a curtain was falling on the pro-life rescue movement—a movement I had been involved in from nearly the beginning, ever since my first arrest at Concord in 1978. Just a few years after FACE became law, the pro-life sit-in movement, in which thousands had participated, essentially dissolved. A bold era in the abortion war was over. Prior to FACE, those who blocked the doors to an abortion clinic usually could expect to receive a city ticket, or at most, a state charge of trespass or disorderly conduct, just like any other protester in any other cause. Now the stakes were much higher. The prospect of spending several months in federal prison was too daunting for the majority of pro-life activists who otherwise would have continued to participate in nonviolent clinic blockades and protests. Even the *New York Times* acknowledged that the new law threatened pro-lifers with severe penalties. The May 12, 1994, edition stated:

> The bill levies Federal prison terms and heavy fines against anti-abortion demonstrators for some non-violent acts—like staging sit-ins and chaining protestors to doorways—that carry mild local or state punishment when any other protest movement employs them.
>
> That provision led opponents today to accuse the measure's more liberal supporters—backers of social protests like the lunch-counter sit-ins of the 1960s civil rights groups—of hypocrisy.

When FACE was first passed in Congress in January of 1994, I sent out a press release which pointed out the discriminatory character of this legislation.

> No other persons who are involved with protests or who use the sit-in or blockade method of redress for injustices are punished by federal penalty as are pro-lifers. The law is blatantly discriminatory. Furthermore, its broad language will place a burden on the free speech rights of pro-life picketers. . . .
>
> Today congressional tyranny has ushered in an age of persecution against those who merely place their own bodies between the abortionist and his unborn victims. If pro-lifers can be turned into felons, those involved with Gay Rights, Animal Welfare, Anti-War, Civil Rights, and Labor had better watch out. They could very well be next.

Other protest groups active in the early nineties who were much more violent than pro-lifers received no special federal attention. In 1992, "ecological terrorists" sabotaged logging operations in the North Woods by damaging logging equipment. According to an Associated Press story, they "punched holes in the radiators of two skidders and dropped BBs and bolts into the $75,000 machines. They removed a transmission line, filled it with compound used for grinding metal, wiped it clean and carefully replaced it." Some activists set fires to department stores that sold fur. Some chained themselves to trees or drove metal spikes into the trees to damage the chainsaws. In December, 1999, a peaceful protest at a meeting of the World Trade Organization in Seattle was interrupted by several environmentalists and anarchists who blocked streets, smashed windows, and set fires. Police cleared the streets with tear gas, pepper gas and rubber bullets, and the National Guard was deployed—but legislation specifically targeting this particular species of "domestic terrorist" never materialized.

With the virtual end of the rescue movement, important pro-life activism was continued by Helpers of God's Precious Infants, 40 Days for Life, Jack Ames' Defend Life, Lila Rose's Live Action, Mark Harrington's Created Equal, Pro-life Action Ministries and similar organizations, including Joe Scheidler's Pro-life Action League. Even Operation Rescue, the Center for Bio-Ethical

Reform, Missionaries to the Pre-born, and my own Citizens for a Pro-life Society carry on opposition to abortion within the boundaries of the legal system as we continue sidewalk counseling, public demonstrations, pickets, educational programs, promotion of pro-life legislation and political candidates, and using the law itself to go after illegal abortion clinic practices.

Only occasionally will pro-lifers risk arrest in organized acts of civil disobedience. A notable example are the Notre Dame 88, pro-lifers including myself, Randall Terry and Joan Andrews Bell, who were arrested protesting Barack Obama's commencement speech at the University of Notre Dame in May 2009. In the twenty-first century, projects like Face the Truth Tours have become a common feature of pro-life activism—in which the poster-size photos of aborted unborn children are displayed along busy intersections. In a response to the needs of women in crisis pregnancies, pro-lifers continued to set up centers to provide help to such women who would otherwise be tempted to seek abortion. Many college-aged pro-lifers pour themselves into politics, working hard to elect pro-life candidates.

Yet even with the clinic blockade movement at a stand-still, advocates of legal abortion have sought to curtail pro-life activism that stayed within the law—enacting buffer-zones around abortion clinics, such as the 2009 Chicago ordinance that forbids sidewalk counselors from being within eight feet of a woman entering an abortion clinic. Other laws have sought to blunt the effectiveness of pro-life crisis pregnancy centers, as in Baltimore where such centers are forced to post signs indicating that they do not offer abortions or make abortion referrals. New York City council members passed such an ordinance in early 2011 against Chris Slattery's Expectant Mother Care centers. Pro-lifers complained that abortion clinics were not similarly required to post services that they did not provide—such as adoption counseling and referrals.

Since 1994, a few rescues have taken place, notably in Philadelphia, which always had a strong activist presence. Linda Gibbons, the well-known Canadian activist, continues her one-woman violation of a Toronto buffer-zone law—which has caused her to be consistently in and out of jail for the last sixteen years. In 2009 a religious congregation was founded in New York called the Order of Mercy at Gethsemane. Its few members are willing, as stated in the order's rule: "to absorb some measure of the cruelty and injustice inflicted on the young unborn. Thus, putting themselves on the side of the outcast they place their bodies before the doors of abortion clinics in solidarity with the unborn about to be aborted. In 2009, the group's founder, Richard Cowden Guido, spent several weeks in jail for what he intended as a personal act of self-immolation on behalf of the outcast victims of abortion. In this way a delicate flame of the rescue movement continues to glow—however faintly.

*   *   *

A month before my release date I sat down to write a letter to Judge Schudson. He was now an appellate court judge and Jeffery Kremers was no longer an attorney in private practice. Wisconsin governor Tommy Thompson had appointed him to a Circuit Court judgeship. In September, 2008, Kremers would reach the prestigious position of chief judge of Milwaukee County.

I told Schudson about the many women in the jail whose lives had crossed mine, about Patrice and Randie and the many women who had confided in me about their abortions. I told him about Kathy, in jail for drunk driving, who occupied the bunk to my right. She had had a baby at sixteen and given it up for adoption and at eighteen she became pregnant again. This time her parents decided she would have an abortion and her father took her "to some woman's house" where she was given pills and with terrible pain birthed a dead four-month old unborn baby into the toilet. She looked at the baby and saw it was a boy. I told Schudson that it was twenty-four years since Kathy had her abortion—how she had confided in me with tears down her face, "I'm even in this jail now because of that abortion—because I'm depressed and I drink."

I then turned my attention to the babies.

I wonder, Judge Schudson, if you will ever really come to understand about the babies. I still have some hope left that you will. But it seems when their dead bodies were presented to you this turned out only to be an occasion for you to wax poetic. In the end your political views obscured the injustice of abortion. Choice—that hideous choice. What kind of world can be founded on a woman's choice, codified by law, to reject her own child? Only a very ugly world. The world of the dead unborn is your world as long as you believe abortion is a right. But this world has nothing to do with real democracy or tolerance. I think it was Abraham Lincoln who said about slavery, "No law can give the right to do what is wrong. The foundation of a free people rests on the nobility of their moral action. . . ."

Some things in life can stir our souls and bring us back to the basic meaning of things. A while ago I heard reports on the radio from Somalia about a soldier's dead body being dragged through the street. I wanted to shut my mind to the thought of it. . . . I happened to see the cover of *Time* magazine with an American soldier's face from Somalia lined with blood and fear on the front cover. I looked at the magazine and inside I saw the soldier's corpse dragged through the streets, dirty, full of open gashes, and bloated-looking. He was tied by his hands and feet. He was surrounded on all sides by jeering, mocking, hostile faces. An old man held up a cane beating the dead body. I knew nothing about this soldier. I knew nothing about his life, his sins or his goodness, but that did not matter. He was another human being, not only dead but encircled by not a single sympathetic eye. His mockers showed how out of relation they were to him.

The soldier's mutilated body transported me back to the dark alleys and loading docks where we retrieved the abandoned unborn. The soldier and the babies look similar. In the naked soldier and the outcast unborn one sees the assault on everything noble, the desecration of all that is sacred, the dissolution of the world. . . .

I have prayed for you and Judge Kremers. I know that according to any objective and real moral standard I am not a criminal and am suffering an injustice. But sometimes being a Christian means going to jail. I hope to be a good influence on the inmates here.

You called me a dangerous person. God should be praised. Perhaps I am.

CHAPTER TWENTY

REQUIEM

"There is no God who condones the taking of an innocent human life. This much we know."
—Barack Obama

"Are memories now so brief," he said,
"And conscience so defiled?"
"Don't you know me as your son?"
"I'm home" said the Holocaust child.
—Nancy Murray

I REMEMBER her face. I remember everything about the woman—her light brown skin, her dark brown eyes, the way she hung her head and tried to fight back her tears. It was a cold October morning outside of the Summit Women's Health Organization. Her boyfriend had just dropped her off at the corner of 6th and Wisconsin, at the foot of a tall office building in downtown Milwaukee.

"I've got to do it," she said. "I know it's wrong, but I *got* to."

"But, Carolyn, you see this picture of what abortion will do to your baby. You know this is a human life, a human being, your own child. Please, let me help you."

The street corner was busy with people hurrying to and fro, and the noise of the traffic competed with the sound of our voices. The world around us was oblivious to the life-and-death struggle playing out on this grey city street. Carolyn started anxiously toward the heavy glass revolving doors, and I followed after her, still pleading.

"Carolyn, at least give yourself one more day to think it over. Your baby's worth at least one more day."

"That's true," she replied, still walking toward the building.

"Come on, Carolyn. Come with me. Let's get a cup of coffee and we'll talk."

But her hand was already on the door. "I'll read your pamphlet. I'll think it over while I'm up there."

In another instant she was inside the building, her figure blending into the darkness of the lobby. I called after her, but she was gone.

So close. She was listening to me. She even told me her name. She had taken my literature. She seemed hesitant to confirm her choice—but in the end she walked through the doors and disappeared. Another loss. Another tragedy. I would feel regret and sorrow for days afterward. And I would mourn for the loss of her baby.

Somehow, almost inexplicably, I missed her child. How could I miss a person never born? I didn't know this life, nor the millions of others who perished in abortion. I did not have what our culture calls a "meaningful relationship" with this unborn baby slated for abortion. But the suffering of my heart told me, on an intimately personal level, that the slain preborn were really here once, and now they were gone, as though banished from the world.

I feel the loss of the aborted most acutely not during times of sorrow but during times of happiness when my soul is stirred by human beauty and the splendor of the created world. In 1986, I attended my first Wisconsin State Fair with my friend Chris Le Blanc. We went to a tent set up by the Mexican Cultural Center to get something to eat. Inside, men and women, matched in pairs and dressed in festive costumes, were dancing to traditional Mexican music. They danced with an explosion of precision, harmony, and joy, their faces wreathed in smiles. As I carefully watched their steps, I was immediately swept into the happiness of the dance and mesmerized until suddenly I felt a deep pain well up within me, and tears came to my eyes. Someone was missing. Indeed, many were missing. Others who should have been there with us. I felt the absence of the aborted unborn as if there was an empty hole in the world that could not be filled. The lively dancers brought me to the edge of it, to mourn.

As a pro-life activist, I am caught in the agony of a desperate time. That moment which crushes the life of the unborn also crushes my heart; and when that moment seizes you, it is no longer possible to live a normal life, as though the world were a normal place. Legalized abortion made me a rebel against society. My life is lived against it, in contradiction to it. I know the absolute absurdity of a world where men and women kill their unborn children and call it a right.

At times I thought I would be a better pro-lifer if I were more detached, that is, if I could stand emotionally aloof from the women and their preborn children. I even prayed for this kind of disconnection. But maybe the only reason a person makes the effort to defend the unborn is precisely because that person knows he or she is attached. I am attached to the woman going into the clinic. I am attached to her baby. I am even attached to the abortionist. The true pro-lifer is invested in all humanity, who can see another personal someone in the smallest speck of human life.

One evening in October, 1987, I happened to pass by the Milwaukee Women's Health Organization on 12th and State. Elinor Yeo's abortion clinic had been permanently closed for weeks. Just a few days after it closed, Citizens for Life held a small celebration on the sidewalk outside. The building was empty now, shut up and dark. I spontaneously decided to pull my car into the clinic's side drive. I had been arrested there in 1986 and how strange it felt to now be on the clinic property with no one there to yell at me or to call the police. I parked in the rear where the employees used to park. I sat in the car for a few moments and prayed for all the women who had entered the clinic's doors and for the children who had died there.

While I sat, I spied a rusty trash barrel in the parking lot. I got out of my car, walked over to it, and peered inside. Five months ago I had helped retrieve aborted babies from the trash behind the Michigan Avenue Medical Center. I had apprehension and fear that perhaps I would find fetal remains here as well. But there were none. At the top of the barrel were cleaning rags and papers and dirt from a vacuum cleaner bag, apparently all thrown out when the clinic staff did their last-minute cleaning. I pushed this trash aside and looked toward the bottom of the barrel. I saw a few used syringes and then I saw suction curettes with blood still inside of them. There was also bloody gauze and soiled blue paper sheets used for lining the surgical tables.

I had never seen a suction curette. I peered at one, struck by the likelihood that it had been used in the killing of an unborn child— that the body of a tiny life had passed through it. I wrapped it up in a piece of newsprint and took it with me as a memorial of that unborn child's death.

As I continued to look in the barrel I came across a piece of paper. Typed on it were instructions on how to prepare the "POCs" for transfer to a pathology lab. The words were hastily written and full of misspellings. The top of the sheet bore the date 11/22/85.

Weigh speciman

Fill out required information on the white slip

Add formalin to cover spec. and swish it around

Remove the tape with name on it from spec. container and put on plastic bag

Drain formalin from speciman and slip the speciman into plastic bag

Seal and put in refrigerator specimans to be sent for path. are prepared in the same way

* * *

On June 2, 1993, I drove home from a hearing at the Milwaukee County Court House at which a 1987 charge of criminal trespass to a medical facility against me was finally dismissed. Jeff Kremers had charged Edmund and me after we had entered the waiting room of Affiliated Medical Services to talk to a woman I had initially spoken with on the street outside of the clinic. I was feeling extremely happy that, after five years of litigation, this case was resolved in my favor. On my way home I again passed by the building that was once the Milwaukee Women's Health Organization, where Citizens for Life had held their small celebration a few years earlier.

I immediately stopped my car. The building was in shambles, less than a third of it still standing. The building that once housed one of Milwaukee's busiest abortion clinics was being demolished. I parked my car on the street and walked over to the crumbling walls. The center of the building was entirely gutted and exposed. With the walls toppled and the roof torn away, the barren, open space beckoned to me, whispering its sorrows and secrets.

I entered the empty space, marked where the procedure rooms used to be, and prayed for all the babies who had died in them, for all the women who had come there, and for all the clinic workers. Now this place of death was being destroyed. Like the unborn killed there, it too would vanish. I was struck by the odd feeling that this place should not be destroyed; some piece of it should stand as a monument to the thousands of lives lost within its walls.

Later that evening I went back to the site. It was dusk and rain was falling as I stood all alone in the heart of the eviscerated building. I picked my way out through the crumbling walls to the back of the clinic. There was a steep stairway leading down to a basement door. I made the descent, peered into the darkness, and studied the shadows. Someone once told me the recovery rooms were down here. There were holes in the ceiling from the demolition and rain was dripping into the empty space below. The silence was broken only by the clear sound of splashing water echoing through the murky shadows.

*　*　*

Sometimes I can still smell the babies. Some odor will unexpect-
edly seem like the smell of blood and formalin and take me back to
them. Sometimes I am still reminded of the little broken bodies.
A child's hand or a baby's foot will bring me back to the alleys and
the loading docks.

Edmund and I often take trips between Milwaukee and Chicago with our children. I look at them nestled in the backseat of the
car, their long-lashed eyes closed in peaceful sleep, and I am drawn
in by their beauty and their innocence. If we go to Chicago or to
my parents' home, we pass by a fork in the expressway where the
building that once housed the Vital Med laboratory still stands. I
know where I am and turn my face to see the door we once passed
through. It led us to the edge of the world, where the broken bodies
of the innocent unborn were cast away.

I turn my face to the building and stare until I can no longer
see it. Our car speeds on with a hundred others, riders unaware
of what they have just passed. If someone looks my way, he will
see a woman cross herself and maybe think it strange. But I mark
the place of the vanished unborn, and offer up a silent prayer in
requiem. My heart affirms, in memory of them, the triumph-song
of life.

ACKNOWLEDGEMENTS

THE author would like to acknowledge the following people who helped bring this book to publication. First, let me thank Jack Ames, founder of Defend Life to whom I am greatly indebted and Rick Rotondi and Robert Gallagher of St. Benedict Press for having the courage and vision to publish this work.

I want to also thank the following persons who read the manuscript and whose suggestions helped perfect it, namely: Mary Meehan, Claudia Michalik, Dr. Janet Smith, Theresa Gase, Jordan Docken, Melissa Peppercorn, Anne Mitzel, Lynn Mills, Tim Murphy, Laura Nelson and Steve Gendregske. I especially wish to thank my student, John Brick, for the enormous contributions he made in editing the manuscript and the editor, Christian Tappe, for his invaluable help.

I am very grateful to Dinesh D'Souza who never gave up on this book, as well as Fr. Frank Pavone and Joseph Scheidler who were a source of constant encouragement. I would like to thank Wes Yoder for his belief in this work.

Finally, I thank my dear husband Edmund for his love and support, and who is so much a part of this story.

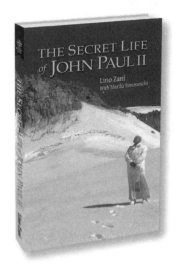

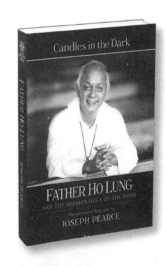